Reading
the
Gospels
in the
Dark

Reading the Gospels in the Dark

Portrayals of Jesus in Film

Richard Walsh

TRINITY PRESS INTERNATIONAL
A Continuum imprint
HARRISBURG • LONDON • NEW YORK

2007

Trinity Press International, P.O. Box 1321, Harrisburg, PA 17105

Trinity Press International is a member of the Continuum International Publishing Group.

Cover art: Actor Jeffrey Hunter as Jesus Christ in *King of Kings* © Bettmann/ CORBIS

Cover design: Wesley Hoke

Photographs found on pages 33, 36, 49, 54, 85, 133, and 157 are reprinted courtesy of PHOTOFEST.

Library of Congress Cataloging-in-Publication Data

Walsh, Richard G.
  Reading the Gospels in the dark : portrayals of Jesus in film / Richard Walsh.
    p. cm.
Includes bibliographical references and index.
  ISBN 1-56338-387-X (pbk.)
  1. Jesus Christ—In motion pictures. I. Title.
PN1995.9.J4 W35 2003
791.43'651—dc21

                                    2003012627

Printed in the United States of America

07 08   10 9 8 7 6 5 4 3 2

It [cinema] is the renewal of Plato's cave, where instead of seeing only shadows, we find illumination in the dark.

Geoffrey Hill, Illuminating Shadows: The Mythic Power of Film, page 21

It is possible to live in myth and without parable. But it is not possible to live in parable alone. To live in parable means to dwell in the tension of myth *and* parable. It is obvious, of course, that one can change from one myth (for example, capitalism) to another (for example, communism), and that every myth can have an antimyth. But a parable is not an antimyth, and it must be carefully distinguished from such. It is a story deliberately calculated to show the limitations of myth, to shatter world so that its relativity becomes apparent. . . . It is in fact the dark night of story, but precisely therein and thereby can it prepare us for the experience of transcendence.

John Dominic Crossan, The Dark Interval: Towards a Theology of Story, page 60

Contents

Preface

Living amidst Stories

. . . Jesus is far too important a figure to be left only to the theologians and the church.[1]

Why bother with Jesus films? As everyone knows, they are artifacts of popular culture, and scholars have far more serious fish to fry. In addition to the fact that postmodernism makes the distinction between high and low culture rather ambiguous, I have three justifications for my investigation.

First, Jesus, along with the hero of the Western in various incarnations, is the American icon. To comment on Jesus film, then, is to consider American mythology and self-identity, if not self-understanding. Chapter 8 summarizes my reflections on this point.

Second, given his (its?) iconic significance, Jesus is a sign contested by various ideologies. We invest Jesus with our own personal meanings and use that construct as an authority for our own programs. Interestingly, while scholarship often obscures its ideological designs, such investments are rather obvious in religious and aesthetic criticism of the Jesus films. Criticism is an attempt to "own" or to disown the films. Chapters 1 and 2 examine such ideological moves and substitute a celebration (for the customary debunking) of the Jesus films.

Third, and most important, I comment on Jesus films simply because I find them—and the conversation partners that I have chosen for them—interesting. Chapters 3 through 7 play out conversations (or comparisons) between a selected film and a gospel. Here, I am trying to realize Burton Mack's fantasy:

> My own fantasy is to enter a hall and find high ceilings, lovely chandeliers, walls lined with bookshelves, wines in the alcove, hors d'oeuvres by the windows, and a wide table down the middle of the room with the Bible sitting on it. And there we are, all of us, walking around, sitting at the table, and talking about what we should do with that book. Some rules are in order. Everyone has been invited. Christians have not been excluded, but they are not the ones in charge. . . . No one has a corner on what the Bible says. We blow our whistles if anyone starts to pout or preach. What we are trying to figure out is why we thought the

Bible so important, whether it is so important, how it has influenced our culture, what we think of the story. . . . Wouldn't that be something?[2]

In short, I invite ancient gospels, modern movies, and scholars to a table like the one Mack imagines. I include non-Christians as I first imagined these conversations because I was dissatisfied with orthodox (ecclesiastical and academic) readings of the Jesus films. Unfortunately, the conversation remains a fantasy, for I orchestrate it and speak for all parties; nevertheless, I have tried not to let the gospels or the scholars dominate the films. In short, I have tried to read the gospels "in the dark" of the theater, not films in the light of the church or the academy.

These chapters, then, are the story of my reading and viewing. I bring a specific gospel and film together because I find the affective experiences I have had of them sufficiently alike to bear comparison. Respectively, the emphasized points of contact are typology, location, precursors, history, and myth. At the end of each of these chapters, I offer some closing reflections on reading the gospel in question in the dark. On occasion, these comments amount to something that I had not previously seen in the gospel. At other times, the movies simply make something already noticed, but often minimized for reasons of decorum, inescapable. On every occasion, the reflections constitute a particular reading, not the truth about the gospel or the film.

According to J. Z. Smith, the unannounced third in any scholarly comparison is the scholar's agenda or ideology.[3] As far as I am aware of it, my own ideology celebrates pluralism and resists mythic univocity. Since Plato, the traditional approach to pluralism is the agonistic attempt to elevate one (our) story at the expense of others. Instead of this mythic imperialism, I suggest that living consciously amidst discordant stories is a more fecund approach today. In our violent times, the "dark night of story" is preferable to and less terrifying than mythic certainty.

Unless specifically noted, citations of movie dialogue are my own. Citations of biblical passages, unless noted, are from the New Revised Standard Version. When I refer to the gospels (Mark, Q, Thomas, Matthew, Luke, John), I think of them as texts, not as authors. Accordingly, I use neuter pronouns for these texts. The movie stills used here are reproduced with the permission of Photofest.

My debt to scholars and teachers is immense. I sincerely hope that my footnotes and bibliography provide proper acknowledgments, because I consider scholarship a conversation, not an authoritative pronouncement. To that end, I dedicate this book to those teachers who have taught me to engage in this conversation: Richard Cutter, Ray Summers, Jack Flanders, Naymond Keathley, Garland Knott, and George Aichele. I hope that I have been faithful to their vision. They would not want me to be faithful to their answers. I would also like to thank Henry Carrigan for believing in and judiciously editing this particular project, and the staff of the Methodist College Library (particularly Susan Pulsipher, Helen Graham, and Kathryn Zybeck) for their invaluable research assistance. Jo Shonebarger also deserves mention for her secretarial assistance.

As always, I would have written no book without the support of my family: Jennifer, Susan, Megan Marie, Michael, and Megan Elizabeth. I appreciate the acceptance and good-hearted tolerance in the refrain heard increasingly around our house of late, "Oh no, not another Jesus movie!"

Notes

1. Jaroslav Pelikan, *Jesus through the Centuries: His Place in the History of Culture* (New Haven, Conn.: Yale University Press, 1985), xv.

2. Burton L. Mack, *Who Wrote the New Testament? The Making of the Christian Myth* (San Francisco: Polebridge, 1995), 310.

3. Jonathan Z. Smith, *Drudgery Divine: On the Comparison of Early Christianities and the Religions of Late Antiquity* (Chicago: University of Chicago Press, 1990), 51.

Chapter 1

Telling Sacred Stories in Cathedral Cinemas

Films are neither icons to be emulated, nor are they distillations of evil. They are cultural products, deeply informed by the perspectives, values, and aspirations of their makers. They beg for creative discussion, for it is finally the uses to which Hollywood films are put that determines their function in American society.[1]

The So-Called Religious Failure of the Jesus Films

Critics delight in debunking Jesus films. The claim that the films are religious failures covers a wide variety of complaints. Under this rubric, some critics deride (all) films as mere art or entertainment. Others express moral, theological, or ideological aversion to (particular) films.

The former criticism is the most serious, but Margaret Miles has convincingly addressed the entertainment fallacy.[2] While the movies are not obviously religious, neither is "religious" art truly religious. Use, not content, renders a painting or a film religious. Only when worshipers bring commitment and imaginative effort to bear does a painting or a film become iconic. As people go to movies to be entertained, they generally do not bring such attention to movies; however, movies can become "religious" if the audience engages them critically. Miles advocates such engagement because she believes that the movies are more than mere entertainments. Their repeated patterns have a lasting "mythic" impact on us.[3]

The other type of complaint agrees that the movies influence us and laments their deleterious impact on our morality or our theology. Such complaints, of course, are clearly situated in the critic's own ideology. Quite simply, the critics advocate an ideology other than what they see in a particular film.[4] Actually, film itself is neither good nor bad, neither religious nor irreligious. As many critics such as Miles suggest, we may well be able to make it part of serious conversations. To pursue that end, I consider the cultural and ideological location of the Jesus films and explore a nonessentialist understanding of religion.

1

American Film and the Portrayal of Religion

Many moviegoers considered the portrayal of religious subjects as irreverent in the early days of film. The Protestant iconoclasm in American culture, the immoral reputation of the theater and actors, and audience discomfort when actors did not look like the audience's mental image of various religious characters all contributed to this sense. Filmmakers and marketers attacked these notions by advertising the spectacular, authentic, and reverent manner of their treatment of religious subjects. For filmmakers, biblical and religious topics guaranteed audience interest and conferred an aura of respectability on their new industry. Accordingly, advertising rhetoric depicted the theater as a church and the film as a sermon.[5]

Film versions of passion plays were quite popular. Generally, filmmakers made little attempt at character portrayal or narration. Instead, film staged pictures from illustrated bibles (particularly the famous Tissot Bible) with titles written in "biblical" language. The plots that gradually developed were primarily stories of divinely inspired conversions.[6]

Such plots continued in the heyday of the reverent religious spectacular. Thus, Cecil B. DeMille's *The King of Kings* (1927), which ushered in this new era, centers its narration on the conversion of important characters (notably, the blind girl and Mary Magdalene). DeMille established the style of the reverent epic with this film and perfected it with other films leading up to *The Ten Commandments* (1956). DeMille and others combined sex, sentiment, and spectacle to titillate and gratify a Protestant audience. Thus, in *The King of Kings*, the provocative, exotic Magdalene titillated the audience, while her conversion to respectable womanhood under Jesus' gaze satisfied their puritanical ethic.

DeMille and others were particularly adept in configuring their religious subjects—whether from the Hebrew Bible, the New Testament, or religious fiction—as if they were Americans. In this way, the epics provided America a mythic (religious) identity as the righteous empire. This identity justified a capitalist, democratic piety and helped America fight the Cold War. Michael Wood says of movies from the 1940s and 1950s, "The movies did not describe or explore America, they invented it, dreamed up an America all their own, and persuaded us to share the dream." As such, the movies of that era are our tradition, our public "classical education."[7]

For a host of reasons, that era and the reverent portrayals of religion ended in the 1960s. Protestant America ceased to exist. Catholic immigrations and increasing attention to civil-rights issues for minorities contributed to an increasingly pluralistic society. Further, foreign films became popular in art houses and influenced Hollywood perceptions of what Americans would pay to see. The end of the studio system and the new ratings system of 1968 encouraged experimentation. The spirit of the times was anti-establishment. Counterculture movements proliferated and were gradually mainstreamed, partly through the influence of Vietnam and Watergate and partly because the hippies grew up.

By the 1980s, although a conservative political and economic reaction had set in nationwide,[8] irreverent portraits of traditional Western religion had become the order of the day. After all, by the 1980s, a secular, pluralist America was unquestionably in place. Filmmakers no longer expected to find a Protestant audience. Instead, they expected to play to various religious and racial minorities who at least had in common a superficial commitment to "politically correct" thinking and foundational commitments to economic success and secularity. Accordingly, films replaced religious authority with psychiatrists, politicians, lawyers, and business executives; films relegated religious groups to the margins; and films attributed religious motivations to hypocrisy and neurosis. In general, film treated Christianity iconoclastically (compare *The Handmaid's Tale, The Rapture, Santa Fe*).[9]

Today, a pluralist America marginalizes Christianity, but film portrays other religions more sympathetically. A disenchantment with modernity and a nostalgia for a simpler past informs movies like *The Gods Must Be Crazy* (not American although hugely popular here) and *Dances with Wolves*. As the West has long believed there is light in the East, film portrays Eastern religions positively. Hollywood is particularly fascinated with Buddhism (for example, *Kundun, Little Buddha, Seven Years in Tibet*). A vague Eastern philosophy or religion undergirds many recent popular films (for example, *The Matrix, American Beauty*). Of the world's great religions, Islam has been treated least sympathetically because of various crises reaching back to the oil embargo of the 1970s. In fact, Arabs have replaced Nazis as the recognizable "bad guys" in film.

In each case, recent film, like older film, renders these religious others according to Hollywood's perception and construction of American mythology. Film homogenizes religious traditions as much as possible,[10] emphasizing a generalized, vaguely religious ethic more than any other component of religion. Probably, the importance of individualism in our mythology contributes to this focus. After all, ethic is more interesting and applicable to solitary individuals than myth, ritual, and communal organizations. Further, in this homogenized religion, the sacred becomes the vaguest possible mysticism (for example, *Powder, Grand Canyon, Michael*). This depiction reflects the importance of Romanticism in forming the American worldview. More importantly, this vague mysticism is more palatable to science, the dominant element in our technological society's worldview (for example, *Contact, Phenomenon*), than are traditional Western theisms. In sum, then, recent film has not turned away from religion; it has portrayed religion in a way marketable to the largest possible pluralist, secular audience. After all, it is rationalized and ethicized religion that has dominated modernity since its earliest days.

Some contemporary films bespeak a slightly different "world," because they exhibit a certain metaphysical anxiety (for example, *The Matrix, The Thirteenth Floor, The Truman Show, eXistenZ, Mulholland Drive, Run Lola Run*). Such films reflect the multiple realities and consequent uncertainties of our postmodern pluralism. Some strive to ease this crisis and justify our technological programs, while others are more disenchanted and deconstructive. In either case, they are not unrelated to the portrayal of religion in contemporary film. At the least, they allow considerations of worldviews other than that of scientific technology (if not of capitalist consumerism).

Jesus Films as Cultural and Ideological Products

This cursory look at the history of film's portrayal of religion identifies four eras, with an emerging fifth: 1) an initial reluctance to portray religion in film; 2) the reverent, spectacular portrayal of Christian religious epics; 3) foreign and countercultural inroads in the experimental 1960s (and early 1970s); 4) a secular and pluralist society's iconoclastic portrayal of Christianity and its gradual acceptance of portrayals of homogenized (modern) religion; and 5) increasing evidence of metaphysical anxiety. Admittedly, these five eras are not exact. There are no clear-cut divisions, and one can easily think of exceptions to the general description in any of the eras. Nonetheless, they are, I think, the identifiable trends and emphases.

The major Jesus films influential in America fit recognizably into these eras.[11] Olcott's *From the Manger to the Cross* (1912), Griffith's *Intolerance* (1916), and DeMille's *The King of Kings* (1927) belong to the era of reluctance. Griffith does not develop the Jesus story. He juxtaposes it with three other stories of innocent victims— a fictional, modern story about two young unfortunates, the Babylonian fall to the Persians, and the sixteenth-century slaughter of the Huguenots—to critique "do-gooders." His artistic film is something of an anomaly among Jesus films because it criticizes imperialism and capitalism, as well as benevolence movements that leave social inequities untouched. Griffith's advocacy of pacifism and his film were largely ignored as America entered World War I.

By contrast, Olcott and DeMille support the values of the American middle class and the established churches. DeMille, in particular, created a portrait of a divine Jesus Christ that was acceptable to popular American religious audiences for decades. In fact, DeMille's silent Jesus was the only popular direct portrayal of Jesus in American film until 1961. In the interim, Jesus appeared indirectly as the "structuring absence" in the stories of his believers (for example, *Ben-Hur, The Robe*).

The real Jesus epics were Ray's *King of Kings* (1961) and Stevens's *The Greatest Story Ever Told* (1965); however, they came too late in the reverent-spectacle era for success. American audiences were interested in other matters and had become far too pluralistic to embrace a version of the Protestant gospel as their metanarrative. Ray, in particular, seems aware of this dilemma. In place of DeMille's divine cipher, he sketches a far more human Jesus. Thus, *King of Kings* is more biographical and historical than *The King of Kings*. Further, his creation of Lucius, the doubting but fair centurion, was an impressive attempt to bring a traditional religious story into scientific modernity for an increasingly secular audience.

Stevens's film is the most American Jesus film. The director of the more famous *Shane* simply created another blockbuster (gospel) Western. He filmed the movie in the American West, used every available Hollywood star, and employed the American poet Carl Sandburg to work on the script. More importantly, Stevens also captured the peculiarly American religion, a matter of personal faith untouched by and itself not touching the world.

Pasolini's *The Gospel According to St. Matthew* (1964), a critically acclaimed foreign film, initiated the countercultural era. Pasolini simply did not play by the rules of the Hollywood spectacular. His was a black-and-white film with eerily long silences, punctuated by nontraditional and highly effective music. Further, Pasolini did not merge the four canonical gospels into one homogenized script as had Hollywood, orthodoxy, and popular Christianity. Pasolini, as his title indicates, followed Matthew closely. Further, he used nonprofessional actors and made no attempt to recreate a first-century Palestine. Instead, he used Italian peasants to re-create a peasant world. These production choices were deliberate, because Pasolini was interpreting the Jesus tradition from and for an Italian Marxist perspective. His Jesus was a revolutionary acting for the people against the middle class and its institutions.

In America, where Pasolini was popular in the art houses and on university campuses, Jewison's *Jesus Christ Superstar* (1973) and Greene's *Godspell* (1973) offered domestic countercultural films. Both were musical plays turned into movies, and both reflected the youth culture of the 1960s. As such, they were anti-establishment (versus the military, industry, and organized religion), but they hardly sponsored revolt or reform. Instead, they helped mainstream the counterculture.

Zeffirelli's *Jesus of Nazareth* (1977) anticipates the swing toward conservatism in the 1980s. As such, his film is somewhat out of place in our five eras of Jesus films, but it was made for Italian and American TV, not for the theater. Although Zeffirelli announced that he intended to create a human Jesus and an ecumenical film, all in the spirit of Vatican II, he actually created a divine Jesus comparable to those of DeMille and Stevens. Certainly, he created a film widely accepted by the religious and palatable to the ecumenical church of his day and thereafter. More people have probably seen Zeffirelli's *Jesus* than any other. Zeffirelli harmonized the Gospels and returned to the melodramatic conversion style of the Hollywood epics. Like the Jesus of Stevens, this Jesus is an invitation to private, personal faith and, accordingly, to an escape from larger social realities. Krish and Sykes's *Jesus* (1979), while based primarily on Luke, is similarly conservative, if not reactionary. Krish and Sykes speak for and to evangelical conservatism, rather than to the ecumenical church.

Monty Python's Life of Brian (British, 1979) belongs to the iconoclastic era. Not generally considered a Jesus film, it returns to the indirect Christ preferred by Hollywood epics. Accordingly, Jesus appears once in the film from afar as he delivers the Sermon on the Mount. The British comedy troupe follows Brian Cohen instead of Jesus. Further, unlike the typical religious spectacular, this movie does not plot Brian's conversion to Christianity. Instead, we have throughout this film an eccentric and iconoclastic look at Christianity and Jesus films. It is as if the troupe were producing a "negative" of the Jesus films. Instead of the hero, then, we are always with followers, particularly with those who misunderstand (for example, the hilarious "blessed are the cheese makers" scene) and with those who would construct a messiah to follow at any price.

Scorsese's *The Last Temptation of Christ* (1988) is equally iconoclastic. It offers a human, tormented Jesus. Intriguingly, Scorsese often films Jesus from above rather than from below, as is the Hollywood tradition. Scorsese shows Jesus consciously "making it (his message and mission) up as he goes," bewildered, tempted, and finally supported by Judas. This characterization has less in common with the Hollywood Jesus film tradition than it does with the tormented heroes and buddies of Scorsese's other films (for example, *Taxi Driver, Mean Streets*).

Arcand's *Jesus of Montreal* (Canadian, 1990) also belongs to the iconoclastic era. Daniel, the hero, is not a first-century Jesus but a twentieth-century actor playing Jesus in a passion play for a Montreal church. Daniel's actions and his rewritten passion play critique various important institutions—notably the church and advertising—and take an iconoclastic look at the church's version of the Jesus story. When placed against the backdrop of more recent films, however, the interesting feature of this Jesus movie is that it anticipates our recent metaphysical anxieties. As the film progresses, it becomes more and more difficult for its actors to distinguish "story" and reality. First, a worshiper cannot distinguish Daniel, playing Jesus in the play, from her Lord. Ultimately, the story also leaks over into Daniel's life as he routs the money-changers (disrupts a commercial), rants an apocalyptic discourse, dies an innocent victim, gives life to others (through organ transplants), and is remembered by his followers. The leakage of the Jesus story into an actor's life has precursors,[12] but Arcand has a twist. His film suggests that liberation—from consumerism and from Hollywood spectaculars—lies not in the church or its story, but in the illusions of art (theater) and its dedicated actors. Thus, Daniel's ethic is largely that of an actor who will not "sell out," and the community that continues Daniel's memory is a theater company.

Young's recent *Jesus* (1999), made for Italian and American TV, does not fit our five-era schema. It remakes the traditional Jesus-as-divine film in a post-Scorsese world. Thus, unlike its precursors, it offers a more human Jesus who struggles with desires for family, with temptation, and with his mission. Unlike Scorsese, however, this Jesus' doubts and temptations are weighted at the beginning, rather than at the end of his ministry. In short, this Jesus matures into the divine man of church tradition. Unlike Scorsese's tormented Jesus, this Jesus sings, laughs, and dances. While speaking for an ecumenical religious tradition (see the importance of Mary), Young offers a Jesus palatable to New Agers and to family-values advocates. This Jesus' primary struggle is "leaving home." In short, it's "family TV." At the turn of the century, it seems rather nostalgic, if not reactionary.

With some equivocations, then, the Jesus films fit fairly well into our five-era schema. In other words, the Jesus films reflect Hollywood's general portrayal of religion at different times in American history. Even the foreign films that have been popular in America (Pasolini, Monty Python, Arcand) reflect currents and tensions in American culture. Figure I sketches these points as we have discussed them, but two other considerations remain important: I) the tradition of Jesus films and 2) the question of ideological perspective.

Figure 1: Jesus Films: History, Tradition, Ideology

Director	Film History	Tradition	Culture	Ideology
Olcott	Reluctance	Precursor	Protestant America	Supportive of Protestant culture
Griffith	Reluctance	Precursor	World War I	Critical of "do-gooders" and advocating pacifism
DeMille	Reluctance	Canonical film	"Protestant kingdom"	Capitalist, middle-class nationalism
Ray	Reverence	Affirmative	Post–World War II America	Secular humanism but respectful of tradition
Stevens	Reverence	Affirmative	Secular America	American gospel of private faith
Pasolini	Counterculture	Demythologize	Foreign infusion	Marxism

Figure 1 continued

Director	Film History	Tradition	Culture	Ideology
Jewison	Counterculture	Musical	1960s "youth"	Domesticated counterculture
Greene	Counterculture	Musical	1960s "youth"	Domesticated counterculture
Zeffirelli	Reactionary	Nostalgic	Ecumenical movement	Orthodoxy
Krish and Sykes	Reactionary	Nostalgic	Evangelistic missions	Conservative Protestantism
Monty Python	Iconoclastic	Burlesque	Comic commentary	Rejection of imperialism
Scorsese	Iconoclastic	Demythologize	1980s "me generation"	Versus spectacular
Arcand	Metaphysical	Demythologize	1980s "me generation"	Versus consumerism
Young	Reactionary	Nostalgic	Millennial reflection	New-Age appropriation of Jesus tradition

First, then, the Jesus films belong to a tradition of Jesus films. They are not creations *ex nihilo*. They are not even, after the early days of Olcott and DeMille, primarily created out of the Gospels, church tradition, and Christian art. The important precursors of later filmmakers are earlier films. In fact, we might see later filmmakers adapting the genre by adopting different moods or orientations. If we take DeMille's *The King of Kings* as the blueprint for the Jesus-film genre, *Monty Python's Life of Brian* is clearly burlesque. Ray and Stevens affirm the generic rules. Pasolini, Monty Python, Scorsese, and Arcand demythologize the genre. Zeffirelli, Krish and Sykes, and Young are overwhelmingly nostalgic.[13]

Second, filmmakers present Jesus according to their personal ideological perspectives. Griffith advocates pacifism and attacks social engineering. DeMille supports American capitalism and the middle class. Pasolini speaks for Italian peasants versus aristocratic and bourgeois regimes. Jewison and Greene reflect the counterculture and oppose the military-industrial complex. Ray is open to secular humanism. Stevens and Zeffirelli speak for "private faith." Zeffirelli and Young are ecumenical, while DeMille is popularly Protestant and Krish and Sykes are evangelical. Monty Python mocks empire (including the church). Scorsese and Arcand criticize Hollywood. Arcand also rejects consumerism.

Audiences, of course, receive the films according to their own ideologies as well:

Representatives of mainline, or liberal, Protestantism often evaluated Jesus films, and Jesus as portrayed in those films, on the basis of the film's social relevance and Jesus' humanness. Representatives of evangelical, or conservative, Protestantism were more concerned with the faithfulness of Jesus films to the biblical text and to Jesus' divinity. . . .

Catholic reaction to Jesus films, at least by reviewers in Catholic publications, has reflected less concern for either social relevance or biblical faithfulness. Catholic reviewers seemed more comfortable than Protestants with Jesus on the screen as image—however provocative that moving image may have been. Reflected here, no doubt, is Catholicism's traditional appreciation for the sacred image of Jesus and his story. . . .

By contrast to these varying Christian appraisals of the cinematic Jesus, the history of Jesus in film has also been a history of ongoing Jewish vigilance against anti-Semitism.[14]

In other words, the Jesus of film is no more innocent than is the Jesus of historical research. If Jesus films are less safe places to construct ideology (and it is not clear that they are), it is only because they are more public than the academy's images of Jesus.

A Matter of Plot: Two Important Reviews

My history of Jesus films, like those of others, is a narrative whose plot fulcrum turns on the cultural changes in America in the 1960s. The theme of this narrative is modernization or secularization. In this story, the portrayal of Jesus shifts in the 1960s (with Ray) from a focus on the divinity (DeMille) to more interest in the humanity of Jesus (Scorsese).[15] Later films emphasizing the (semi-) divine Jesus seem anachronistic and nostalgic (Stevens, Zeffirelli, Krish and Sykes). One can tell this same story quite differently, however.

Living after the end of the (Protestant) American metanarrative, Stern, Jefford, and DeBona tell the tale nostalgically. Accordingly, they assert that DeMille's film would likely draw "more laughter than applause" today, and they also observe that Stevens and Zeffirelli can offer a "divine" Jesus only by restricting the matter to "private faith." This approach abandons history for "myth," by which they mean Gnosticism/Docetism, the long-standing opponent of incarnational orthodoxy.[16] Accordingly, they celebrate those Jesus films that they can read as critical of this heresy (for example, Scorsese, Arcand).

Their resulting story is the familiar tale (myth) of a fall into decadence from a lost golden age.[17] That lost golden age is the time of the Christian metanarrative. Contemporary society and its films represent decadence. Stern, Jefford, and DeBona add a postmodern twist, however, by refusing to call for a return to the Christian metanarrative. Because a pluralist society exists, they speak for a particular micro-community, that of incarnational Christians, struggling to survive in the face of consumerism's proliferation of images. Understandably, their avowed purpose is to help such beleaguered communities understand and purify their image of Jesus. Although they admit a historical imaging process, they do not accept postmodernism's unending semiosis. Instead, they defend the Christian tradition, an "eternal gospel," and "the God beyond all imagining."[18]

By contrast, W. Barnes Tatum reads the history of Jesus films hopefully. In fact, Tatum uses Jesus movies to introduce his readers to historical-critical approaches to Jesus and the Gospels.[19] Accordingly, Tatum considers in detail the films' use of the Gospels as sources and the films' verisimilitude.[20] On the question of sources, Tatum identifies a harmonizing and an alternative approach. The former draws somewhat eclectically on all four gospels (Olcott, DeMille, Ray, Stevens, Zeffirelli). The alternative approach focuses on one gospel (Pasolini, Krish and Sykes), juxtaposes the Jesus story with a modern story (Griffith, Arcand), or replaces the Gospel with a modern fiction (Jewison, Greene, Scorsese). While the harmonizing approach leads to dramatic coherence, the alternative path interests Tatum more because of its potential for sensitivity to the historical Jesus.[21] Unfortunately, Tatum feels that the films have failed here; however, he hopes that someone may make a film "that *explicitly* claims to base its characterization of Jesus on the results of life-of-Jesus research."[22]

Tatum's resulting story is that of liberal Protestantism's classic quest for the historical Jesus.[23] Modernity does not trouble this story because a modern method—the historical-critical method—deals with the gap between culture and tradition by creating the historical Jesus of Nazareth. That figure is liberal Protestantism's apologetic response to modernity and its move toward a postmillennial kingdom, created by human hands, on earth. As he has an answer waiting for it, then, Tatum accepts modernity more easily than Stern, Jefford, and DeBona; nonetheless, he is no more postmodern than they. Their incarnate Christ stops the process of signification. Tatum uses the historical Jesus similarly.

Together, these two important reviews of Jesus films constitute a textbook example of Peter Berger's claim that the historic (world) religions have responded to modernity in one of two ways: defensive rejection of the modern world in favor of tradition (Stern, Jefford, and DeBona) or accommodation of the tradition to modernity (Tatum).[24] For our purposes, this dichotomy suggests that the appraisal of the religious value of the Jesus films rests upon general attitudes toward modernity.

Telling Sacred Stories in Cathedral Cinemas

While critics often define modernity as antithetical to religion,[25] we need not do so unless we define religion itself in essentialist terms as some kind of metaphysical dualism.[26] After all, in addition to the continuance of traditional religion, new religious forms steadily appear.[27] Further, as we have seen, religion still appears in Hollywood film. Of course, that religion is not traditional Western monotheism or a religion appealing to academics and intellectuals; it is popular religion, religion "carried on outside the formal structures provided by most societies for such activities."[28] In fact, watching film has certain similarities to participating in religious ritual:

> We pay our votive offerings at the box office. We buy our ritual corn. We hush in reverent anticipation as the lights go down and the celluloid magic begins. Throughout the filmic narrative we identify with the hero. We vilify the antihero. We vicariously exult in the victories of the drama. And we are spiritually inspired by the moral of the story, all while believing we are modern techno-secular people, devoid of religion. Yet the depth and intensity of our participation reveal a religious fervor that is not much different from that of religious zealots.[29]

Furthermore, M. Darrol Bryant describes film as the central ritual of our technological civilization. Film (technology) continues the alchemist dream to transform nature and achieve immortality by providing

> . . . a magically transformed and ordered world where the discontinuity between desire and reality is overcome. In the movies, boy gets girl, the lawman gets his man, the mistreated gets revenge. In film intimate and harmonious contact with the elemental powers that order things is reestablished: the human world is brought into line with the forces that rule our lives. We can thus see in the popular response to cinema a desire to reconnect the ordinary world with a more magical realm.[30]

The hero's technological adeptness (compare Neo in *The Matrix*) often provides the salvific connections to this transformed world. As a result, the ritual of film affirms our technological culture.[31]

While Christ figures may be technological adepts, Jesus is not, so Jesus films relate more obviously to civil religion and to privatized faith. Civil religion is a quasi-religious regard for the state, the beliefs and practices shared by the people of a nation, a kind of social faith and ritual.[32] For Bellah, the tenets of the American civil religion are essentially those identified by Rousseau: the existence of God; the life to come; the reward of virtue and the punishment of vice; and the exclusion of religious intolerance. To this, Bellah adds only the motif of God's special concern for and action in American history (manifest destiny) to arrive at an American "faith"[33] and the sense that America is God's people/nation.

Hollywood's religious and biblical spectaculars from the 1920s to the 1960s visually reinforced this faith and America's capitalist empire. As is well known, Bruce Barton, who construed Jesus as the founder of modern business, advised DeMille on the script for *The King of Kings*, and, not surprisingly, the film omits Jesus' ascetic teaching in order to offer a Jesus palatable to middle-class Protestant America. In short, DeMille "capitalizes" Jesus. For DeMille, Jesus is not a peasant but the icon of the American middle class. The later Jesus epics follow similar patterns. To find a Jesus truly critical of capitalism, one has to turn to foreign filmmakers like Pasolini and Arcand.

Behind DeMille and his successors—particularly the Cold War biblical epics—stand the Puritan notions that wealth represents divine favor and that wealth should be possessed dutifully, not hedonistically. Hedonistic luxury, not wealth, is wrong. Thus, DeMille opens *The King of Kings* with the exotic luxury of Mary Magdalene. When she meets Jesus, with a wager of a purse of gold in the balance, he cleanses her of the seven deadly sins, and she becomes a chaste (nun-like) follower. Later in the film, both Caiaphas and Judas provide foils for Jesus' moderate path. For them, religion is about wealth and power. For Jesus, it is about fatherly love. The family values here do not require abandonment of business; they simply require the proper ordering of spirituality, family, and business. DeMille's paternalistic Jesus incarnates the appropriate order. Fittingly, DeMille concludes his film with the risen Christ towering over—if not baptizing—an industrialized city.

The epics of the 1950s continued DeMille's pattern. For them, the Romans play the role of profligate hedonists while Jesus represents the appropriate attitude toward money and business. Repeatedly, wealthy, aristocratic Romans are "saved" by learning to possess empire and wealth rightly. Neither wealth nor empire is wrong.

Further, the Cold War films blatantly equate Christianity and the American "empire." DeMille puts the issue most blatantly in his sermonic introduction to *The Ten Commandments* (compare Richard Burton's voice-over narration beginning *The Robe*). For DeMille, Moses versus Pharaoh equals the United States versus the Soviet Union.[34] For the biblical epics, Christian (Republican) Rome is the mythic reconciliation of ideal and actuality: Christianity provides the transcendent, ethical ideals; Rome provides the practical imperial necessities. America is the modern Christian Rome, the kingdom of God on earth.

As America became more pluralist in the 1960s, the use of the biblical epic and the Jesus film to support American civil religion gradually diminished. Subsequent Jesus films, then, increasingly evidence the privatization and subjectivization that are characteristics of modern religion. For modernity, religion no longer provides the social glue, so religion is something about which an individual has endless choices. It is a vehicle for individual expression. Religion becomes virtually synonymous with family values, personal psychology, and peace of mind.[35] The films of Stevens, Zeffirelli, and Krish and Sykes fit this model. Their Jesus is an invitation to personal exploration, to finding oneself in the American West, in affirmations of tradition, or in the personal Jesus of evangelistic piety. They offer retreats from, not engagements with, larger society. Scorsese's Jesus differs, but he, too, is an exercise in psychological depth, not in social or traditional commitments.

If we think of religion in terms of its modern forms, then, we have little reason to condemn the Jesus films as religious failures. They function as part of American civil religion (DeMille, the 1950s epics). They justify expressive individualism (Jewison, Greene) and invite a private, internalized faith (Stevens, Zeffirelli, Krish and Sykes, Scorsese). Against this background, some even provide alternative—if not prophetic—critique (Pasolini, Monty Python, Scorsese, Arcand).[36] What they do not do is provide theologically correct statements of orthodox Christology—an invention of the fourth and fifth centuries—or provide an unassailably accurate Jesus of Nazareth (the so-called historical Jesus)— the project of the liberal Protestantism of the nineteenth century. As these films are twentieth-century products, we can hardly expect them to do so unless we have essentialist notions about the Jesus story and/or religion. The Jesuses of DeMille, Ray, Stevens, and others are of their time and society, and ideals or icons for their time and society. They act, as Geertz would have it, both as models of and models for society.[37] Thus, an ascetic pacifist has been and is the iconic hero of a capitalist empire.

Conclusion: A Matter of Ownership

That the Jesus films are different from our own ideologies, from orthodox Christianity, from historical Jesus research, and from the Gospels does not mean they are religious failures. In fact, it is exactly their "difference" that opens up the religious (or mythic) possibilities of interpretation and the creation of livable space. While this is not classical transcendence, in these gaps and incongruities we can create meaning.[38]

The Jesus films are religious failures if we operate with an essentialist understanding of religion. They fail if we look to them for a hierophanic revelation of the wholly other. They fail if we expect them to reject prophetically the culture that produced them. They fail if we see them as modern and see modernity as inimical to religion. They fail if we are not sensitive to their role in American mythology, civil religion, and private quests for faith. They fail if we see no place in religion for art and entertainment. In short, they fail religiously if we expect them to present (the) true, unadulterated religion.

If we expect from the Jesus films a presentation of the one, true religion, the ideology of the film will have to match our ideology. If we operate in this fashion, we, as interpreters, will vanish behind covert equations of our interpretations and film/reality/truth/religion. If we do so, we attempt to stop semiosis with our interpretation. In short, we claim to own the Jesus story (and Jesus films). In postmodern pluralism, such attempts are immoral and impractical.

Instead of owning the Jesus story, then, we should rather "own"—honestly admit—our own ideological interpretations (our religious, mythic work). Accordingly, I cannot simply assert that the Jesus films have religious value. I can only claim that they may have religious value as they become part of an interpretative comparison. My goal here has been to deny essentialist views of religion, modernity, and Jesus films. I have attempted to denude their "natural" status and to disclose their cultural and ideological locations. As a critic, I am most concerned with the ideology of criticism, so I confess that my own stance has been postmodern and pluralist. While I wish to interpret the Jesus story and Jesus films, I do not want to own them. I will simply lay them alongside gospels.

A Postscript: By Way of Further Confession

I have not argued the relative religious merits of the Jesus films, but the reader may well guess my own favorites from my confessions to this point. Given the pluralist culture in which I live, I have a tendency to favor those films presenting multiple stories (for example, Griffith, Greene, Arcand), those highlighting the importance of interpretation (Python, Arcand), and those suggesting multiple realities (Scorsese). Of course, if one deconstructs a film's mythic whole, almost any of these films reveal multiple realities. Ray's Lucius, Stevens's Lazarus, Jewison's Judas, and Scorsese's buddies (Jesus and Judas) are important mythic switching points that easily come undone. At least, they reveal important tensions that the respective films strive to harmonize between science and religion, capitalism and religion, hippies and the establishment, and humanity and divinity.

I have not yet included DeMille, Pasolini, Zeffirelli, Krish and Sykes, and Young in this postscript. For me, these provide "difference" sufficient to provide religious value at a discourse level rather than at a content level. The existence of each director's film creates interesting disjoints, for example, if one compares it to its primary sources (for example, Christian art and DeMille; Pasolini and Matthew). The discourse of TV—the interruption of the story by commercials—also provides a postmodern discourse of competing stories for Zeffirelli and Young. In my videotape copy of Young's film, this competition reaches quite amusing levels. Special-effects resurrection scenes and prayerful worship end the movie's story, but a commercial for the videotape ($29.98 at 1-888-CBS-8881) follows immediately. Religion and capitalism are together again, even if they are strange bedfellows.

Notes

1. Margaret R. Miles, *Seeing and Believing: Religion and Values in the Movies* (Boston: Beacon, 1996), 193.

2. Clifford Geertz, *The Interpretation of Cultures* (New York: Basic, 1973), 112, distinguishes the aesthetic perspective—"engrossed with surfaces with no concern for practical significance"—from the religious perspective—committed to the "really real." That distinction privileges one aesthetic perspective (like that in Susan Sontag, *Against Interpretation and Other Essays* [New York: Farrar, Straus & Giroux, 1966], 3–14) and one religious perspective (that of a premodern believer). Geertz's own understanding is more like those of Durkheim and J. Z. Smith, "postmodern" views of religion that are less easily distinguished from the aesthetic because they do not rely on conventional notions of transcendence.

3. Miles, *Seeing and Believing*, 186–90.

4. Michael Medved, *Hollywood vs. America* (New York: HarperPerennial, 1991), 3–10, 275–85; and Richard C. Stern, Clayton Jefford, and Guerric DeBona, O.S.B., *Savior on the Silver Screen* (Mahwah, N.J.: Paulist, 1999), 10–23, 321–33, criticize Hollywood film, respectively, in favor of conservative morality and theology. Liberals also challenge Hollywood films on ideological grounds, contending, for example, that they reflect a "hegemonic discourse which ultimately supports the status quo of classist, racist, and sexist ideologies (to name the most significant)" (John Lyden, "To Commend or to Critique? The Question of Religion and Film Studies," *The Journal of Religion and Film* 1, no. 2 [1997]: n.p. [cited on 15 August 2001] from http://www.unomaha.edu/~wwwjrf/tocommend.htm).

5. The various essays in Roland Cosandey, André Gaudreault, and Tom Gunning, eds., *Une Invention Du Diable?* (Sainte-Foy, Canada: Les Presses De L'Université Laval, 1992), are very helpful for this period. See especially pp. 187–96, 200–3.

6. See ibid., 112–20, 275–310, 353–58.

7. *America in the Movies*, 2nd ed. (New York: Columbia University Press, 1989), 1–23, 189–96. Wood's work is a major precursor of Bernard Brandon Scott's *Hollywood Dreams and Biblical Stories* (Minneapolis, Minn.: Fortress, 1994). In this era, the movies combined Puritan theology, Victorian ethic, and nationalistic propaganda in a melodramatic formula. According to Ronald Holloway, *Beyond the Image: Approaches to the Religious Dimension in Cinema* (Geneva: World Council of Churches, 1977), 9–43, 75–104, the resulting "dream cult" hypnotized audiences and prevented contact with the real world and negotiation of its problems. For Holloway, foreign films and Chaplin encouraged engagement rather than passivity in this era (ibid., 61–73, 141–62).

8. For a treatment of the change of American values between the 1960s and 1980s via the movies, see Tom O'Brien, *The Screening of America: Movies and Values from Rocky to Rain Man* (New York: Continuum, 1990). For other discussions of film in this era, see Miles, *Seeing and Believing*; Scott, *Hollywood Dreams and Biblical Stories*; and Medved, *Hollywood vs. America*.

9. These two sentences summarize Miles, *Seeing and Believing*, 5–25, 48–67.

10. DeMille merged Judaism, Christianity, and Islam into an American religion in *The Ten*

Commandments. The Prince of Egypt homogenizes even more than DeMille's film. There is little recognizably religious and even less recognizably Jewish about this film. Compare Jennifer Rohrer-Walsh, "Coming of Age in *The Prince of Egypt*," in George Aichele and Richard Walsh, eds., *Screeing Scripture: Intertextual Connections Between Scripture and Film* (Harrisburg, Pa.: Trinity Press International, 2002), 279–300, for a reading of this film in terms of American mythology. Recent films also Americanize Eastern religions (e.g., *American Beauty; The Tao of Steve*). The Indian hero of *The City of Joy*, for example, becomes an "American" hero through his struggle to achieve political and economic independence. The American (doctor and) rebel who assists him correspondingly learns something about communal values. East may meet West, but they do so in such a way as to support our central commitments: for example, capitalism, science, and individualism.

11. W. Barnes Tatum, *Jesus at the Movies: A Guide to the First Hundred Years* (Santa Rosa, Calif.: Polebridge, 1997), 2–5, 195–97, has a very helpful treatment of the history of Jesus films. He identifies a four-stage process—reluctance, reverence, diversity, and scandal—to which I am clearly indebted. Stern, Jefford, and DeBona, *Savior on the Silver Screen*, also provide a wealth of historical information on the Jesus films. Roy Kinnard and Tim Davis, *Divine Images: A History of Jesus on the Screen* (New York: Citadel, 1992), 13–18, provide a short overview.

12. See, e.g., Nikos Kazantzakis, *The Greek Passion*, trans. Jonathan Griffin (New York: Touchstone, 1953), or the film version of the novel, *He Who Must Die*. In a sense, this leakage is also part of *Jesus Christ Superstar*. This film begins with a troupe of actors going into the Israeli desert to perform a passion play. When the play is over and the actors board the bus, the actor playing Jesus is not among them.

13. Here, I am following the lead of John Cawelti, "*Chinatown* and Generic Transformation in Recent American Films," in Barry Keith Grant, ed., *Film Genre Reader II* (Austin: University of Texas Press, 1995), 234–43, who argues, using the Western as an example, that filmmakers adapt established film genres toward burlesque (*Blazing Saddles*), nostalgia (*True Grit, Raiders of the Lost Ark*), demythologization (*Chinatown, Bonnie and Clyde*), or affirmation (*The Wild Bunch*).

14. Tatum, *Jesus at the Movies*, 197. Film critics have bestowed most praise on *The Gospel According to St. Matthew* and *Jesus of Montreal* (*Intolerance* deserves, at least, honorable mention) and have rejected *King of Kings* and *The Greatest Story Ever Told* most completely. *The King of Kings* long had popular and (Protestant) religious favor. More recently, the religious have treated *The Gospel According to St. Matthew* and *Jesus of Nazareth* most favorably and criticized *The Last Temptation of Christ* most vociferously.

15. See Kinnard and Davis, *Divine Images*, 13–16.

16. Stern, Jefford, and DeBona, *Savior on the Silver Screen*, 48, 153–59, 224–28, 285–95, 321–33.

17. Compare Robert L. Wilken, *The Myth of Christian Beginnings* (Garden City, N.Y.: Doubleday, 1971); and Richard Walsh, *Reading the Bible: An Introduction* (Notre Dame, Ind.: Cross Cultural Publications, 1997), 474–85.

18. Stern, Jefford, and DeBona, *Savior on the Silver Screen*, 3, 11–16, 217, 333.

19. Tatum, *Jesus at the Movies*, 2–5, 186–88, 195–97.

20. Tatum analyzes films according to a fourfold question: "To what extent is this film about Jesus not only *cinematically* interesting, but *literarily* sensitive to the gospel sources, *historically* probable, and *theologically* satisfying?" (ibid., 12). Questions two and three are the historical-critical heart of the matter.

21. Ibid., 14.

22. Ibid., 203. In the 1990s, director Paul Verhoeven met several times with the Jesus Seminar to discuss plans for such a movie.

23. The religious character of Tatum's hope is most evident in his analysis of Arcand's film. While that film has a protagonist who acts as a historical critic to rewrite a passion play for modernity, Tatum does not celebrate this aspect of the film. Instead, he challenges its rejection of the Gospels for archaeology and its demythologizing. In short, he dissents from Daniel's historical criticism on ideological grounds (see ibid., 179–92).

24. Compare Peter Berger, *The Sacred Canopy: Elements of a Sociological Theory of Religion* (Garden City, N.Y.: Anchor, 1969), 155–71; and *idem, A Rumor of Angels: Modern Society and the Rediscovery of the Supernatural* (New York: Anchor, 1990), 1–27. This distinction parallels Troeltsch's famous definitions of sects and churches. Compare Clive Marsh and Gaye Ortiz, eds., *Explorations in Theology and Film: Movies and Meaning* (Oxford: Blackwell, 1997), 21–34, 245–55. In George M. Marsden's history of religion in America (*Religion in American Culture* [San Diego, Calif.: Harcourt Brace Jovanovich, 1990], 178, 238–78), the distinction between defenders and accommodators is far more important than any denominational designation.

25. Film is the quintessential modern medium. It is the result of science, technology, and capitalism (and can now be packaged for individual consumption). While other twentieth-century visual arts eschewed realism, film capitalized on realistic (although often romanticized) photography. Further, for Hollywood film, the narrative conventions have been and remain essentially those of the other modern art form, the novel. Recent film in the era of metaphysical anxiety, however, is more postmodern. Some early film, before the conventions of realistic photography and the novel took hold, also seems so. Arguably, commercial TV, with its rapidly shifting montage of images, is a more postmodern medium than film.

26. Historically, of course, European modernism challenged the Western monotheisms at ideological and institutional levels. Western monotheism's dualistic metaphysic hierarchically privileges the spirit over the physical. By contrast, modernity's metaphysic is relentlessly materialistic. Historically, Western monotheism has supported social hierarchies privileging priests and divine-right monarchs. By contrast, modernity's social tendencies have been relentlessly egalitarian, ultimately privileging the individual (or the bourgeoisie). Further, Western monotheism arranged the world both intellectually and institutionally according to authority (either that of the divine or earthly sovereign). By contrast, modernity arranges everything rationally according to notions of cause and effect (science) or bureaucratic social arrangements.

27. See James C. Livingston, *Anatomy of the Sacred: An Introduction to Religion,* 3rd ed. (Englewood Cliffs, N.J.: Prentice-Hall, 1998), 75–85, 177; and Michael Molloy, *Experiencing the World's Religions: Tradition, Challenge, and Change,* 2nd ed. (Mountain View, Calif.: Mayfield, 2002), 455–89.

28. Peter Williams, *Symbolic Change and the Modernization Process in Historical Perspective* (Englewood Cliffs, N.J.: Prentice-Hall, 1980), 228.

29. Geoffrey Hill, *Illuminating Shadows: The Mythic Power of Film* (Boston: Shambhala Publications, 1992), 3. See also the various essays in John R. May and Michael Bird, eds., *Religion in Film* (Knoxville: University of Tennessee Press, 1981); and Joel W. Martin and Conrad E. Ostwalt, Jr., eds., *Screening the Sacred: Religion, Myth, and Ideology in Popular American Film* (Boulder, Colo.: Westview, 1995).

30. "Cinema, Religion, and Popular Culture," in May and Bird, *Religion and Film*, 109–10.

31. Ibid., 112.

32. For more complex definitions and dissenting views, see Donald G. Jones and Russell E. Ritchey, eds., *American Civil Religion* (New York: Harper Forum, 1974). A recent synopsis is available in Robert Nisbet, "Civil Religion," in Mircea Eliade, ed., *Encyclopedia of Religion* (New York: Macmillan, 1987), 3:524–27.

33. Robert N. Bellah, *Beyond Belief: Essays on Religion in a Post-Traditional World* (New York: Harper & Row, 1970), 168–72. The faith that Americans hold in common changes over time. See Marsden, *Religion in American Culture*, 17–18, 42–43, 75–76, 214–15, 273–74; Robert M. Pirsig, *Lila: An Inquiry into Morals* (New York: Bantam, 1991); and Robert N. Bellah, Richard Marsden, William M. Sullivan, Ann Swindler, and Stephen M. Tipton, *Habits of the Heart: Individualism and Commitment in American Life* (Berkeley: University of California Press, 1985), 27–51.

34. Thus, DeMille introduces the concern of *The Ten Commandments* as "Whether man ought to be ruled by God's law or by the whim of a dictator like Rameses? Whether men are property of the state or free souls?" In case anyone misses this blatant moralizing, DeMille further opines that the same battle continues today (in the Cold War). Appropriately, the movie climaxes with the divine gift of the law at Sinai (which looks remarkably like the Paramount mountain!). As Seporah [sic] thereafter describes Moses as God's torch lighting the way to freedom, Moses poses in a fashion reminiscent of Lady Liberty. While Moses' final words—"Go, proclaim liberty to all nations"—allude to Jesus' Great Commission (Matthew 28:16–20), they also translate it into DeMille's law-and-order gospel.

35. Berger, *The Sacred Canopy*, 127–53, describes modern religion as a cheap form of family psychotherapy.

36. Notably, foreign films dominate this group. Incidentally, these are also the films most often approved by critics, whose self-identity is typically one of conscious alienation.

37. See Geertz's *The Interpretation of Cultures*, 91–94.

38. I follow here Jonathan Z. Smith's understanding of religion as interpretation or the production of a map by which to live. See, e.g., *Map Is Not Territory: Studies in the History of Religion* (Leiden: Brill, 1978), 88–103, 289–309; and *idem, To Take Place: Toward Theory in Ritual* (Chicago: University of Chicago Press, 1987), 1–23. I find *Map Is Not Territory*, 289–309, the most concise statement of Smith's understanding of religion. For an expanded treatment, see his *Drudgery Divine: On the Comparison of Early Christianities and the Religions of Late Antiquity* (Chicago: University of Chicago Press, 1990). Smith has developed his view of religion in conscious dialogue with

and critique of Eliade's famous notions of hierophany (see Mircea Eliade, *The Sacred and the Profane: The Nature of Religion,* trans. Willard R. Trask [New York: Harcourt Brace & World, 1959]). In a recent public lecture, Smith nicely illustrated his view by use of Borges' amusing "On Rigor in Science," a story about cartographers who made a map so like that which it mapped as to be unusable (see Jorge Luis Borges, *Dreamtigers,* trans. Mildred Boyer and Harold Morland [Austin:: University of Texas Press, 1964], 90). See the appendix below for a discussion of the portrayal of the sacred in film.

Chapter 2

Films without Heroes

Hence, the principal watchword for any photographically-based rendering of Christ as character was "reverence." To my knowledge, no filmed representation of Christ up to and including that found in From the Manger to the Cross *transgressed this understood cultural prohibition, to the extent that Christ becomes* the structuring absence within his own life story. *In stylistic terms, this translates into no attempt being made to invest Christ with the dimensions of character psychology. . . .*[1]

The So-Called Aesthetic Failure of the Jesus Films

When it comes to Jesus films, we prefer other stories. This preference is one of the ultimate bases of the judgment that the Jesus films are aesthetic failures. The other basis of the criticism is our ideological distance from the Jesus films. Thus, Stern, Jefford, and DeBona "guess" that a contemporary audience would be more likely to laugh at DeMille's *The King of Kings* than to applaud.[2] Having shown some of the religious spectacles to contemporary college students, I am inclined to agree. Students "appreciate" these films only if someone places them in a fairly detailed context. Otherwise, contemporary audiences find the films dated, sentimental, and "kitschy." The soft lighting, upward (to Jesus) camera angles, angelic choirs, and dazed faces are, as one recent student remarked to me, "just too much."

Today, audiences expect better technology and special effects and better (more sexy and/or violent) stories, all of which they can easily find in the action-adventure or blockbuster form.[3] While Jesus remains a cultural icon even in pluralist America, he is no longer a figure about whom the audience shares enough belief to justify the spectacle's astronomical expense. In the post-Christian situation, criticism of the aesthetic quality of the Jesus films is virtually a given.[4] We pluralists reject the spectacles because we do not wish to have the Protestant American metanarrative foisted on us.

We may also be ill disposed to the Jesus films because they are melodramas. Everyone receives his/her just deserts. Despite his unjust death, the hero's significance lives on through his resurrection, through his influence on his followers, or through his followers' (that is, Christianity's) triumph over Rome. The

21

villains (particularly Judas) also "get their comeuppance." In fact, the plot of the Jesus films often turns on the dramatic conversion (read "salvation" for true melo-dramatic effect) of some follower(s) and/or the degradation of some enemies.

Of course, this criticism applies to film broadly, because melodramatic for-mulas dominate Hollywood film. The good guys win; the hero never dies; and the boy gets the girl. Exceptions occur, but the pattern remains. Thus, while the hero of *Sommersby* does die, the film's denouement suggests the redemptive nature of the hero's death. The film's French precursor, *The Return of Martin Guerre*, sim-ply does not do so. Anecdotally, I remember watching Zeffirelli's *Hamlet* in the theater and hearing a woman opine at the film's end, "But, it's so sad; they all died." A heartfelt and genuine remark to be sure, but one nurtured by film's melodramatic, not tragic, conventions.

Criticism of the Jesus films for their compliance with Hollywood's melo-dramatic patterns may be somewhat unrealistic. Moreover, the criticism of melodrama reveals aristocratic prejudices, because Western critics have histori-cally preferred tragedy's "high art" to the popular forms of melodrama or com-edy. *Sullivan's Travels* takes as its premise just such prejudices. The story's hero, who has made many successful zany comedies, aspires to make the great American film. He goes on the road incognito to gather material, but one catastrophe after another besets him. Winding up in prison, he sees the joy that one of his come-dies brings to his fellow inmates during a viewing in an old, rural church. Ultimately, of course, he learns that his comedies have significance because they bring temporary release to people, and he returns to film more comedies. In short, *Sullivan's Travels* accepts, only to pillory, aristocratic prejudices against com-edy and melodrama.

Again, criticism of the melodrama depends on a particular worldview. To judge them unrealistic or fantastic by comparison to tragedy (or to some other pattern) depends on prior assumptions about the nature of reality. Such judg-ments likely depend upon whether one has a "healthy minded" or "sick-souled" view of life generally.[5] Of course, the melodramatic conversion formula of the Jesus films does look less realistic in post-Christian American than in the days of the Protestant American metanarrative. Since American culture has moved away from Christianity rather than toward it, American history has simply not replicated those conversion stories.[6]

In addition to blockbusters and tragedy, some of us also prefer the Gospel to Jesus films. Those trying to move from Gospel to film do face almost insu-perable problems:

Any film-maker approaching the life of Christ—be he exegete or hack—
is confronted with the same problem: the impossibility of piecing together

a screen play using only the dialogue and specific information available in the New Testament. From this simple fact emerge all kinds of agonizing and insoluble dilemmas. Shall we write "additional dialogue" for Christ? What kind of small talk did He make, for example, at the marriage feast of Cana? Shall we provide motivation where none exists specifically, e.g., for Judas' betrayal? How shall we establish the social, political, religious, etc., conditions of the world into which Christ came?[7]

Filmmakers have responded to this problem by filling in the gaps in the Gospels with fictionalized screenplays (or by inserting the Jesus story into another story). Those seeing the Gospel as truth decry these additions, apparently without recognizing that the Gospels are themselves already fictionalized to a greater or lesser extent. We, of course, notice and object to such fiction according to our own ideological light. Unless our worldview demands it, then, the Jesus films need not be faithful to the (true or fictional) Gospels.

Finally, we may not like the Jesus films because their stories are either too unfamiliar or too familiar for us. With respect to the first possibility, the Jesus films are noticeably different than other films. Their "hero" is neither an action hero nor the leading man of a romance. Jesus is pacifist and celibate.[8] Sex and violence, which we desire in our films, are absent or marginalized. Violence is in the hands of Jesus' opponents. Sex belongs to the enemy as well, as in DeMille's Mary Magdalene and in the Romans of the biblical epics, or is the road not taken, as in Scorsese's tempting visions.

Alternatively, the films are too familiar. We have heard this story before, and our society, born in revolution and trained by Madison Avenue, is fascinated by the new. Of course, film itself offers us relatively few plots: a hero wins; a boy gets a girl; a flawed character learns from his mistakes and becomes whole; and so forth. What film really offers is new incidents—special effects, interesting characters, and exotic locales—in a comfortably familiar structure (genre, plot).[9] With the Jesus story, then, our complaint is not that we know the plot. We always know the plot at the movies. It is simply that the "past" dominates the Jesus story so completely. If a director is to offer us new yet unobjectionable incidents, he/she must be incredibly imaginative. The fate of Scorsese's film is an instructive warning here. Not surprisingly, then, film has generally turned away from the relatively sparse Jesus story to Christ-figure films and to stories of other characters—real or fictional—that append on the Jesus story. These heroes, while suggesting Jesus by allusion or proximity, are more easily manipulated than the divine or iconic Jesus. Accordingly, eccentric characters and plots characterize the Jesus films (see figure 2).

Cinematically, spectacle dominates the films of DeMille, Ray, Stevens, Monty Python, and Scorsese. These films invest rather heavily in setting and scene, in elaborate re-creations of first-century Palestine, in battle scenes (Ray), and in panoramic photography (Stevens), rather than in the character of Jesus. Special effects (DeMille, Krish and Sykes, Zeffirelli) and song-and-dance routines (Jewison, Greene, Monty Python) are other centers of cinematic interest.

Narratively, the films are also not about Jesus. They are about innocents in all ages (Griffith), about other first-century Jews (Ray, Monty Python), about peasants in all times (Pasolini), or about Christ figures (Arcand). Their stories focus on miraculous deliverances (Griffith) and dramatic conversions (DeMille, the biblical epics, Zeffirelli). They present ideas, rather than stories (Stevens, Pasolini, Krish and Sykes, Greene). At times, they are simply about the struggle to understand Jesus (Ray, Jewison). Scorsese and Young are the exceptions. They focus literary attention on Jesus simply by placing him in a similarly difficult position. He is the one who struggles to understand (God).

Figure 2: Cinematic and Literary Focus

Film	Cinematic Focus	Story
Griffith	Disasters, escapes, and hope	Miraculous salvation of innocent couple
DeMille	Special effects	Conversion of Magdalene and degradation of Judas
Biblical epics	Spectacle	Conversion of main character
Ray	Spectacle, battle scenes	Judas' choice between Barabbas and Jesus
Stevens	Spectacle, Western scenes	Presentation of Jesus' ideas
Pasolini	Peasant life	Destruction of peasants by institution
Jewison	Song-and-dance routines	Struggle of Magdalene and Judas to understand Jesus
Greene	Song-and-dance routines	Enactment of parables and death of clown
Zeffirelli	Special effects; conversions	Conversion of apostles
Krish and Sykes	Special effects; conversions	John 3:16
Monty Python	Eccentric spectacle	Rome's unconscious destruction of nobodies
Scorsese	Spectacle and visions	Jesus' unsuccessful flight from God
Arcand	Struggles of troupe	Daniel's struggle for artistic purity and resulting death
Young	Family scenes	Jesus' coming of age

When it comes to Jesus films, then, we prefer to see Marcellus, Demetrius, Ben-Hur, Daniel Coulombe, and Maximus (Russell Crowe in *Gladiator*). We prefer these stories because we prefer the Hollywood hero to Jesus. We want interesting, identifiable heroes in film. Jesus is not that. We know him too well for him to interest us, but he is also too different from us to interest us. He has solved our problems—for example, of sex and violence—and is beyond them and us. Whether divine or icon, he is ideal, not real. Accordingly, we cannot identify with him except as the ideal other. He is not sufficiently human. Not surprisingly, then, cinematic and literary attention turns elsewhere. Jesus in film is objectified and externalized; he is the "lost original" of the Christ-figure films; he is the touchstone that generates various responses. As *Life of Brian* makes wonderfully clear, the Jesus films are follower films.

Spectacle and Epic: Externalized Heroes

Jesus is nonheroic for us because we have lost our sense of epic. According to Holman and Harmon, an epic is "A long narrative poem in elevated style presenting characters of high position in adventures forming an organic whole through their relation to a central heroic figure and through their development of episodes important to the history of a nation or race."[10] The crucial issues here are: 1) poetry; 2) lofty characters; and 3) cultural significance. Leaving aside poetry, Borges claims that the last epics were Hollywood spectaculars and, more specifically, Westerns:

> In a way, people are hungering and thirsting for epic. I feel that epic is one of the things that men need. Of all places (and this may come as a kind of anticlimax, but the fact is there), it has been Hollywood that has furnished epic to the world. All over the globe, when people see a western—beholding the mythology of a rider, and the desert, and justice, and the sheriff, and the shooting, and so on—I think they get the epic feeling from it, whether they know it or not.[11]

Borges said these words in the late 1960s. Since then, film has changed. Despite recent revivals, the change is obvious in many of the Westerns of the 1960s and 1970s, which detailed the end of the West/the Western (for example, *The Wild Bunch, Butch Cassidy and the Sundance Kid, The Shootist*). Compared to the classic Western, these Westerns seem "mean" and small. The epic world of the classic Western seems far away, for we no longer share their worldview.[12] Our pluralist culture, after the demise of the Protestant American metanarrative, does not have *a story* of national or cultural significance. Pluralism has many stories. They may reflect similar or limited (Hollywood) patterns, but incidents change endlessly in a fashion pleasing to our "revolutionary" and individualistic culture.

Further, epic heroes are not modern individuals. Achilles, Odysseus, Aeneas, Jesus, Shane—like their spectacular settings—are larger than life. They are monumental, external, without (understandable) motivations. Like all ancient characters, they are "flat," static, unchanging. They do not develop and surprise, like "real" individuals.[13]

A number of factors overdetermine this epic externality. First, the story and characters of epic are well known to their audiences. Epic poets begin *in medias res* and rely on audiences that delight in minor variations in the telling of the tale. That such characters' stories are well known, however, means that they do not really develop. They appear full-blown, developed, and complete. They are dominated by the past, their own and that of the cultures for whom they are emblems. Second, the epic poems are for the most part products of honor-shame (or Rome's pious duty) cultures. In such cultures, persons are what their peers deem them to be. People know themselves literally "through the eyes of others." In contrast to the intensely subjective modern world, ancient characters and stories have little "inside" to reveal. Third, the "development" of an ancient hero, then, is simply a matter of shifting (normally ascending) social locations, the rise to his appropriate career (for example, as king), and its fruition or his demise. It is not his development as a character or person that is interesting, but this ascending or descending plot. Plot dominates character. In fact, the important issue is normally the hero's fate (Achilles, Aeneas, Jesus) or his social location (Odysseus, Shane). Finally, the question of (ideological) interpretation does not arise with ancient epic. The singer and the audience share a common worldview. The hero, then, does not articulate his own personal position; he represents a known cultural value. The epithet does not merely describe the exemplary epic hero; the hero is reducible to the epithet: Raging Achilles, Cunning Odysseus, Pious Aeneas. The epithet says it all.

The Jesus of film—certainly of the spectaculars—is also so reducible (see figure 3). He is the Son of God, the innocent victim, the rebel, the social critic, the teacher, or the searcher. Beyond that, we know little about Jesus' interior life—even in Scorsese's visions—or his development. He is sheer externality. We know him only as he is seen by others (see the discussion of touchstones below) or in what he says or does. More importantly, his story is well known. He is dominated by his past, by his cultural significance, and by his fate. We know this story all too well even if we cannot explain its reasons or motivations. Only his fate explains his end. Thus, to this day, we cannot explain why Jesus died otherwise.

In fact, the Jesus of film differs notably from the epic hero only in his "meaning." Since the pluralization of America, Jesus does not have a culturally determined significance. Now, his "meaning" is a matter of ideology, context, and genre (see figures 1 and 3). His epic past and his continuing iconic significance leave Jesus as an external object, rather than as a modern character.

Figure 3: The Epithets and Genres of Jesus Films

Film	Genre	Epithet[14]
Griffith	Passion play + Christ figure	Innocent victim
DeMille	Visualized Bible	Son of God
Biblical epics	Biblical epic	Son of God
Ray	Biblical epic	Innocent victim/Ethical teacher
Stevens	Biblical epic	Ethical teacher/Son of God
Pasolini	"Documentary"	Social critic
Jewison	Passion play, musical	Rebel
Greene	Musical + passion play	Rebel
Zeffirelli	TV miniseries	Son of God
Krish and Sykes	"Documentary"	Son of God
Monty Python	Ironic epic	Innocent victim
Scorsese	Buddy movie	Searcher
Arcand	Passion play + Christ figure	Social critic
Young	Family TV	Modern hero

Our culture has quite different heroes,[15] who are more "realistic" to us. They resemble the hero of the novel more than the hero of the epic. We have more in common with Leopold Bloom (the hero of Joyce's *Ulysses*) than with Odysseus.[16] The hero of the novel and of much of film is the common man or woman. This person is inevitably out of joint with his/her situation, either being too much or too little for his/her location (for example, the heroes of Peter Weir's *Witness*, *Dead Poets Society*, and *The Truman Show*). This disjoint does not, however, create a study in the hero's social location or fate. The novel's hero is not constrained by his past. Instead, the hero has possibilities. We do not know his/her story (although we probably know the structural pattern). Unlike the epic, the novel has plot interest.[17] The novel and most film, unlike the epic, is an "invented" story.[18]

Further, the novel—whether it opts for an omniscient or limited narration—provides intensive, prolonged "inside views" of its hero. In fact, some twentieth-century novels are simply the hero's stream of consciousness. Here, subjectivity is everything. Two important consequences follow. First, this internalized character does not see himself/herself through the eyes of others. He/she has a divided self—a public and a private self. Character, not plot, makes the novel. Further, this character develops and changes through time. In fact, Scholes and Kellogg follow Forster in distinguishing the novel from ancient literature as "life by time" rather than "life by values."[19] Second, this hero has an ideological position to express.[20] Where the epic hero lives according to cultural values, the novel's hero takes a personal "stand" (expresses herself/himself) that generally does not agree at a critical point with his/her particular culture's worldview. As a result, we do not share these heroes' ideologies without thought. They, as they live, and we, as we read, interpret.

We easily identify with such characters, however. After all, they and we are creations of modernity. Their subjectivity matches our individualism. Their potential—their separation from a determining past—fits our sense of life's plasticity. The fact that there are multiple, unending stories to be told—instead of only one epic—also fits our pluralistic society.

The Jesus of the (epic) Gospels and of the spectaculars does not fit this ethos at all. He is not a common man (for our culture). He is an icon. He does not develop. His story is not new. His story is dominated by the past and by fate (God), not by his character. He has no subjectivity. Accordingly, we simply do not "get" him.

Of course, this distance is true for all (ancient)[21] epic heroes. My students do not "get" Achilles—no matter how much I talk about honor-shame cultures—nor Aeneas—no matter how much I talk about Roman piety. For them, Achilles and Aeneas are not heroic. Achilles is a whiny "drama queen," and Aeneas is a "heartless bastard." These are decidedly epithets, but hardly those attached to the same figures by ancient audiences and modern scholars. Similarly, the Jesus of the spectacles does not seem heroic to us. Exteriorized and idealized, he is a cardboard cutout. For contemporary audiences, he is not alive because he has no interior.

Ancient heroes live for modernity only when someone retells their stories as the adventures of every person. In such revisions, the hero's journey and struggles become symbolic of our struggle with inner demons. The mighty hero becomes the king within each of us. Myth and epic become psychology.[22] Scorsese and Young both move in this modern direction. Although Scorsese bases his story on a modern novel, his focus on a flesh-spirit dualism seems antiquated in the modern West. More importantly, Scorsese's Jesus remains too riven. His "success" comes too late to convince us of his heroism.

Only Young, then, renders Jesus as a successful modern hero. Young presents Jesus' story as his separation from his intimate, happy family and his close friends, Lazarus and Mary. Jesus is happy working with his father and contemplating marriage to Mary. Only when his father dies does his mother demand that he find his own unique answers. Thereafter, Jesus—although still happy and dancing—begins gradually and hesitantly, with his mother's support, to understand and follow his career. Notably, it is another death, that of his friend Lazarus, that sparks the final stage of his career. His own death in Jerusalem is decidedly penultimate, because several lengthy resurrection scenes, a climactic upper room encounter with all the disciples and his mother, and a special-effects departure reconfigure that death as triumph.

This story is a standard hero tale. The hero separates himself from his youthful embeddedness, undergoes various trials and temptations, and finally takes on his heroic (kingly) career. Following contemporary trends, Young has modernized this tale into a Freudian family drama. Thus, Jesus becomes messiah only when he "gets over" his father Joseph. Further, he never truly leaves his mother Mary. She is there as his mentor to the very end. Mary's continuing importance suggests, however, that Young is not completely satisfied with the Freudian drama, and that emphasis, along with Jesus' departure for the "spirit world," may indicate a Jungian conclusion. According to Jung, ego formation and separation are the work of the first half of life. In the second half of life, the hero reconnects with his unconscious. Jesus, then, fulfills both halves of the contemporary, psychological hero story by divorcing himself from his earthly father and by reuniting thereafter with his mother (a symbol of the unconscious for Jung) and with his heavenly father.[23]

As a result, Young's Jesus is not an epic hero, but a modern, psychologically developing hero à la Campbell and Jung. Accordingly, his journey is not outward into exotic lands, but inward into his inner psychological depths. As a result, despite the special-effects miracles, Young's Jesus has become a generic figure. His story is everyone's journey from Freudian childhood to Jungian maturation (if we make it that far). He differs from us only in special effects. He is no longer monumental.

The "Lost Original": Christ-Figure Films

Interestingly, Scorsese and Young have not been well received. Jesus remains too epic and iconic for such modernization. As most filmmakers and audiences desire a modern hero, Jesus generally becomes the "lost original." Christ figures efface and replace him. Ironically, historical critics claim that the church(es) similarly effaced Jesus, who was merely a precursor of the New Testament, Christianity, and the church, with the Christ of faith.[24] Of course, the critics claim to restore this "lost original" with their researches, but they actually replace the Christ of faith with modern, ideologically constructed Jesuses.[25] Christ-figure films stand, then, in a long tradition of replacement.[26]

In an oft-quoted essay on Christ figures in American fiction, Robert Detweiler distinguishes four different permutations of Christ (note that Jesus has already vanished) in literature: sign, myth, symbol, and allegory.[27] First, he isolates sign. Sign denotes while myth, symbol, and allegory connote. While signs are typical of evangelistic propaganda, myth, symbol, and allegory are more appropriate for imaginative creation. Second, he distinguishes direct (allegory) and allusive (symbol, myth) references to Christ and his story.[28] Finally, Detweiler separates signifiers that are marginal to their literary context (symbol) from those that dominate their context (myth). Detweiler, of course, provides many concrete examples of these distinctions: for example, the minister in *A Singular Life* (sign); Jim Casey in *The Grapes of Wrath* (myth); Jim Conklin in *The Red Badge of Courage* (symbol); and Billy Budd in *Billy Budd* (allegory). Detweiler also observes that with the demise of the Christian metanarrative, the Christ symbol is endlessly manipulatable.[29] When the Christian metanarrative dominated the West, Christ did not "mean" so variously.

Theodore Ziolkowski expands Detweiler's transformations. Less concerned with faith than Detweiler, he freely talks about Jesus, not Christ. Actually, his concern for issues of setting and time leads him to make a major distinction between two categories that I would label "Jesus" and "Christ." Additional concerns for setting and for degree of reference lead to subdivisions of these two major categories and the creation of an intermediate category. The first major category (Jesus) includes fictional biographies and stories of Jesus *redivivus*. The former fictionalizes the story of Jesus in its own setting (for example, *The Last Temptation of Christ*). The latter imagines Jesus' reappearance in a more recent time (for example, "The Grand Inquisitor"). The second major category (Christ) incorporates pseudonyms of Christ and fictional transfigurations of Jesus. The former depicts a hero who has some thematic connection—for example, as a redeemer—to Jesus. In the latter, Ziolkowski's own area of interest, a fiction's characters and actions reconfigure persons and events associated with the Gospels. Between the two major categories stands the *imitatio Christi* story in which the hero deliberately endeavors to live like Jesus.[30]

In essence, Ziolkowski's "Jesus" category deals with stories and signifiers that Detweiler ignores. His *imitatio Christi* resembles Detweiler's sign. His pseudonyms of Christ are like Detweiler's myth, and his fictional transfigurations of Jesus like Detweiler's allegory. Ziolkowski also observes that the transfigurations (either myth or allegory) can be offered in various spirits from faith to parody. In fact, he concludes that the history of the ideological manipulation of "Jesus" is roughly from tract to parody.[31] This trend, of course, reflects the demise of the Christian metanarrative.

For Baugh, the Christ figure has a theological as well as an artistic appeal:

> The Christ-figure is neither Jesus nor the Christ, but rather a shadow, a faint glimmer or reflection of him. As a fully human being, the Christ-figure may be weak, uncertain, even a sinner, that is may have all the limits of any human being in the situation at hand. The Christ-figure is a foil to Jesus Christ, and between the two figures there is a reciprocal

relationship. On the one hand, the reference to Christ clarifies the situation of the Christ-figure and adds depth to the significance of his actions; on the other hand, the person and situation of the Christ-figure can provide new understanding of who and how Christ is: "Jesus himself is revealed anew in the Christ-figure."[32]

By contrast, the Jesuses of film are dangerously unorthodox.[33] His remarks intrigue, because they suggest that Christ figures surreptitiously co-opt the Jesus signifier for some ideological program or imaginative work. The absent Jesus lurks in the background as an indisputable warrant. In fact, I am tempted to conclude that Christ-figure movies employ a rhetoric that resembles, while reversing, that of historical criticism. In both cases, that effaced—respectively, Jesus and Christ—authorizes the replacement, and the replacement becomes a safe haven for ideological work.[34] Historical criticism foregrounds Jesus, but the disappearing Christ authorizes historians' reconstructed Jesuses and their new ideologies. Without the depth of divinity or icon, the sign is hardly worth manipulating. Conjoining Christ-figure movies and historical criticism calls our attention to the reversibility of this semiotic process.[35]

With its embarrassing number of Jesuses (and/or Christs), Arcand's *Jesus of Montreal* exposes this semiotic process. In a roughly sequential order, the viewer sees a videotape of the Jesus of a traditional passion play, various Jesuses as Daniel researches a new play, the critically constructed Jesus of a "Deep Throat" librarian, and various statues and other iconic representations of Jesus. The troupe also tries out different Jesuses as they rehearse different methods of acting their new play. The new passion play presents the Jesus of Daniel's historical researches. When the authorities are shocked, they stop Daniel's play and revive the old passion play. Meanwhile, Daniel himself has begun to appropriate characteristics of Jesus, and he becomes a Christ figure himself. Finally, in a revealing conversation with Daniel, the priest Le Clerc admits that the church has known for a long time that it has obscured Jesus with Christ. Le Clerc, however, contends that this opiate is necessary for the people.

Arcand's "Jesus" is an endlessly manipulated sign. Unless it is Daniel as Christ figure, Arcand privileges none of them, and we are left with a confusion of signs and with a "stories alongside" pluralism. Further, unlike some, Arcand moves publicly back and forth between Jesus and Christ, exposing their connection and reversibility and the ideological work therein. Arcand's film, then, reminds us that Jesus is always an interpretative ideological construct and that Christ lurks to authorize Jesus (or vice versa).

In fact, if we "look hard" enough, we can see "Christ" casting its shadow upon and effacing the character of Jesus in most Jesus films. We can start with Tatum's distinction between Christ-figure films—films in which characters or events "substantially recall" the story of Jesus—and Jesus films, which he nicely designates as "bathrobe dramas."[36] This pithy tag notes that Jesus films are frequently set in a simulacrum of first-century Palestine. By this standard, Jewison, Greene, and Arcand made Christ-figure films, not Jesus films, because their films are not set in first-century Palestine.

The Christ figure also replaces Jesus when a film presents the Christ of the church, rather than a credibly human Jesus. Thus, the films of DeMille, Stevens, Zeffirelli, Krish and Sykes, and Pasolini efface Jesus with Christ, the ideological representative of the Protestant American metanarrative (DeMille, Stevens), of the ecumenical movement (Zeffirelli), of conservative evangelicalism (Krish and Sykes), or of Christian myth (Pasolini). Young's film probably also belongs here, as he offers Jesus by turns as the divine Christ of tradition and as the generic (psychological) everyman. Both moves efface Jesus' character.

Finally, Christ—not Jesus if we require a developed character for that sign—appears in several Jesus films at the level of Detweiler's symbol. He is a marginal character or sign providing interpretative depth and resonance for another story. Quite simply, Jesus is not the protagonist in Griffith, the biblical epics, Monty Python, or Arcand.

Only Ray and Scorsese remain. In this context, Ray's film is remarkably like that of Arcand, because Ray's Lucius highlights the conflict between tradition—the Protestant American metanarrative—and modernity's pragmatic, scientific worldview. Like Arcand, then, Ray's concern is semiotics, the debated character of the sign Jesus and its interpretation, not the character of Jesus. Finally, Scorsese himself denied that he had made a Jesus film. His opening titles claim that the film is based on Kazantzakis' novel of the same name and that it reflects the eternal conflict between the flesh and the spirit. Despite the film's simulacrum of first-century Palestine, this conflict is no more imaginable in that context than is the neo-Platonic Christ of the creeds.

On the bases of setting, protagonists, and ideological context, then, most Jesus films are Christ-figure films. Their Jesuses are not characters. I will tentatively except Ray, Scorsese, and Pasolini from this judgment. Even in them, however, Jesus is actually a cipher-sign, trailing behind it the divine or iconic Christ (Scorsese, Pasolini), or simply a site allowing reflections on the semiotic process itself (Ray; compare Arcand). In the other cases, Christ more completely overshadows Jesus.[37]

For the Jesus films, Jesus simply denotes Christ. The effaced Jesus functions not as a character but as a cipher for the depth, resonance, and authority of Christ. This constant interplay between Jesus and Christ reminds us that no "lost original" really exists; there are only signs in various contexts and intertexts; or, as Arcand makes wonderfully clear, there is only unending semiosis. In the

Jesus films, context and ideology—contests for power—are more important than (Jesus') character.

Our search for Jesus in film chases shadows and whispers. Jesus in film has no concrete reality; he is only a signifier; he is an intertext connecting a long history of stories and traditions or, better yet, a palimpsest upon which other searchers have written their own scripts.[38]

Jesus as Talismanic Touchstone

Film, with the exceptions of Scorsese and Young, simply does not delineate Jesus by the dimensions of character psychology. If we expect film to do so, we will be disappointed. Fascinated by Jesus' brilliant absence, we miss the fact that this absence structures the film. In short, in Jesus films, as in the Gospels, Jesus is mere talismanic touchstone. He is a reified blank. As other characters assign meaning to him, they display themselves.[39] To understand the Jesus films, we have to look away from Jesus to the stories of conversion and degradation swirling around his structuring absence.

The camera focuses on Ben-Hur, as we glimpse the hand of Jesus.

Film's reduction of Jesus to touchstone becomes quite clear when Scorsese restructures the pattern. He creates Jesus as a character by rendering God as the touchstone. Jesus himself becomes a follower of or a searcher for God. In fact, throughout most of Scorsese's film, Jesus tries vainly to escape God. In that respect, *Barabbas* is a more important precursor for Scorsese than *The King of Kings*. Scorsese arrives at this radical (for Jesus films) re-centering partly by camera work. As we have seen, DeMille introduced Jesus to the audience through the healed eyes of a blind girl. He and his successors consistently photograph Jesus from below. By contrast, Scorsese introduces us to Jesus asleep on the ground. We see him from above from a "divine perspective," and we hear his agonized "inside voice" as he reflects on the painful visions that represent God for him. Jesus has tried to rid himself of these voices by fasting and prayer. In fact, in the first extended action in the movie, Jesus makes crosses and helps the Romans crucify messianic pretenders in order to flee from God. He wants God to hate him. For him, God is fear. We also learn that he cannot escape this God. Thus, despite his attraction to Mary Magdalene, his devastating visions mean that she is simply not an option.

Various desert retreats and the interaction of Judas help Jesus define his mission and purpose, but his message confusingly evolves from (fear to) love to axe to death. On the cross, forsaken by God, Jesus has his last temptation. A young girl (Satan) invites him to leave the cross for a "normal" family life with various wives. In his vision, Judas convinces him that he has erred, and he returns to the cross to die as the messiah. For Scorsese, Jesus' death provides only his own "salvation." Here, then, Scorsese has transposed not only the touchstone pattern; he has also transfigured the cross. The cross remains revelatory, but only for Jesus. At the cross, Jesus is not forsaken (contrast Mark 15:34). Instead, he finds God—or at least what he thinks God demands of him. The successful nature of Jesus' quest (and his smiling death) stands in stark contrast to the ambiguous end of *Barabbas*: "Darkness . . . I give myself up into your keeping." Against the gospel tradition, however, Scorsese's cross unsettles. Jesus is no longer the touchstone. This Jesus struggles to define himself. Given his previous vacillation on this point, the smiling, strobe-light end is not very reassuring.

"Four Versions of Judas"

Most often, Jesus films create story by turning to other characters.[40] Most often, they turn to Judas.[41] With these films, as in Borges' "Three Versions of Judas," the Jesus story becomes the Judas story. Borges tells the tale of a modern gnostic who dismisses the gospel story of the betrayal of a public teacher by a handpicked disciple as incomprehensible. In response, he tells three increasingly fantastic stories: 1) of a Judas who was the human response to the divine Christ; 2) of a Judas who strove to be worthy of the divine revelation through a spiritual asceticism (the betrayal); and 3) of a Judas who was himself the incarnation.[42] The Jesus films are not so fantastic, but they are intrigued with the human Judas.

DeMille greatly expands the traditional betrayer by situating greedy Judas between equally greedy Caiaphas and the ethereal Jesus. Thus, Judas wishes to use Jesus' first miracles to make money. Further, at a climactic moment, DeMille juxtaposes Judas and Jesus. In the cleansed temple, before an adoring crowd, Jesus holds a lamb and refuses monarchy while Judas despairingly holds a crown. Thereafter, Judas betrays Jesus to Caiaphas for money. As Jesus dies, DeMille pairs Judas, who hangs himself with the rope used to bind Jesus, and Caiaphas, whose final prayer goes unheard as he watches the rent Temple veil burn. This "traditional" Judas is safely outside Christian orthodoxy.

Ray motivates Judas differently. In the manner of the biblical epics, Ray imagines Jewish freedom fighters struggling against the arrogant Roman Empire. Having watched other biblical epics, the viewers know, of course, that Jewish freedom fighters were not what overcame Rome. Rather, it was the message of Jesus Christ. When Ray's Judas faces a choice between the messiah of war (Barabbas) and the messiah of peace (Jesus), his choice seals his fate in the eyes of the better-informed audience. Judas vainly tries to chart a middle way between Jesus and Barabbas as he and Barabbas plot the nonviolent acclamation of Jesus as king in the Temple. Unbeknownst to Judas, however, Barabbas's real intention is war. While Jesus preaches peace in the Temple, the Romans destroy Barabbas's army. Judas, then, betrays Jesus to force him to use divine miracles against Rome. Instead, Jesus dies. In an important scene, Judas and Barabbas watch the crucifixion from afar as Barabbas wonders aloud why that man dies in his place. Later, but still during the crucifixion, Barabbas finds Judas hung, removes him from the tree, and holds him in a bleak Pietà. While more human than the Judas of the Gospels and of DeMille, this Judas still remains safely outside the Christian myth. In negative, he may be a dim analogue to Borges' spiritual ascetic, sacrificing himself in order to bring Jesus to Judas's understanding of the divine mission.

Jewison's Judas is far more fantastic. His is the voice that competes with Jesus' throughout the musical.[43] His constant theme is that Jesus is "just a man," because he wishes to strip the dangerous, messianic myth from the man Jesus. Like the priests with whom he allies, Judas finds Jesus a threat to Jerusalem's precarious order. Finally, he betrays Jesus because he thinks this is Jesus' own wish. Jewison's Judas is angry, fated. He, more than Jesus, is a victim. Feeling used, he hangs himself, claiming that God murdered him. Surprisingly, however, Jewison "resurrects" Judas for a heavenly song-and-dance routine featuring the title song, "Jesus Christ Superstar," as Jesus goes to the cross. In fact, at that crux, the camera focuses on Judas's resurrection rather than on Jesus' passion. Clearly, Judas and Jesus have swapped places. Jewison's Judas may not be Borges' divine Judas, but he is close. This Judas fantastically deconstructs the Christian myth.

Jewison's Judas corrects Jesus.

In contrast, Scorsese does not elevate Judas over Jesus. Instead, he treats them as "buddies." For Scorsese, Judas is as important a motivator as God for Jesus. In fact, other than Jesus, Judas is the first character that we see in the film. He bursts into Jesus' house to upbraid him for conspiring with the Romans. Later in the film, after Jesus has had several confusing visions, Judas arrives to kill Jesus. He does not only when Jesus tells him that the two of them together are God's plan. Thereafter, Jesus and Judas are on the most intimate of terms. In fact, Scorsese often photographs them (once asleep) together. In Jerusalem, Jesus decides God intends that he die. Judas is crucial to this plan, so Jesus reminds Judas that he promised to kill him and tells him that he (Judas) is God's instrument. Jesus even opines that Judas has the harder job. As in Jewison's film, Scorsese's Judas makes an important appearance during Jesus' crucifixion. In

Jesus' dream fantasy, he arrives, with the smell of smoke about him, in Jesus' home to report the destruction of Jerusalem. Motivated and enlightened by Judas, Jesus returns to the cross and his destiny. Again, while not exactly Borges' first Judas, this Judas is close to that character. It takes both of Scorsese's buddies to "get the (divine) job done."

These films find human interest in Judas. They focus on his understandable, if mistaken, human struggles with religion, wealth, ambition, and violence. Accordingly, their Judases are neither the traditional demonic figure mysteriously opposing a divine savior nor a gnostic/divine figure mirroring a divine/human Jesus. Instead, their Judases live in the human realm between demonic and divine others, between Christian myth and Borgesian fantasy.

Films without Heroes: Puppets on a String

When film does not efface Jesus with the more human Judas (or Brian), it replaces him with the institutional Christ (as we have seen). In Zeffirelli's movie, this replacement is most blatant. As Jesus slips away, the triumphant, apostolic church takes center stage.

In part one of his movie, Zeffirelli painstakingly portrays first-century Judaism—including synagogue services, debates over Torah and the Prophets, a betrothal, a wedding, a circumcision, a bar mitzvah, and a funeral. Zeffirelli's imaginative re-creation focuses on the marriage of Joseph and Mary and the early life of "their child." Notably, however, the Scriptures quoted and debated are more often about prophecies of the messiah than about living according to Torah. In short, Zeffirelli presents a Christianized form of Judaism. Everyone— even political leaders—waits for Jesus (the messiah). Part one's climax dramatizes the point when, in synagogue sermons, Jesus declares prophecy fulfilled. The majority of listeners violently reject him; only a minority accept him. Part three of the movie replays this same pattern in Jerusalem. Although the Sanhedrin rejects Jesus, Nicodemus watches the cross from afar, intones Isaiah 53, and whispers, "Born again." In sum, Zeffirelli is not depicting first-century Judaism; he is celebrating Christianity's replacement of Judaism.

In part two, Zeffirelli displays the apostolic character of this Christianity. Jesus is there, but he is not the narrative concern. The plot turns on the fate of John the Baptist and of Zealots who wish to use the Baptist's death as a pretext to revolt. Jesus' disciples are related to this revolt tangentially. Vignettes characterizing the disciples à la tradition provide additional "human interest": John is the man of the spirit; Andrew is the witness; Peter is the fiery fisherman; Matthew is the tax collector; Thomas is the doubter; Simon is a Zealot; and Judas is a manipulative intellectual. Zeffirelli makes the most of a rivalry between Peter and Matthew, which he resolves with Jesus' parable of the prodigal son (hardly a matter of apostolic management in Luke), and of the relationship of Simon and Judas to the Zealots. Part two has a twofold climax: the apostolic mission and the resurrection of Lazarus. This climax foreshadows respectively the mission and message of the apostolic church.

Part three's passion play visualizes the church's (death-) resurrection proclamation. Once again, the story is really about Judas. Believing he is following Jesus' wishes (anticipating Scorsese's Judas), Judas betrays Jesus to help him toward his peaceful monarchy (pace Ray's Judas) by providing him the opportunity to convince the Sanhedrin of his identity. Jesus' death destroys Judas's hopes, and Judas comes to his traditional fate.

Zeffirelli displaces Judas somewhat by inventing Zerah. In fact, Judas is Zerah's dupe (compare Stevens's use of the Dark Hermit). Like Jesus, Judas disappears. With Zerah, Zeffirelli offers a passion play in which none of the traditional characters—Judas, Jews, or Romans—are culpable. Thereby, Zeffirelli sanitizes the apostolic church's story for a pluralist age. Zeffirelli's film, perhaps more than any other Jesus film, thrives on absence. Judas, Judaism, and Jesus vanish beneath the monolithic, imperialistic, apostolic (should we say "divine"?) church (and Zerah, the excluded other). Surprisingly, Zeffirelli's conclusion foregrounds this disappearing act. The resurrection scenes confer authority on the church, but the film's last shot is of "empty" grave clothes at an "empty" grave.

Monty Python's Life of Brian exposes this magic trick with its own supercessionist parody. The troupe replaces Jesus Christ with Brian, just an ordinary, first-century Jew. To that end, the film concentrates its references to the Jesus story early (the magi, the Sermon on the Mount, the healings).[44] Thereafter, the film concentrates on Brian's passion because of his unfortunate involvement with various Jewish liberation movements. Notably, Monty Python's first-century Judaism is decidedly less monolithic than Zeffirelli's.

Brian escapes from the Romans, having been imprisoned in a failed attempt to kidnap Pilate's wife, only to fall afoul of various popular religious movements. He is mistaken for a prophet and then for a messiah. Parodying Christian sectarianism, Brian's followers disintegrate into rival parties, some of whom claim that the sandal is Brian's symbol and others the gourd. When Brian refuses to explain his teaching, they press him for his "secrets." When Brian denies that he is a messiah, they claim that only the true messiah would deny it. When he admits that he is the messiah to get rid of the crowd, the group unites to destroy the one unfortunate soul, the heretic, who doubts Brian's messianic identity.

All of this is a delightfully witty critique of followers, of people's desires for saviors and messiahs, and of their ability to make them out of virtually anything, even Brian or Jesus (compare *Being There, Santa Fe*). One of the most amusing moments in the film is when Brian tries to dismiss his followers by telling them, "You're all individuals." As if that is not ironic enough, the crowd then responds in unison, "We're all individuals."[45]

Here, of course, there is no monolithic apostolic church. Instead, the film offers multiple messiahs, as many as the crowds can conjure up, and even more sects that follow them. Thereby, the film exposes the church's construction of Jesus as messiah. *Life of Brian* reminds us of the absent hero and vacuous signifier at the heart of the Jesus films. If we remove the church's story or Judas's story from other films, no hero remains. As *Life of Brian* wittily reveals, the Jesus films are follower films. In film, as in Western culture and gospel, Jesus is sign, not character. Apart from Christianity, Jesus is a blank upon which anything (even Brian or Judas) can be written. The Jesus films, then, are films without heroes.[46] The manipulation of signs—interpretation—remains.

Notes

1. Charles Keil, "*From the Manger to the Cross:* The New Testament Narratives and the Question of Stylistic Retardation," in Cosandey, Gaudreault, and Gunning, eds., *Une Invention Du Diable?* 114. Emphasis added.

2. Stern, Jefford, and DeBona, *Savior on the Silver Screen*, 48.

3. While *Demetrius and the Gladiators* may not play well today, *Gladiator* does. For a comparison of the new spectacles with the old, see Steve Neale, *Genre and Hollywood* (London: Routledge, 2000), 91–92.

4. See Bruce Babbington and Peter William Evans, *Biblical Epics: Sacred Narrative in Hollywood Cinema* (Manchester and New York: Manchester University Press, 1993), 1–7.

5. See William James, *The Varieties of Religious Experience: A Study in Human Nature* (Cleveland, Ohio: Fountain Books, 1977), 92–171.

6. Incidentally, while the Christian melodrama is not a realistic portrayal for pluralist Americans, the melodrama seems an appropriate choice for the Jesus story, because the Christian Bible and the canonical version of the Jesus story have a comic (I prefer melodramatic) worldview. Compare D. D. Raphael, *The Paradox of Tragedy* (Bloomington: Indiana University Press, 1960), 37–68; Northrop Frye, *The Great Code* (New York: Harcourt Brace Jovanovich, 1982), 169–98; and Conrad Hyers, *The Comic Vision and the Christian Faith: A Celebration of Life and Laughter* (New York: Pilgrim, 1981). David M. Gunn, "The Anatomy of Divine Comedy: On Reading the Bible as Comedy and Tragedy," *Semeia* 32 (1984): 115–16, has insightful objections.

7. Moira Walsh, in Tatum, *Jesus at the Movies*, 7. On the difficulty of moving from Gospel to film, see ibid., 6–12; Lloyd Baugh, *Imaging the Divine: Jesus and Christ-Figures in Film* (Kansas City, Mo.: Sheed & Ward, 1997), 3–6; and William R. Telford, "Jesus Christ Movie Star: The Depiction of Jesus in the Cinema," in Marsh and Ortiz, eds., *Explorations in Theology and Film*, 124–30. Film's

realistic photography presents its own problems. Some actor must play Jesus; therefore, what star—and the new "thing" that we often go to see at the movies is some favorite star's new role—plays Jesus? The very physical presence of the star will carry the intertextual allusions of all his/her other roles and his/her own persona with it and impact the Jesus story accordingly.

8. See Telford, "Jesus Christ Movie Star," 128–29.

9. Compare Robert E. Scholes and Robert Kellogg, *The Nature of Narrative* (Oxford: Oxford University Press, 1966), 238–39.

10. Hugh C. Holman and William Harmon, *A Handbook to Literature*, 6th ed. (New York: Macmillan, 1992), 171.

11. Jorge Luis Borges, "The Telling of the Tale," *Atlantic Monthly* (September 2000): 65.

12. The spectacle continues as the action/adventure (or blockbuster). Such films frequently privilege action or special effects (that is, incident) over narrative unity. Further, while the action/adventure has cultural significance (or evidences a mythology), it often has an ironic (and individualistic), rather than epic, sense. Maximus (and even Ben-Hur) is more clearly a detached individual than are Gilgamesh, Achilles, and Aeneas. While rumors of new Jesus spectaculars persist, after the relative "failures" of Ray and Stevens, directors have turned to other venues for Jesus films—to the musical, to TV, to independent production, and to Christ-figure films. The era of the biblical spectacle ended with the increasing popularity of TV, the increasingly youthful and anti-traditional audience of film, and the liberalizing of censorship. See Babbington and Evans, *Biblical Epics*, 1–24; and Telford, "Jesus Christ Movie Star," 115–19.

13. The classic distinction between "flat" and "round" (lifelike) characters is found in E. M. Forster, *Aspects of the Novel* (New York: Harcourt, Brace & World, 1954), 103—18. Forster, ibid., 118, summarizes succinctly, "The test of a round character is whether it is capable of surprising in a convincing way. If it never surprises, it is flat. If it does not convince, it is a flat pretending to be round. It has the incalculability of life about it—life within the pages of a book." For a debunking of the notion of "real" characters, see William H. Gass, "The Concept of Character in Fiction," in Michael J. Hoffman and Patrick D. Murphy, eds., *Essentials of the Theory of Fiction* (Durham, N.C.: Duke University Press, 1986), 267–76. Seymour Chatman, *Story and Discourse: Narrative Structure in Fiction and Film* (Ithaca, N.Y.: Cornell University Press, 1978), 107–38, provides a nice introduction to the debate between structuralists (who see character as a plot function) and "realists" (who see character as a simulacrum of a person). While most scholars agree that ancient characters are flat, Robert Alter, *The Art of Biblical Narrative* (New York: Basic Books, 1981), 114–30, finds biblical characters surprising because they are animated by a rhetoric of divine sovereignty and human freedom.

14. Tatum, *Jesus at the Movies*, provides distinctive "tags" for each Jesus film that distinguish the various Jesuses more specifically: e.g., DeMille, healer; biblical epics, crucified redeemer; Ray, messiah of peace; Stevens, incarnate Word; Zeffirelli, suffering servant; and Scorsese, reluctant messiah.

15. Aeneas is as clearly Roman as Odysseus is Greek, as Rama is Indian, and as Shane is American. Thus, William Doty, *Mythography: The Study of Myths and Rituals*, 2nd ed. (Tuscaloosa: University of Alabama Press, 2000), 64, says, "The history of the ways the heroic is defined

will be as well the history of the definition of selfhood: active or passive, conquering or receptive, critical toward or accepting of traditional models, and so on. . . ." See also *idem*, "From the Traditional Monomythic Hero to the Contemporary Polymythic Hero/ine," *Forum* 8 (September/December 1992): 337–69; and Dean A. Miller, *The Epic Hero* (Baltimore: Johns Hopkins University Press, 2000), 1–69.

16. For helpful discussions of the epic and the novel, see Scholes and Kellogg, *The Nature of Narrative*; and M. M. Bakhtin, "Epic and Novel," in Hoffmann and Murphy, eds., *Essentials of the Theory of Fiction*, 48–69. The contrast between Bloom and Odysseus comes from Scholes and Kellogg, *The Nature of Narrative*, 164.

17. Bakhtin, "Epic and Novel," 59, 63–64.

18. Borges, "The Telling of the Tale," 64, says that we began to invent artificial and trivial stories about ordinary people in ordinary situations at the end of the eighteenth century.

19. *The Nature of Narrative*, 169. See Forster, *Aspects of the Novel*, 44–68.

20. Bakhtin, "Epic and Novel," 64–65.

21. I add "ancient" because my students seem to "get" Luke Skywalker, Neo, Maximus, and Frodo Baggins. They do not "get" the hero of the classic Western. I am still musing over this difference. Is it simply a phase in popular genres? Is it that ancient epic, Jesus films, and the Western are passé while science fiction and fantasy are fashionable? Maximus seems to belie that answer. Is it a move from utilitarian to expressive individualism? Once again, Maximus (and others) seemingly belies the answer, but perhaps we "get" him because we see his apparently stoic life as an expressive lifestyle choice, rather than something dictated by God/culture (as in the Jesus story). Notably, Neo becomes the hero of *The Matrix* only after the Oracle deceives him about his "fate." He can be the modern hero only if he is not fated. He must choose his destiny.

22. Joseph Campbell, *The Hero with a Thousand Faces* (Princeton, N.J.: Princeton University Press, 1972), 256. Rollo May, *The Cry for Myth* (New York: Dell, 1991), claims that psychotherapy has replaced mythology in modernity. For a critical analysis of the three major analyses of hero myths—Campbell, Rank, and Raglan—see Robert A. Segal, *Theorizing about Myth* (Amherst: University of Massachusetts Press, 1999), 117–41. Only Raglan takes a nonpsychological approach. Liberal Christianity also takes a modern approach by conceiving Jesus as model (to be imitated), rather than as transcendent savior.

23. Compare Segal, *Theorizing about Myth*, 84–86, 99–115, 125–29.

24. See Rudolf Bultmann, *Theology of the New Testament*, 2 vols., trans. Kendrick Grobel (New York: Scribner's, 1955), 1:3, 33.

25. These Jesuses are often indistinguishable from the heroes of novels (see, e.g., Ernst Renan, *The Life of Jesus* [New York: Modern Library, 1927]).

26. On Christ-figure films, see Neil P. Hurley, "Cinematic Transfigurations of Jesus," in May and Bird, eds., *Religion in Film*, 61; Peter Malone, *Movie Christs and Antichrists* (New York: Crossroad, 1990); and Baugh, *Imaging the Divine*, 109–237.

27. Robert Detweiler, "Christ and the Christ Figure in American Fiction," *The Christian Scholar* 47, no. 2 (1964): 113–19.

28. This distinction dominates the brief discussion in Tatum, *Jesus at the Movies*, 209–14.

29. Detweiler, "Christ and the Christ Figure in American Fiction," 112–13, 120–21. Hurley, "Cinematic Transfigurations of Jesus," 62–66, distinguishes the religiously faithful from the culturally iconic presentations.

30. Theodore Ziolkowski, *Fictional Transfigurations of Jesus* (Princeton, N.J.: Princeton University Press, 1972), 3–29.

31. See ibid., 270–98.

32. Baugh, *Imaging the Divine*, 112.

33. Ibid., 109–12, 234–37.

34. Compare John Dominic Crossan, *The Historical Jesus: The Life of a Mediterranean Peasant* (San Francisco: HarperSanFrancisco, 1991), xxviii, who says, "It is impossible to avoid the suspicion that historical Jesus research is a very safe place to do theology and call it history, to do autobiography and call it biography."

35. To change the image, we might simply say that "Jesus" is intertextual. That sign cannot appear without trailing other signs, texts, and contexts, most notably the notion of Christ. Put differently, Jesus is like a well-known actor that we have seen many times before. When we see him in a new role, his old roles attend us like some dimly seen choir of angels.

36. Tatum, *Jesus at the Movies*, vii, 209.

37. Some films doubly efface Jesus, replacing him not only with the Christ, but also with an actor playing Jesus (Jewison, Arcand), a clown (Greene), other innocent victims in history (Griffith, Ray, Pasolini), or Brian (Monty Python).

38. Jorge Luis Borges' short piece, "The Approach to Al-Mu'tasim," in *Ficciones*, trans. Anthony Kerrigan (New York: Grove, 1962), 37–43, provides a nice illustration (by analogy) of this unending, interchanging semiosis. Borges' narrator-reviewer describes a "fictional" novel, *The Approach to Al-Mu'tasim*, whose hero obsessively searches for the "more complex interlocuter" suggested by his conversations with the vile. The novel ends as the hero enters a room from which the voice of Al-Mu'tasim has issued. Borges' narrator-reviewer describes this novel as a sophomoric allegory of the mystic's quest for God. From a "lost original," an earlier version of this novel known only to himself, this narrator re-creates a "better story" in which Al-Mu'tasim is himself searching for someone (the historical Jesus?) and so on ad infinitum, creating a story about an endless succession of searchers (read "interpreters"). The interpreters, of course, become "sophomoric" mystics, and we have returned to the story's beginning without knowing it. The interchanging semiosis includes all, and no sign's meaning remains stable.

39. Melville's famous whale functions similarly. Thus, my wife, who teaches *Moby-Dick*, repeatedly tells her students, "It's just a whale." Despite lengthy chapters on the whale's "meaning" (e.g., "The Quarter-Deck," "Moby Dick," and "The Whiteness of the Whale"), Moby Dick has no final signification. Instead, against the blank of Moby-Dick, Melville spins a tale about life's opacity and our tendency to assign meaning (to signify). These assignations reveal more about our character than that of the touchstone. See the chapter entitled "The Doubloon." Therein, after Ahab nails a doubloon to the mast for he who first espies Moby, a series of soliloquies by various characters reveal their inmost selves.

40. The biblical epics and Christ-figure films create new stories. Jesus films often create new characters (e.g., Ray's Lucius, Stevens's Dark Hermit, and Zeffirelli's Zerah). They also expand gospel characters like Mary Magdalene (in DeMille, Jewison, Scorsese), Mary, the mother of Jesus (along with Joseph in Young), Pilate, Herod, various religious leaders (in numerous films), John the Baptist (Ray, Zeffirelli), and Lazarus (Stevens).

41. On the developments of Judas's story in the Gospels and in scholarship, see Frank Kermode, *The Genesis of Secrecy: On the Interpretation of Narrative* (Cambridge, Mass.: Harvard University Press, 1979), 75–99; Stern, Jefford, and DeBona, *Savior on the Silver Screen,* 169–71; and William Klassen, *Judas: Betrayer or Friend of Jesus?* (Minneapolis, Minn.: Fortress, 1996).

42. The story is in Borges, *Ficciones,* 154–56.

43. The actor playing Judas has the superior singing voice. Why would one cast so? The actor playing Jesus has a higher voice and the actor playing Judas has a lower voice. Does this suggest a contrast between the spiritual (or mythical for Jewison) and this-worldly practicalities? Is it important that a black actor plays Judas?

44. On the intra-Christian character of *Life of Brian,* see Carl Dyke, "Learning from *The Life of Brian:* Saviors for Seminars," in Aichele and Walsh, eds., *Screening Scripture,* 229–50. Notably, Monty Python replaces Jesus with Brian, but Christ, even if it is the Christ of the Hollywood epics, remains. The result throws an eccentric light on the interplay of the "Christ" and "Jesus" signs that I have discussed before. In fact, Monty Python's replacement (amusingly) deconstructs the standard switches.

45. This scene is a far simpler demonstration that individualism is a corporate myth than is Bellah et al., *Habits of the Heart.*

46. I allude here to Thackery's *Vanity Fair,* subtitled *A Novel without a Hero.*

Chapter 3

On Earth as in Heaven:
Jesus of Montreal and Mark

This type of interpretation [typology] obviously introduces an entirely new and alien element into the antique conception of history. For example, if an occurrence like the sacrifice of Isaac is interpreted as prefiguring the sacrifice of Christ, so that in the former the latter is as it were announced and promised, and the latter "fulfills" (the technical term is figuram implere) *the former, then a connection is established between two events which are linked neither temporally nor causally—a connection which it is impossible to establish by reason in the horizontal dimension (if I may be permitted to use this term for a temporal extension). It can be established only if both occurrences are vertically linked to Divine Providence, which alone is able to devise such a plan of history and supply the key to its understanding. The horizontal, that is the temporal and causal, connection of occurrences is dissolved; the here and now is no longer a mere link in an earthly chain of events, it is simultaneously something which has always been, and which will be fulfilled in the future; and strictly, in the eyes of God, it is something eternal, something omni-temporal, something already consummated in the realm of fragmentary earthly event.*[1]

Reading Mark and *Jesus of Montreal*

As a gospel, Mark announces the good news of Jesus' proclamation of the kingdom of God in Galilee, but Galilee is not receptive—or, at best, is only partially receptive—to the kingdom. In particular, the powers-that-be resist Jesus' kingdom. While the people are intrigued, Jesus goes largely unrecognized (save by the demons) until, at the story's peripatia, Peter acknowledges Jesus as the messiah. Then, Jesus immediately and repeatedly instructs his disciples on his upcoming death. The disciples do not understand his ironic reversal of the notion of messiah; nonetheless, they follow him to Jerusalem. Although he is acclaimed as king by the people, the powers-that-be conspire to crucify Jesus. Before his death, Jesus predicts an apocalypse that will consume these powers. Although Jesus is deserted by his disciples and by God, a Roman centurion acknowledges him as the Son of God at his death. Women watch from afar, visit his empty tomb where a mysterious man informs them of his resurrection, and flee in frightened silence. So ends Mark's good news.

In Denys Arcand's *Jesus of Montreal*, an actor, Daniel Coulombe, modernizes a traditional passion play at a priest's invitation. Daniel, an artist of integrity, assembles a bedraggled troupe and researches Jesus and the passion. His inquiry leads to a dramatically nontraditional play featuring a radical version of scholarship's historical Jesus. An appalled church resists Daniel's modernization with predictable consequences. Maintaining his artistic integrity, Daniel persists with a renegade production of the play against the church's wishes and, in the process, is mortally wounded. Before he dies, he deliriously predicts the apocalyptic doom of his society. After his death, his remains are literally and symbolically divided as his organs are harvested and his troupe shares in the largess of his legacy.

Despite their historical, cultural, and generic differences, Mark and *Jesus of Montreal* create similar affective, aesthetic experiences for their readers and viewers.[2] Both live in and create apocalyptic worlds. Both have unlikely, surprising heroes. Both confuse boundaries chaotically. Both stories function imperialistically. At least, their stories linger. Finally, both depend heavily on typological hermeneutics.

Doomed Temples and *The Decline of the American Empire*

Apocalyptic seers live in worlds of "radical exile"[3] in which their world has become entirely corrupt. None of the traditional institutions provide avenues to good lives any longer. Accordingly, apocalyptic seers create (or come from) sects, movements that have separated from the larger society. They separate, of course, in order to become pure, and then, to maintain their purity. They are the righteous vis-à-vis the impure, corrupt social and natural world. Accordingly, the seers envision that larger world in bestial, demonic, or mechanistic (in recent Hollywood apocalypses) terms and their own sects as truly human.[4] The seers demand allegiance to the sectarian tradition and hostility to the world as proof of sectarian purity. Generally, the tradition comes from a bygone day, and, accordingly, the sect has a nostalgic longing for "the good old days." Given the world's unrelieved corruption, the seer himself/herself and his/her visions are the sole avenues to life-giving knowledge. The seer often makes these visions available for the faithful in a book. On occasion, the visionary book is attributed pseudonymously—in keeping with sectarian nostalgia—to some ancient worthy. The book (and/or the seer's vision) is typically about the other, heavenly world that actually controls this world or about the upcoming end of this age or of history itself. In their happy purity, the sect voyeuristically awaits this end and the world's damnation.

Biblical scholars generally date "classic" apocalypses to a fairly specific time period, from the second century B.C.E. to the second century C.E. In the Christian canon, Daniel 7–12 and Revelation are the classic examples of apocalypses, but Paul and Mark are also notably apocalyptic in worldview. The classic apocalypses reflect the frustrations of natural, traditional religions in the face of new world empires. In the old natural religions, political, economic, and religious authorities were one or at least worked together harmoniously. In that situation, to be good religiously meant to prosper politically and economically. The new empires destroyed that cozy arrangement and installed their own ways of being and having it good. One either adapted to this situation or one—particularly one who strove to maintain traditional purity—risked falling behind the success curve. The result, for the intransigent, was a clash of myths. Apocalypses like Daniel 7–12 and Revelation imagine this clash in gruesome, gothic detail. They also await, in a highly reactionary mode, the restitution of their lost natural religion.[5]

Such clashes extend beyond these four centuries. Bryan Wilson, for example, depicts more recent colonial resistance to empire as manifestations of apocalyptic sectarianism.[6] Millennial movements—in which some pure sect damns the world and awaits the end—are also quite common in the history of Christianity. American Christianity, partly because of its inherently sectarian nature, has been particularly prone to such apocalyptic visions.[7]

Accordingly, Hollywood has made many movies about end-time catastrophes. Despite their capitalist and imperial might, Americans are often uncertain about the future because of modernization, mechanization (including computers), nuclear weapons, ecology, big business, big government, and so forth. Typically, Hollywood apocalypses imagine catastrophes brought about by or imminent because of some human or natural actions. They also imagine that these catastrophes can be avoided or reversed by practical, generally technologically adept heroes. Instead of a supernatural replacement of a demonic world, Hollywood imagines the human restoration of a fundamentally good (present American) society. In short, Hollywood apocalypses tend to name and localize American anxieties and to imagine their successful denouements. In fact, we might think of Hollywood apocalypses as managing frustrations with "the American Dream." In Hollywood apocalypses, business ultimately goes on as usual. Ancient apocalypses are more fatalistic and hope for more radical change.[8]

Hollywood's hero movies also have this "modern" apocalyptic flavor. In a typical hero movie like *Shane,* a good society has gone bad. Evil ruffians and institutions rule the day, but a hero comes to town. The hero may suffer, but he maintains his integrity. In fact, quite often the hero is the last remaining bastion of purity and goodness. When matters are bleakest and the odds seemingly insurmountable, the unlikely hero restores—usually violently—a lost paradisal order.[9]

In this modern sense, Arcand's *Jesus of Montreal* is apocalyptic.[10] The world and its institutions are corrupt, as various scenes indicate. First, in a secret meeting with a "Deep Throat" academic, Daniel learns that scholars know the "truth" about Jesus but remain silent because of their fear of the church. Second, two crucial, connected scenes expose the corrupting influences of consumer society. In a modern replica of Jesus' temptation, Richard Cardinal—a svelte, sleazy lawyer—entices Daniel to cash in on his temporary fame. The price, of course, is Daniel's artistic integrity. Later, Daniel, à la Jesus' "cleansing of the temple," upsets a beer commercial in order to save his disciple Mireille, the model, from degradation. These two scenes suggest that everything in Montreal (and the rest of the world, I suppose) is for sale, even a model's body and an artist's integrity. Third, before the final performance of the modernized passion play, Father Le Clerc admits to Daniel that his revised play is closer to the "truth" than the church's message is; however, Le Clerc justifies the church's lies by claiming that the faithful need illusions.

The major institutions of Montreal—the academy, the law, business, advertising, and the church—are corrupt and devoid of life-giving power. Not surprisingly, then, *Jesus of Montreal* begins with the performance of a Dostoevskian play reflecting on the death of God. One character, played by Pascal, claims that the other's denial of God's existence has led him to commit murder. Then Pascal hangs himself, rejecting God and embracing the void.

As the audience (characters within the film) reflects upon this play, a woman announces that she wants Pascal's "head." She means, of course, that she wishes to uses Pascal's image for an advertising campaign. The character conversing with her laments that Pascal is too "pure" (artistically) to do commercials. The camera then switches to Pascal, who points Daniel out to his troupe of admirers as the one greater—in artistic integrity—than himself. Clearly, Pascal is an anti-type of John the Baptist. Unlike the Gospels' Baptist, however, Pascal does not maintain his integrity. At the film's end, his "head" is on a subway billboard. Pascal has betrayed art.[11] As a result, Arcand's world is more degraded than that of Mark.

The Dostoevskian play in *Jesus of Montreal* adapts the complicated relationships between two of the brothers in *The Brothers Karamazov*, Smerdyakov (Pascal) and Ivan.[12] Smerdyakov, the bastard son of Fyodor Karamazov, takes Ivan's "death of God" ethic seriously and kills their father. Failing to gain his brother's acceptance and approval, Smerdyakov hangs himself in despair. Dostoevsky, however, only reports Smerdyakov's hanging. Further, Dostoevsky does not end his novel with that event. He has the other brothers' stories to tell, so he traces Ivan's temporary insanity, Dmitry's unjust condemnation for his father's death and subsequent imprisonment, and Alyosha's graveside hopes. The story of the last two brothers suggests pointedly that new life can come through a purifying suffering (compare his *Crime and Punishment*).

By ending with the hanging, Arcand creates a bleaker, more clearly existentialist tale. Arcand's Smerdyakov, like a modern existentialist, embraces his own death (and the void) by denying any supporting essentialism. He becomes authentically himself by willing his own death. Dostoevsky's eschatological hope—and that of ancient apocalyptic—has vanished in Arcand's adaptation.[13]

Arcand's tenuous hope lies in art's purity, a hope endangered by Pascal's apostasy. The film's denouement, which includes a meeting between Daniel's disciples and the sleazy lawyer to discuss capitalizing on Daniel's legacy, further diminishes such hopes. Sectarian purity exists only temporarily, because Daniel's troupe apostatizes beyond his death. Thereafter, hope flickers only in Mireille's refusal to join the troupe's capitalization of Daniel.[14]

The radical exile of *Jesus of Montreal* is not only less hopeful than ancient apocalyptic, it is also less nostalgic.[15] The nostalgia is largely confined to the rewritten passion play, which Daniel modernizes but does not abandon. Of course, given his ecclesiastical patron and specific commission, he is not really at liberty to do so.

Further, the mortally wounded Daniel's subway rant is more damning of the surrounding world than is its Markan precursor.[16] Abandoned by his male disciples, Daniel discusses the meaning of life with his female disciples in the subway and predicts the demise of these buildings (compare Mark 13:2). When he

Daniel's apocalyptic rant before Pascal's "head," the abomination of desolation.

sees Pascal's "head" on a billboard, he retches, warns the people in the subway of the abomination of desolation, and instructs them to flee (compare Mark 13:14–18). He predicts the arrival of false prophets, the shaking of the powers of heaven, and the judgment (compare Mark 13:21–25). Because no one knows the time, he tells those who hear, "Watch" (compare Mark 13:34). Then Daniel collapses, never to speak again.

Comparing this speech to Mark 13 is quite revealing.[17] First, this abomination of desolation is the Baptist's betrayal of artistic integrity, rather than the profanation of the Jerusalem Temple. Second, all references to the Gospel, the Son of Man, and God are missing in Daniel's thoroughly secular apocalypse. Daniel's auditors have only their own human strength to rely on (in contrast to Mark 13:11, 20, 27). As a result, *Jesus of Montreal* lives in a more unrelieved exile than does Mark. At least Mark's disciples can rely on God, as Jesus does in Gethsemane, and can hope that God might shorten the time of the apocalyptic woes (Mark 13:20).[18] Accordingly, Arcand's mysterious young man in white (a doctor) announces Daniel's death, not his resurrection, to the women disciples (contrast Mark 16:5–7).

In contrast to Arcand's call to existential self-fashioning, Mark offers an eschatological gospel of divine salvation. Jesus proclaims this kingdom in both Galilee (Mark 1:14–16) and Jerusalem (Mark 11:1–10); however, the kingdom does not arrive.[19] Conflict dominates both the Galilean and Jerusalem ministries (Mark 2:1–3:6; 11:27–12:40). In Galilee, when Jesus first enters a synagogue, he exorcises a demon (Mark 1:21–28, 39). Clearly, these holy places are corrupt. Jesus' exorcism of "Legion" (Mark 5:1–20) damns Roman military and political institutions (and Roman occupation of Palestine) as well. Arriving in Jerusalem, Jesus continues to damn corrupt institutions. Intercalated around the "cleansing of the temple" (11:12–24), the cursed fig tree depicts Jesus' disgust with Jerusalem's institutions. In fact, this intercalation and the Markan apocalypse (Mark 13) render Jesus' Temple act a symbolic destruction of the Temple, rather than a "cleansing."[20]

Like apocalyptic and Arcand, Mark imagines a pure sect in the midst of this corruption. Here, too, people leave their quotidian lives to follow the hero (Mark 1:16–20; 3:13–19). If they are not the botched and the bungled,[21] neither are they the elite. Only a common commitment to the will of God holds the sect together (Mark 3:31–35). They are the good ground to which Jesus entrusts the secrets of the kingdom (Mark 4:1–34).[22]

As in Jesus of Montreal, the sect does not withstand the apocalyptic crisis well. Only Jesus—abandoned by everyone including God at the gospel's climax— and the women who watch from afar (compare Daniel's female disciples) are true believers. Jesus' male disciples, like Daniel's, vanish. We should not be surprised, for even though they were privy to the kingdom's secrets in Galilee, they remained blind, deaf, and hard-hearted (Mark 8:14–21). Not incidentally, Jesus uses similar language to describe outsiders in Mark 4:12.[23] Despite identifying Jesus as the messiah and being privy to lengthy instructions about the upcoming passion, the disciples never understand Jesus' teaching (Mark 9:32; 10:32–45). During his passion, then, they betray, deny, and flee (Mark 14:17–72). At the gospel's end, they are not (yet?) recouped.[24]

Nevertheless, Mark has more hope than Arcand.[25] Historical critics generally date Mark ca. 70 C.E. They do so largely because of Mark 13, which appears to be a fair description of events around Jerusalem at that time. If so, Mark deliberately connects Jesus' proclamation of the kingdom in Galilee with his death, the destruction of the Temple, and the hope of a renewed kingdom in Galilee shortly thereafter. As a result, Mark has no resurrection appearances.[26] Mark expects parousia appearances in Galilee instead. For Mark, no real time exists between Jesus' death, Mark's writing, the Temple's destruction, and the arrival of the apocalyptic kingdom. Mark's readers, like Markan disciples, wait for Jesus in Galilee (Mark 16:7).[27] Put differently, Mark's end (Mark 16:7) repeats (and transforms, without fulfilling) Jesus' proclamation of the kingdom's arrival in Galilee (Mark 1:15).

All this is more hopeful than the frustration of Arcand's worlds, a frustration that becomes almost unbearable in *The Decline of the American Empire.*[28] That movie, which some critics have called an intellectual's *The Big Chill,* traces the weekend retreat of eight friends, several of whom teach in a university history department. The movie begins and effectively ends with a taping of the female historian's (Dominique) comments about her new book, *Changing Concepts of Happiness.* Dominique contends that civilizations decline to the extent that notions of personal happiness permeate culture. Thereafter, the film's relentless focus on the eight friends' unending conversations about sex[29] makes the decline of the American empire painfully obvious. As the movie moves to its denouement, Dominique's interview is played for the gathered friends. When Louise, Remy's nonacademic wife, objects to Dominique's pessimism (she, without irony, recommends the search for personal happiness), Dominique retaliates by making an offhand comment about her affair with Remy. In the movie's painful conclusion, Louise learns too much about Remy's affairs, Remy tries to hold on to Louise, the nonattached friends hug, and the attached friends look on wistfully. In contrast to many Hollywood films, then, Arcand's *The Decline of the American Empire* explores the fragility of romance and love as the sole bulwark versus apocalyptic crisis.

Because all these people do is talk,[30] they effectively watch the world "go to hell." In *The Decline of the American Empire,* this passivity reflects fatalism and a tinge of intellectual superciliousness (precisely what Louise objects to in Dominique's analysis). While less supercilious, *Jesus of Montreal* is equally frustrated.[31] If Burton Mack's analysis of Mark is correct, Mark's voyeurism—like that of Tertullian, who believed that the joys of heaven would include watching the suffering of the damned—is more maliciously gleeful.[32] Regardless, both *Jesus of Montreal* and Mark effectively end with the hero's angry damnation of the world.[33]

He Who Must Die

Natural religions expect their faithful to prosper. People who do well will have the good life. Apocalyptic sectarians do not live in such happy worlds. The mark of the faithful for such believers is suffering, not success. As corruption and evil rule the world, apocalyptic heroes die (or narrowly escape). Not surprisingly, then, passion dominates both Mark and *Jesus of Montreal*. Mark has, in fact, been described as a passion narrative with an extended introduction. That Jesus' final words are "My God, my God, why have you forsaken me?" (Mark 15:34), that the climactic confession of Jesus' identity comes from a Roman at the cross (Mark 15:39), and that Mark has no resurrection appearances concentrate attention on the passion dramatically.

Jesus of Montreal focuses attention similarly. The movie begins with a play climaxing in a suicide. Thereafter, the movie's content is a modernist revision of a passion play, and the movie climaxes with the hero's unfortunate death.

The meaning of this death is ambiguous. On the one hand, Daniel is the victim of bad luck. No one intends to kill Daniel. A scuffle knocks over his cross, and, unattended, he dies. On the other hand, the movie provides a rich interpretative context for this death in the passion play and in Daniel's increasing Christ-likeness. This context suggests that Daniel dies, in part, because he is like Christ. In fact, his fate resembles that of the hero of *He Who Must Die*.[34] Chosen by the authorities to play a role, the role escapes its limits and consumes its actor. Daniel is innocent in that he does not deserve death (if anyone does),[35] but he is also heroic in that his fate comes upon him while he pursues his artistic integrity. Nonetheless, his death is neither theologically purposeful nor redemptive.

Mark also presents Jesus' death on two levels. On the one hand, Jesus' death is the result of the murderous designs of the powers-that-be (Mark 3:6; 14:1–2). As such, his death is that typical of the apocalyptic righteous in a corrupt world (Mark 8:34–9:1). On the other hand, Jesus' death is also the result of God's predetermined plan. In addition to various allusions to prophecies, Mark's Jesus predicts—in too precise detail—his death (Mark 8:31; 9:31; 10:32–45; 12:1–12; 14:8, 17–25) and various events attending his passion (for example, the disciples' betrayal, flight, and denial). For Mark, it is this divine fate that matters. God, not the authorities, determines Jesus' death. Thus, after Jesus announces his death, both Jesus and his opponents move toward the same end. Ironically, his opponents assist him. Ironically, his disciples do not. Ultimately, Jesus' opponents, not his disciples, confess his identity at the cross and bury him.

Accepting his divine fate at Gethsemane (Mark 14:32–42), Jesus achieves heroic stature. Incidentally, Jewison's montage of crucifixion paintings in *Jesus Christ Superstar* nicely dramatizes this moment in Gethsemane. When even corrupt officials cannot put him to death, Jesus seals his own fate with his only public admission of his identity in the entire gospel (Mark 14:61–62). Elsewhere, this matter has been a (divine) secret.[36]

In Schweitzer's reading of the passion, however, Jesus' fate takes on its own ambiguities. Without apocalyptic support, Jesus' fate is as pathetic as Daniel's:

> Soon after that comes Jesus, and in the knowledge that He is the coming Son of Man lays hold of the wheel of the world to set it moving on that last revolution which is to bring all ordinary history to a close. It refuses to turn, and He throws Himself upon it. Then it does turn; and crushes Him. Instead of bringing in the eschatological conditions, He has destroyed them. The wheel rolls onward, and the mangled body of the one immeasurably great Man, who was strong enough to think of Himself as the spiritual ruler of mankind and to bend history to His purpose, is hanging upon it still. That is His victory and His reign.[37]

Despite Schweitzer's final paean to Jesus' iconic significance, his fated delusionary reanimates the Markan Jesus' final words—"My God, my God, why have you forsaken me?"[38]—and reminds us that the apocalyptic kingdom did not arrive in Galilee after either Mark 1:15 or 16:7–8. D. D. Raphael offers a similarly unadorned reading of Mark:

> Imagine a pagan hearing the history of Jesus, and dismissing as superstition both the supernatural interpretation of it and the report of a miraculous resurrection. If such a pagan were a dramatic artist, he could make of the story a Tragedy of the highest order. The hero shows great human qualities, inspires high hopes in his followers, comes into conflict with the powers that be, and perishes with a cry of despair. . . .[39]

Jesus of Montreal reminds us that Mark can be read in this "pagan" way, either pathetically or tragically, rather than apocalyptically (the last reading includes the resurrection, an apocalyptic concept). Of course, neither Daniel nor Mark's Jesus is quite the Brian of *Monty Python's Life of Brian,* because Brian is simply the victim of imperial indifference to the colonized (not even a victim of "fate").[40] That fate Crossan nicely captures with the chilling title, "The Dogs beneath the Cross." Both Daniel and Mark's Jesus are more heroic; nonetheless, the absence of an apocalyptic finale for either renders their heroism strikingly masochistic. Their pursuit of integrity is a "death wish."[41]

Further, the denouements of both stories render these death wishes rather questionable. Daniel's disciples quickly betray his artistic integrity by making a lucrative pact with Cardinal, the sleazy lawyer that Daniel resisted. Mark's Jesus is similarly betrayed. Mark's apocalyptic readers either vanished or were consumed by an imperial, institutional church at home in the world.[42] If the two-source hypothesis is correct, Matthew and Luke effectively subsumed Mark's apocalyptic message with resurrection narratives authorizing the apostolic church.[43] The additions to Mark (Mark 16:9–20, and the shorter ending) treat the text

DeMille's (far too) domesticated dog(s) beneath the cross

of Mark itself similarly. In short, Jesus died, but à la Schweitzer, the world "rolled on." It soon included an imperial, apostolic church. Arcand's *Jesus of Montreal*, like Dostoevsky's "The Grand Inquisitor," Kazantzakis' *The Greek Passion*, Dassin's *He Who Must Die*, and Pasolini's *The Gospel According to St. Matthew*, reminds us that ecclesiastical empires are as deadly as Roman ones. Arcand's Le Clerc, in particular, is a chilling figure raising the question of the imperial church's betrayal of Jesus.[44]

Confused Boundaries: Insiders, Outsiders, Who Can Tell?

Apocalyptic times are confusing because the old boundaries demarcating identity have been destroyed. Apocalyptic arises from times of anomie, from times when it appears that the world (*cosmos*) is lost. Further, sectarian withdrawal inherently creates a "war of myths" with the paramount culture.[45] Various powers contend for the right to define reality and identity. Incidentally, by this definition, contemporary pluralism is equally apocalyptic. At the least, various agencies compete to define our realities. In addition to our pluralism, however, ancient apocalyptic also has the perplexing problem of the divine sovereignty. Ultimately, the divine sovereignty ideology means that no one can know his/her fate before the apocalyptic finale (compare Matthew 13:24–30). With Herodotus's Solon, apocalyptists call no one happy before he/she is dead.

As an apocalyptic gospel, then, Mark wreaks havoc with boundaries. Twice, possibly three times, the gospel changes the rules and presents expected insiders as outsiders. First, the religious leaders are left outside Jesus' secrets and those who do God's will (Mark 3:20–4:34). While demons dwell in the synagogues and Jesus marks the Temple for destruction, Jesus incorporates the disciples and other outcasts. Then, however, Mark disowns these very disciples. After two sea crossings and miraculous feedings, Jesus describes his own disciples as outsiders (Mark 8:14–21). Thereafter, the disciples increasingly fail to "disciple." Their tasks are left to the enemy and to women (including the anonymous woman of Mark 14:3–9).

Mark's characterization is not specifically opposed to the disciples. They are not notably bad; they are simply human. Thus, Mark is misanthropic.[46] Mark devalues humans before the apocalyptic God. Thus, without God, no one survives apocalyptic crisis (for example, Mark 9:29; 10:27; 13:20).[47] In short, a capricious divine sovereignty rules Mark's world (Mark 4:10–12).

Even Mark's central thesis that Jesus is the messiah (the kingdom-bringer) who dies (the apocalyptic moment) is beyond human ken. "Death" deforms the category of "messiah" beyond recognition; therefore, only revelation imparts Mark's secrets of the kingdom.[48] Appropriately, Mark bookends his teaching on the dying messiah (Mark 8:22–10:52) with two miracles of divinely restored sight (Mark 8:22–26; 10:46–52). If one "gets" Mark, it is as if the blind suddenly see.[49] Notably, the first miracle is a "double-touch" healing, the only one in the gospel tradition. Analogously, Mark offers a twofold revelation: 1) Jesus is the messiah (Mark 1:1–8:30); and 2) the messiah is he who must die (Mark 8:31–16:8). The anointing—for burial, not rule (Mark 14:3–9)—nicely encapsulates this counterintuitive message.

Ultimately, the divine sovereignty imperialistically incorporates the reader as well (see below). Mark threatens to change the insider-outsider boundaries a third time because it leaves its readers with an important question: Will they survive the apocalyptic crisis? If we look back through Mark, we find other times when the reader is left outside. For example, in Mark 4, Mark explains only one of the parables, but the gospel claims that Jesus explained all the parables for the disciples (Mark 4:34). Further, Mark never explains the leaven of the Pharisees, which the disciples do not understand, for the reader (Mark 8:15). Where, then, is the reader in Mark's boundary games? Is he/she a disciple or not?[50]

Jesus of Montreal plays similar games. The movie starts simply enough, and in good gospel fashion, with the rejection of the expected insiders—the institutional church and its clergy—for a miscreant group of ragtag outsiders, Daniel and his disciples. Like Mark's gospel, however, the movie continues to play with boundaries. The most notable shift is, of course, the frequent transgressions of the boundary between the play within the movie and the movie's primary reality, Daniel's life. Thus, a delusional worshiper mistakes Daniel, while he plays Jesus in the passion play, for Jesus. Further, and more important, Daniel increasingly becomes a Christ figure.[51] Daniel's transformation allows the movie to play with Daniel's disciples in the same way that Mark does with Jesus' disciples. Are they inside—do they remain true to Daniel's artistic integrity—or outside—do they betray him—at story's end? As we have seen, Arcand's film is less hopeful than Mark. Arcand allows no character to promise a reunion. For Arcand's film, no superintending divine sovereignty rescues frail humans. Arcand's imagination is more catastrophic than apocalyptic (compare *The Decline of the American Empire*),[52] because only apocalyptic crisis, not an apocalyptic God, remains.

Without divine sovereignty and incensed by a corrupt church (and other equally failing institutions), Arcand's film plays still more imaginative insider-outsider games. For Arcand, religion is out and art is in. Religion, particularly as an institution, is passé. Art alone can resist commercialism's corrupting influence, but only if the artist has integrity. Such integrity entails sacrifice and martyrdom.

As we have seen, Daniel's integrity renders his fate somewhat heroic. Existentialism leaves more room for such than does divine sovereignty. Arcand's turn to artistic integrity recalls Camus' hope for absurd creation. In an absurd world, Camus believes that one has certain options: one can commit suicide, one can commit philosophical suicide (by considering the absurd divine as do Job, Kierkegaard, and Dostoevsky), or one can become an absurd hero as do Don Juan, actors, conquerors, and artists. Although Arcand flirts with suicide in the opening play, *Jesus of Montreal* ultimately depicts Daniel as an absurd creator:

> Of all the schools of patience and lucidity, creation is the most effective. It is also the staggering evidence of man's sole dignity: the dogged revolt against his condition, perseverance in an effort considered sterile. It calls for a daily effort, self-mastery, a precise estimate of the limits of truth, measure, and strength. It constitutes an ascesis. All that "for nothing," in order to repeat and mark time. But perhaps the great work of art has less importance in itself than in the ordeal it demands of a man and the opportunity it provides him of overcoming his phantoms and approaching a little closer to his naked reality. . . .
>
> Thus, I ask of absurd creation what I required from thought—revolt, freedom, and diversity.[53]

By contrast, in Camus' terms, Mark's apocalyptic affirmation of the divine sovereignty is philosophical suicide.

Arcand's use of art to replace religion ignores the differences between the aesthetic perspective as an engrossment with surfaces, and the religious perspective as a concern with the really real.[54] Of course, sans divine transcendence, surfaces are all. Accordingly, Camus' absurd creation forgoes "myth" for "no other depth than that of human suffering."[55] Arcand's *Jesus of Montreal* agrees.

"Let the Reader Beware": Imperialistic Stories[56]

In the absence of transcendent truth, those disenchanted with their reality (myth) seek meaning in "stories alongside." Thus, multiple stories in Mark and *Jesus of Montreal*[57] jostle one another, interpret one another, and seemingly go on forever. In essence, their stories will simply not stay "put."

First, both film and gospel have stories within that provide interpretative keys for their whole. Such devices are, of course, not rare in either literature or film.[58] *Jesus of Montreal* offers two such stories: the opening Dostoevskian play and Daniel's modernized passion play. The first situates the film in a death-of-God world and prepares the viewers for its ultimate celebration of existential heroism. The play's suicide makes a nice foil for Daniel as his act of absurd creation trumps the character's suicide and as his integrity surpasses that of the actor who is his John the Baptist precursor. The modernized passion is equally interpretative. As Tatum observes, that play demythologizes the Jesus story. No transcendent meaning remains.[59] This Jesus is thoroughly human. His birth is illegitimate, his death is fated by indifferent institutions, and his resurrection is a late-arriving interpretation of the disciples. Accordingly, when Daniel becomes that Jesus' successive Christ figure, we expect no apocalyptic resurrections. Daniel is on his existential own.

Mark also provides interpretative stories.[60] The parable of the rejected, murdered son of the vineyard (Mark 12:1–12) nicely summarizes Jesus' reception and subsequent fate in Jerusalem (compare Mark 14:3–9). It also serves as a plot device, hardening the lines of opposition and further provoking the murder plot. By far the most important interpretative story, however, is the parable of the soils (Mark 4:1–12).[61] The parable anticipates in advance the diverse responses to Jesus' kingdom message (the different ground upon which the seed falls) and provides the catalogue that disowns the disciples. More importantly, the "hard words" that constitute the basis for that disowning (Mark 4:11–12) reveal Mark's apocalyptic, divine sovereignty worldview as clearly as *Jesus of Montreal*'s internal plays reveal its existentialist worldview.

Second, the protean stories of Mark and *Jesus of Montreal* endanger the reader. They threaten to consume the reader/viewer, as Cortázar's short story, "Continuity of Parks," illustrates nicely. A harried businessman finds an opportunity to finish an intriguing murder mystery. He sits down in his favorite green velvet armchair and gradually "falls into" the words of the novel. Cortázar ensnares the reader in this second narrative level and then ends the whole piece with the murderer entering a house: "No one in the first room, no one in the second. The door of the salon, and then, the knife in hand, the light from the green windows, the high back of an armchair covered in green velvet, the head of the man in the chair reading a novel."[62] The confusion between the reader and the book read haunts the reader of Cortázar's piece. At least, it haunted me when I first read the short story in a green armchair in a lonely house on a dark, stormy night. The device of transgressing narrative levels suggests, of course, that texts and readerly reality are not distinct. Texts have a way of bleeding over into our own story.

The Bible's rhetoric tends toward such imperialism. It eschews discursive rhetoric for incorporating demand (scholars like to call it kerygmatic rhetoric). Thus, for example, the Deuteronomic legislation addresses people who have never been in Egypt as those that YHWH delivered from Egypt and made covenant with at Horeb (Deuteronomy 5). The delivered died in the wilderness, and Deuteronomy restates the law for the new generation as if they had participated in the original covenant. To this day, the celebration of Seder continues the mantra that God brought us (not some past generation) out of Egypt. Northrop Frye makes similar observations about the structure of the Christian Bible: "We suggested earlier that the Bible deliberately blocks off the sense of the referential from itself: it is not a book pointing to a historical presence outside it, but a book that identifies itself with that presence. At the end the reader, also, is invited to identify himself with the book."[63] It is this imperializing quality that Hans Frei points to when he opines that before modernity, Westerners "lived" within the Bible (between Acts and Apocalypse).[64]

Mark's open ending provides a particularly blatant example of this imperialism. Mark predicts the reunion of Jesus and the disciples in Galilee. A mysterious young man entrusts this good news to women who flee in frightened silence (Mark 16:7–8). Most readers have read this end (Mark's last word is the Greek conjunction *gar*, "for") as fraught with ellipses.[65]

According to Petersen, Mark's "true" end is the apocalyptic discourse in Mark 13.[66] In short, what comes after frightened women—that is, the implied end—is the litany of events prophesied in Mark 13. If so, the reader of Mark (at least a reader ca. 70 C.E.) expects Jesus' return to Galilee for the reader as well as for the disciples. Mark does not need resurrection appearances, because the gospel anticipates the present apocalyptic crisis envisioned by Mark 13 to come to a quick, divine end. No wonder, then, that the gospel speaks directly to its reader: "Let the reader beware" (Mark 13:14). Presumably, Mark warns the reader of a present apocalyptic crisis (compare Mark 13:37, "And what I say to you I say to all: Keep awake").

The promised kingdom did not arrive, so we can hardly read Mark apocalyptically today. That ideology no longer makes sense of Mark's dying messiah.

Canonical readers, of course, are little troubled here, for they simply supply the canonical ending (Matthew and Luke bookend and contain Mark), the apocalyptic resurrection narratives that authorize an imperial church. If we are wary and awake, however, we can avoid such imperial consumption by reconsidering Mark in light of Raphael's pagan, Schweitzer's failed fanatic, Monty Python's Brian, and Arcand's Daniel.

Jesus of Montreal consumes differently. It does not ingest our world as Mark 13 and the canonical resurrection narratives do (although it does bid us beware our consumption by consumerism). In fact, at first blush, the narrative transgressions remain within the movie. Thus, the modernized passion play suborns the reality of at least one worshiper (who mistakes Daniel for Jesus) and of Daniel himself as he becomes a Christ figure. The modernized passion play, however, also consumes the traditional passion play. It ingests (apocalyptic) divine sovereignty and excretes existentialism. Arcand's film consumes the imperial Gospel, deals with its threat, and renders it palatable to modernity. If that troubles us no more than Cortázar's "Continuity of Parks," it is because we already live in a secular world. When *Jesus of Montreal* consumes its various Jesuses, it mirrors our world; it does not threaten to change it. As James Morrow assumes in his amusing novel, *Towing Jehovah*, we have already been dealing with the problem of disposing with the divine body. Like Daniel, we are already alone and trying to make our way as suicides or absurd heroes in apocalyptic worlds sans apocalyptic gods.

On Earth as in Heaven: Typology as Generative Hermeneutic

All these moveable, consumable stories bring us to the generative hermeneutic at the heart of apocalypse and of *Jesus of Montreal:* typology. Typology connects two events separated in time through divine providence—as the epigraph to this chapter indicates—or by an interpreter's assertion of such providence. According to Northrop Frye, this hermeneutic is endemic to the Christian Bible: "Evidence, so called, is bounced back and forth between the testaments like a tennis ball; and no other evidence is given us. The two testaments form a double mirror, each reflecting the other but neither the world outside."[67] The double mirror, of course, is a formal basis for the Bible's imperialism. Let the reader beware. Unless someone like Arcand exposes the trap, no one escapes.[68]

Apocalyptic's type is the ancient combat creation myth or some earlier prophecy. Its visions are the anti-type interpretation. A superintending providence (or seer's assertion of such) connects these two disparate stories and, accordingly, apocalyptic's nostalgia for some lost past (for example, Eden or the natural religion of a small kingdom) with the future hope (for example, heavenly garden or revived natural religion). More importantly, the superintending providence means that it is and will be "on earth as in heaven." Wars on earth reflect and are settled by wars in heaven. More importantly, as Revelation makes dramatically clear, worshiped heavenly sovereignty (Revelation 4–5) will ultimately be worshiped earthly sovereignty (Revelation 21–22). The kingdoms and beasts that rule the world only appear to do so. The worship of the sectarian community reveals this divine truth in advance.[69]

Mark provides the definitive interpretation (the anti-type) for various earlier events and texts. Mark's primary typology, however, connects the death of Jesus with the fate of Jerusalem's Temple and that of the gospel's early readers. For Mark, Jesus is not the victim of indifferent or hostile authorities. Jesus' death is divinely ordained. It initiates the apocalyptic crisis in which the reader lives, that is, Mark 13. This connection is hardly rational. It depends on apocalyptic visions of the sovereignty of God.

This visionary claim, however, is actually hermeneutic and rhetoric (ideology). Frye clarifies what is at stake here by comparing typology to another rhetoric, that of causality, which he considers an "analogy of typology":

> Causality, however, is based on reason, observation, and knowledge, and therefore relates fundamentally to the past, on the principle that the past is all that we genuinely or systematically know. Typology relates to the future, and is consequently related primarily to faith, hope, and vision. . . .
>
> Another distinction between causality and typology is of great importance. Causal thinking tends not to move out of the same dimension of time: especially in third-phase causality, the causes have to be in the same temporal plane as their effects, or they are not genuine causes. Ascribing a disease to the will of God or to the malice of a witch is not causal thinking. Typology points to future events that are often thought of as transcending time, so that they contain a vertical lift as well as a horizontal move forward.[70]

While both rhetorics construct meaningful "history," only typology demands or asserts divine providence.

Arcand's *Jesus of Montreal* exposes Mark's divine providence for the hermeneutical act and rhetorical claim that it is. The film does so by consuming Mark's type and anti-type. Mark's Jesus and apocalyptic crisis have become the type for Daniel's existential crisis, but no divine sovereignty, or any other essentialism, connects Daniel with Mark's (or any other) Jesus. Daniel simply has circumstances (not a "fate") that include the Jesus of the passion play and against which he defines himself. He only appears to belong to apocalyptic's suffering righteous or to Jesus' martyr disciples (compare Mark 8:34–9:1). In the absence of divine sovereignty (apocalyptic ideology), he can only belong to Camus' absurd world or that of science's mechanistic materialism. Arcand's absurd hero, in true existentialist fashion, rejects scientific essentialism as well. His life is no more caused by scientific reason than it is by divine providence. Thus, Jesus is neither the divinely given type nor the cause for Daniel's "Christ-likeness." In fact, Arcand's film leaves the "reason" for Daniel's Christ-likeness wonderfully unexplained.[71] Here, Jesus is (actually Jesuses are) simply precursor(s). Typology, still ostensibly employed, comes undone. The Jesus story, in all its forms—as modernized passion play as well as Daniel's replication of bits of Jesus' story— becomes profane. Apocalyptic becomes existential crisis. Perhaps we should simply imagine these Jesuses, like Sisyphus, happy.[72]

Reading Mark in the Dark: Absurd Creators

Moreover, our conversation with *Jesus of Montreal* and Mark invites us to consider Mark's Jesus in the same (existentialist and artistic) vein. Given the nonoccurrence of the apocalyptic kingdom in Galilee, Mark's Jesus, like Schweitzer's deluded fanatic, remains "hanging upon it (the cross) still." This comparison has unsettling consequences for a canonical or traditional academic reading of Mark.

First, without the expected apocalyptic finale or the canon's replacement of that non-event with resurrection narratives authorizing Jesus' successors (like that of Mark 16:9–20), Mark is not melodramatic or comic. Jesus is not vindicated, and Mark is as pathetic or tragic as Raphael's imagined "pagan reading" of Mark indicates. Like Arcand's cross, Mark's cross ceases to have clear theological and redemptive meaning. If Mark's Jesus remains heroic, he is so, like Daniel, in terms of his relentless commitment to his own program or in terms of his integrity in the face of suffering and despair. Positively, then, this Jesus does remind us of happy Sisyphus, for he deals with (and teaches us to deal with?) frustration and mortality in a death-of-God world.[73]

Second, without apocalyptic finales and canonical institutions, we may wish to reconsider Mark's Jesus as an *artistic* creator. Perhaps his program is not so far from Daniel's after all.[74] The disjoint between the two depends on a distinction between the religious and aesthetic perspectives. In a world without transcendence, in a world of "surfaces," the artistic play with surface may prove more inviting than an apocalyptic seer might imagine. Further, in our world of capitalism and consumption, the aesthetic perspective's nonpragmatism may also provide temporary (and helpful) escape and/or release. In short, perhaps we should think of Mark's Jesus as performing his life/death or his kingdom in an existential or artistic fashion.[75]

Third, in the dark, the identity of the Markan Jesus becomes quite ambiguous. Jesus, the mysterious young man, and Mark predict Jesus' arrival in Galilee (Mark 14:28; 16:7). As he did not arrive, what are we to make of this Jesus? In light of the nonoccurrence, the dominical words of Mark 13:5–6, 21–22 have a subversive (perhaps frightening) quality. Do Jesus, the young man, and Mark become false prophets? Which Jesus—he of Mark 13:5–6, 21–22 or he of 14:28—do we believe? Canonical resurrection narratives nicely resolve this issue. Reading Mark in the dark with Arcand reopens it.

Notes

1. Erich Auerbach, *Mimesis: The Representation of Reality in Western Literature*, trans. Willard R. Trask (Princeton, N.J.: Princeton University Press, 1968), 73–74.

2. After I had written the first draft of this chapter, I came across Arcand's claim that Mark inspired his film. See Bart Testa, "Arcand's Double-Twist Allegory: *Jesus of Montreal*," in André Loiselle and Brian McIlroy, eds., *Auteur/Provocateur: The Films of Denys Arcand* (Westport, Conn.: Greenwood, 1995), 110 n. 11.

3. Leonard L. Thompson, *Introducing Biblical Literature: A More Fantastic Country* (Englewood Cliffs, N.J.: Prentice-Hall, 1978), 197–212, 218–21.

4. Contending parties frequently dismiss the other's humanity in the language of war or conflict. Not incidentally, some scholars claim that apocalyptic (or the prophetic notion of the "Day of Yahweh") originated in holy-war ideology.

5. For fuller description and bibliography, see Walsh, *Reading the Bible*, 310–28, 362–80, 448–73, 486–504. In addition, see Wes Howard-Brook and Anthony Gwyther, *Unveiling Empire: Reading Revelation Then and Now* (Maryknoll, N.Y.: Orbis, 1999); and Tina Pippin, *Apocalyptic Bodies: The Biblical End of the World in Text and Image* (London/New York: Routledge, 1999).

6. See Bryan Wilson, *Magic and the Millennium* (New York: Harper & Row, 1973), for a taxonomy of such sectarian movements.

7. See Catherine Albanese, *America: Religions and Religion*, 2nd ed. (Belmont, Calif.: Wadsworth, 1992), 275–343; and Robert Jewett, *The Captain America Complex*, 2nd ed. (Santa Fe, N.M.: Bear & Co., 1984).

8. Compare Scott, *Hollywood Dreams and Biblical Stories*, 193–217; Conrad E. Ostwalt Jr., "Hollywood and Armageddon: Apocalyptic Themes in Recent Cinematic Presentation," in Martin and Ostwalt, eds., *Screening the Sacred*, 55–63; and Richard Walsh, "On Finding a Non-American Revelation: *End of Days* and the Book of Revelation," in Aichele and Walsh, eds., *Screening Scripture*, 1–23.

9. See Robert Jewett and John Shelton Lawrence, *The American Monomyth* (Garden City, N.Y.: Anchor, 1977).

10. Of course, Arcand's film is not a Hollywood production. It is Canadian. On occasion, it reflects, and on other occasions, it reveals Hollywood patterns. See also n. 45 below.

11. Greene's *Godspell* had previously combined the Baptist and Judas in one character.

12. Book 11 reports the last conversations between Smerdyakov and Ivan and Smerdyakov's death. Ivan elaborates his "death of God" ethic in a conversation with another brother, Alyosha, in Book 5.

13. Stern, Jefford, and DeBona, *Savior on the Silver Screen,* 307–13, read the movie as a conflict between existentialist and eschatological faith.

14. André Loiselle and Brian McIlroy, "Introduction," in Loiselle and McIlroy, eds., *Auteur/ Provocateur,* 3–6; and Testa, "Arcand's Double-Twist Allegory," 90–106, point out the potentially redemptive character of art in Arcand's work. Arcand himself says, "What gives me hope, the solution I have found, is cinema" (in André Loiselle, "'I Only Know Where I Come from, Not Where I Am Going': Conversations with Denys Arcand," ed. and trans. André Loiselle, in Loiselle and McIlroy, eds., *Auteur/Provocateur,* 157). Nevertheless, the "dialogic" quality (see Loiselle and McIlroy, "Introduction," 2) of Arcand's work leaves this ambiguous.

15. Arcand has said, however, that he was exploring religion's impact on his youth and his later apostasy while making the film. See Loiselle, "'I Only Know Where I Come from, Not Where I Am Going,'" 155–56.

16. Arcand describes the Jesus of Mark 13 as delirious. See Adam Barker, "Actors, Magicians, and the Little Apocalypse," *Monthly Film Bulletin* 57 (January 1990): 4.

17. According to Loiselle and McIlroy, "Introduction," 5, Arcand uses the parallels between Jesus and Daniel "to emphasize the essential differences between their projects."

18. After Jesus' command to watch in Mark 13:32–37, he prays in Gethsemane while his disciples sleep (Mark 14:32–42). This contrast suggests that Jesus is, but they are not, ready for apocalypse.

19. Mark reiterates the proclamation of the kingdom's arrival in Galilee with 16:7. That Galilee replaces Jerusalem (and that the Baptist works in the wilderness) suggests the corruptness of the Markan world. For discussions of the theological displacements of Mark's settings, see Willi Marxsen, *Mark the Evangelist: Studies on the Redaction History of the Gospel,* trans. James Boyce, Donal Juel, and William Poehlmann with Roy A. Harrisville (Nashville, Tenn.: Abingdon, 1969), 30–116; and Elizabeth Struthers Malbon, *Narrative Space and Mythic Meaning in Mark* (San Francisco: Harper & Row, 1987).

20. See E. P. Sanders, *Jesus and Judaism* (Philadelphia: Fortress, 1985), 61–76. Sanders is more concerned with the historical Jesus than with Mark. For me, the issue is a matter of literary context. The Temple act is in an apocalyptic gospel; moreover, a cursed fig tree sandwiches it, and the prediction of the Temple's demise follows it.

21. Eastwood's *Bronco Billy,* with its ragtag troupe surrounding the titular hero, makes a nice interlocutor for both Mark and *Jesus of Montreal.* Notably, Daniel finds the members of his acting troupe among the dregs of the acting profession.

22. Apparently the sect includes Jews and Gentiles, because there are two miraculous feedings, one on both sides of the Sea of Galilee. The geography of Mark's Galilean ministry is, however, famously confused (or confusing). Other markers of Gentiles include the inclusion of the Syro-Phoenician woman, Jesus' travels to Tyre and Sidon, and his abandonment of Jewish purity regulations (Mark 7).

23. See Robert M. Fowler, *Loaves and Fishes: The Function of the Feeding Stories in the Gospel of Mark,* Society of Biblical Literature Dissertation Series 54 (Chico, Calif.: Scholars, 1981).

24. Scholars disagree on the fate of Mark's disciples. Theodore J. Weeden, *Mark: Traditions in Conflict* (Philadelphia: Fortress, 1971); and Werner Kelber, *Mark's Story of Jesus* (Philadelphia: Fortress, 1979), argue that Mark deliberately separates the disciples from Jesus in order to support a non-Petrine Christianity. Vernon K. Robbins, *Jesus the Teacher: A Socio-Rhetorical Interpretation of Mark* (Philadelphia: Fortress, 1984), thinks the disciples, like Socrates' dialogue partners, stumble and bumble for pedagogical reasons. They allow the Markan Jesus to explain and re-explain his position for the readers of Mark. Thomas E. Boomershine, *Mark the Story-Teller: A Rhetorical-Critical Investigation of Mark's Passion and Resurrection Narrative* (Ph.D. diss., Union Theological Seminary, 1974); and Elizabeth Struthers Malbon, *In the Company of Jesus: Characters in Mark's Gospel* (Louisville, Ky.: Westminster John Knox, 2000), argue that the disciples provide lessons for readers in what Malbon calls "fallible following." I find the disciples caricatures of Mark's apocalyptic worldview. No one, not even a disciple, survives without relying on God in such worlds (cf. Mark 9:27; 10:27; 13:20, 32–36).

25. Mark also has more nostalgia. The wilderness prophets, Elijah and Elisha, are particularly important precursors for Mark. See Burton L. Mack, *A Myth of Innocence: Mark and Christian Origins* (Philadelphia: Fortress, 1988), 91–93, 216–19. Mark, however, does not have as much nostalgia as Jewish apocalypses typically do.

26. Mark ends at 16:8. For evidence for and discussion of the significance of this ending, see Bruce M. Metzger, *A Textual Commentary on the Greek New Testament* (New York: United Bible Societies, 1971), 122–26; and J. Lee Magness, *Sense and Absence: Structure and Suspension in the Ending of Mark's Gospel* (Atlanta, Ga.: Scholars, 1986).

27. See Marxsen, *Mark the Evangelist,* 111–16, 151–206. That the disciples are in Galilee waiting for Jesus depends not on their character but on Jesus' predictions. All Jesus' other passion predictions come true in Mark. See Norman Petersen, "When Is the End Not the End? Literary Reflections on the End of Mark's Narrative," *Interpretation* 34 (1980): 163–68.

28. John Harkness, "The Improbable Rise of Denys Arcand," *Sight & Sound* 58, no. 4 (Autumn 1989): 235, 238, says that the keynote of Arcand's early films is despair.

29. The working title of the film was "Indecent Conversations."

30. Arriving unexpectedly, Diana's blue-collar lover comments precociously that he heard the men talking about sex all day and expected an orgy, but he found only "fish-pie."

31. I do not disagree with those who see *Jesus of Montreal* as a move from the cynicism of *The Decline of the American Empire* toward hope. See Arcand's comments in Loiselle, "'I Only Know Where I Come from, Not Where I Am Going,'" 157–58. Nevertheless, as we have seen, that hope is ambiguous.

32. See Mack, *A Myth of Innocence,* 353–76.

33. For Mark 13 as Mark's "end," see Petersen, "When Is the End Not the End?"

34. Jules Dassin's 1957 film of this name is about a passion play become reality in twentieth-century Greece. The film was based on Kazantzakis' novel, *The Greek Passion.*

35. I am reminded of William Munny's (the character played by Eastwood) line in *Unforgiven* on the deaths of various characters, "It's not about deserve. . . ." Arcand asserts that Daniel's fate was sealed from the inception of the film because our society has no other end for one who will not compromise. He also claims, however, that he tried to undercut the tragedy of this death. See Loiselle, "'I Only Know Where I Come from, Not Where I Am Going,'" 157. Perhaps he has in mind the comic undertones of the passion.

36. Robert Tannehill, "The Gospel of Mark as Narrative Christology," *Semeia* 16 (1979): 37–95, claims that Mark's passion educates the reader in Markan discipleship. To follow Jesus, the disciple must give up his/her desire to avoid death (cf. Mark 8:34–9:1). Thus, the gospel repeatedly leads the reader to think that Jesus will avoid death, only to deny that "hope." Apocalyptic heroes and disciples die. Similarly, Crossan, following George W. E. Nickelsburg ("The Genre and Function of the Markan Passion Narrative," *Harvard Theological Review* 73 [1980]: 153–84), finds two generic precursors for Mark's passion narrative: 1) innocence rescued; and 2) martyrdom vindicated. Mark follows the latter pattern. The Gospel of Peter is an example of the former (see Crossan, *The Historical Jesus,* 383–91; idem, *The Cross That Spoke: The Origins of the Passion Narrative* [San Francisco: Harper & Row, 1988]). On the ambiguity of Jesus' identity even at Mark 14:61–62, see n. 48 below.

37. Albert Schweitzer, *The Quest of the Historical Jesus: A Critical Study of Its Progress from Reimarus to Wrede,* trans. W. Montgomery (New York: Macmillan, 1968), 370–71.

38. Vincent Taylor, *Jesus and His Sacrifice: A Study of the Passion Sayings in the Gospels* (London: Macmillan, 1937), 158–62, cites three interpretations of Mark 15:34: 1) the cry indicates that God abandoned Jesus to suffer as a substitute for sinners; 2) the cry is an abbreviated statement of faith citing Psalm 22; or 3) the cry is a statement of desolation.

39. D. D. Raphael, *The Paradox of Tragedy,* 53.

40. John Dominic Crossan, *Jesus: A Revolutionary Biography* (New York: HarperSanFrancisco, 1994), 123–58, offers frightening insights into the imperial indifference and degradation of the cross. The films of Ray and Pasolini also dramatize this aspect of Jesus' death by connecting it with the death of others.

41. See Fred Burnett, "The Characterization of Martin Riggs in *Lethal Weapon 1:* An Archetypal Hero," in Aichele and Walsh, eds., *Screening Scripture,* 251–78; and Miller, *The Epic Hero.*

42. On apocalyptic Mark and the imperial church, see Mack, *A Myth of Innocence;* and idem, *Who Wrote the New Testament? The Making of the Christian Myth* (San Francisco: Polebridge, 1995).

43. On the resurrection narratives as authorizations of the church, see Crossan, *The Historical Jesus,* 395–416. For a more dismissive view of the narratives, see H. S. Reimarus, *Fragments,* ed. Charles H. Talbert; trans. Ralph S. Fraser (Chico, Calif.: Scholars, 1985), 240–48; or Scorsese's portrayal of Paul's message in *The Last Temptation of Christ.*

44. Testa, "Arcand's Double-Twist Allegory," 110, describes Le Clerc's speech as "a humiliated rendition of Dostoyevsky's arrogant discourse of the Grand Inquisitor."

45. See Amos Niven Wilder, *Early Christian Rhetoric: The Language of the Gospel* (Cambridge, Mass.: Harvard University Press, 1971); and *idem, Jesus' Parables and the War of Myths: Essays on Imagination in the Scripture* (Philadelphia: Fortress, 1982). Mack, *A Myth of Innocence,* reads Mark as the product of various Jesus communities' attempts to define themselves vis-à-vis ancient Jewish groups. Mark 3:20–35 and Mark 7 are important here. Peter Wilkins, "No Big Picture: Arcand and His U.S. Critics," in Loiselle and McIlroy, eds., *Auteur/Provocateur,* 113–35, discusses Arcand's films as a Canadian response to the imperialism of the American media. Stern, Jefford, and DeBona, *Savior on the Silver Screen,* 321–33, use the film to express their own concerns about the media's proliferation of such images.

46. Berger, *The Sacred Canopy,* 53–80, calls such attitudes "masochistic." He describes theodicy both as the intoxication of surrender to the other and as a pact with death. It takes God "off the hook" by putting humans "on the hook." In light of Mark, perhaps we should rephrase this as "on the cross."

47. The Markan character prepared for apocalypse is Jesus. He alone watches and prays (cf. Mark 13:32–37 and the Gethsemane scene in Mark 14:32–42), but he dies forsaken.

48. George Aichele, *Sign, Text, Scripture: Semiotics and the Bible* (Sheffield: Sheffield Academic Press, 1997), 83, states, "The messianic titles that accumulate in Mk 1.1 are eventually undermined at 8.29–31, 14.61–62 and elsewhere in the Gospel of Mark." Compare *idem, Jesus Framed* (London: Routledge, 1996), 21–26. These deformations render Jesus' identity ambiguous or, in Aichele's terminology, "fantastic."

49. DeMille's *The King of Kings* has a comparable use of Mark as a character. Mark, a lame boy healed by Jesus, brings a young blind girl to Jesus. We, the audience, see Jesus first through this girl's restored sight. DeMille's Jesus, however, is not a dying, apocalyptic messiah. He is a miraculous, divine man.

50. Aichele, *Jesus Framed (passim),* argues that readers of Mark (and other texts) are always outside. He queries, ibid., 41, "Can the entire text of Mark be read as a disturbing attempt to say "nothing to anyone" (see also Mark 8:30)? Is Mark a text which, finally and forever, keeps a secret?"

51. Testa, "Arcand's Double-Twist Allegory," 105, describes *Jesus of Montreal* as an *imitatio Christi,* rather than a modernized Jesus story. See the discussion in Chapter 2 above. Baugh, *Imaging the Divine,* 113, treats it as a transitional film between his Jesus films and Christ-figure films.

52. See Wilder, *Jesus' Parables and the War of Myths,* 165, for this distinction.

53. Albert Camus, *The Myth of Sisyphus and Other Essays,* trans. Justin O'Brien (New York: Vintage International, 1991), 115, 117. Throughout his essay Camus follows Nietzsche's famous elevation of aesthetic over ethic. See ibid., 93. We could see Arcand's *The Decline of the American Empire* as an exploration of Don Juan's absurd freedom. For an intriguing comparison of the Jesus of the Gospels to Camus' absurd hero, see Burnett, "The Characterization of Martin Riggs in *Lethal Weapon 1.*"

54. Geertz, *The Interpretation of Cultures,* 111–12.

55. Camus, *The Myth of Sisyphus and Other Essays,* 117–18.

56. Given the intimate connections between this section and the last, I forgo the general apocalyptic introduction here, but imperialistic and protean story does characterize apocalyptic generally. First, apocalypses rewrite older texts. As a genre, apocalypse transfers the ancient combat creation myth that dominated the ancient Near East—the quarrel of a god with a (dragon) monster—to the future. More specifically, various apocalypses rewrite their precursors. For example, Daniel rewrites Jeremiah's seventy years of exile (Jeremiah 25:11–12; 29:10) as seventy weeks of years (Daniel 9:2, 24–27). Daniel's visions presume to inhabit the last week and thus play repeatedly with seven years and fractions thereof. Revelation rewrites and relocates this last week (e.g., Revelation 11). As we have already seen, *Jesus of Montreal* rewrites Mark's "abomination of desolation," itself a relocating of Daniel 9:27. In short, apocalyptic story never ends. It is always recalculable. Second, then, apocalyptic symbolism is notoriously plastic. The heavily coded symbols mean virtually whatever an interpreter wants them to mean. The manifold signifieds of Revelation's 666 are a typical case.

57. See Chapter 2 for a discussion of the multiple "Jesuses" in *Jesus of Montreal.* Loiselle and McIlroy, "Introduction," describe the style of Arcand's film as dialogic. He has repeatedly claimed that his fictional films have no message and that interpretation is up to the viewer. See Loiselle, "'I Only Know Where I Come from, Not Where I Am Going,'" 142–43, 156–57. Given the title of this book, I understandably appreciate this comment from Arcand: "To tell you the truth, I never try to do anything specific with my films. I never know where I am going; I am always in the dark when I shoot a film" (in ibid., 145).

58. At random, I remember Idgy's story in *Fried Green Tomatoes,* the heroine's dream in *Final Fantasy,* and the lobsterman's explanation of the part of a lobster trap called "in the bedroom" in the film of the same name.

59. Tatum, *Jesus at the Movies,* 182–86. Demythologizing is, of course, Bultmann's famous interpretative program. Like Bultmann, Daniel/Arcand has restated the Gospel in existential terms; however, Bultmann keeps a transcendent element that Arcand does not (cf. Rudolf Bultmann, "New Testament and Mythology," in Rudolf Bultmann, *Kerygma and Myth: A Theological Debate,* ed. Hans Werner Bartsch; trans. Reginald H. Fuller [New York: Harper & Row, 1961], 1–44). Certainly, there is no theological meaning to Arcand's cross.

60. Mark often intercalates (or sandwiches) stories so that they resonate with one another. We have already observed the intercalation of the cursed fig tree and the Temple act in Mark 11:12–24. Mark also places Peter's denial (Mark 14:66–72) between Jesus' confession and silence at his trials (Mark 14:53–65; 15:1–5). For discussion of Mark's intercalations, see Howard Clark Kee, *Community of the New Age: Studies in Mark's Gospel* (Philadelphia: Westminster, 1977), 54–56; and Kermode, *The Genesis of Secrecy,* 125–45.

61. For an elaborate exposition of these parables as the key to Mark, see Mary Ann Tolbert, *Sowing the Gospel: Mark's World in Literary-Historical Perspective* (Minneapolis, Minn.: Fortress, 1989).

62. In Julio Cortázar, *Blow-Up and Other Stories,* trans. Paul Blackburn (New York: Pantheon, 1967), 65.

63. Frye, *The Great Code,* 137–38. See also ibid., 27–52.

64. Hans Frei, *The Eclipse of Biblical Narrative* (New Haven, Conn.: Yale University Press, 1974), 1–16.

65. If the two-source hypothesis is correct, Matthew and Luke supplied their own endings. In Mark's own textual history, two different people took it upon themselves to supply endings. The NRSV prints both the so-called shorter (in footnote) and longer (as Mark 16:9–20) endings. See Metzger, *A Textual Commentary on the Greek New Testament,* 122–26.

66. Petersen, "When Is the End Not the End?"

67. Frye, *The Great Code,* 78.

68. George Aichele, *The Control of Biblical Meaning: Canon as Semiotic Mechanism* (Harrisburg, Pa.: Trinity Press International, 2001), exposes such imperialism in the semiotic machine known as "canon."

69. See Walsh, "On Finding a Non-American Revelation."

70. Frye, *The Great Code,* 82. Compare W. T. Stace, *Religion and the Modern Mind* (Westport, Conn.: Greenwood, 1980), 15–30, for a comparison of religion's teleological worldview with science's mechanical one.

71. That Daniel's life becomes "Christ-like" seems an intriguing reversal of Schweitzer's dictum that scholars recreate Jesus in light of their own ideals. As we have observed, however, Daniel's revised passion play creates an existential Jesus reflecting the overall worldview of Arcand's film. Thus, at that level, Schweitzer's dictum still applies. Existential Jesuses were, of course, all the rage during the time that Bultmann and his students dominated New Testament studies. In my opinion, Arcand's Jesus is (Jesuses are) far more existential than those of the Bultmannians. For Arcand, Jesus' situation (and that of Daniel) is not about life before divine demand, but absurd creation in an absurd world.

72. Camus, *The Myth of Sisyphus and Other Essays,* 123.

73. Negatively, this Jesus is masochistically obsessed with death and writes his own death (life?) script by following the stories of previous martyrs too closely (just as Daniel follows the script of the passion play too closely [but less purposefully]). See nn. 36, 41, 53, 59, and 71, above. I have reduced this negative possibility to a note here because I am reading Mark and *Jesus of Montreal* together and Arcand is slightly more hopeful than this interpretation.

74. Despite the reflections in n. 14 above, Arcand does not distinguish religion and art so sharply. George Aichele has suggested that the juxtaposition of advertising and idolatry (in the commercials in the film) and the fact that the same musicians sing in the church (in the opening) and in the subway (in the conclusion) raise the question of the connection between (pure) art and (true) religion in the film.

75. See Chapter 4.

Chapter 4

Location, Location, Location: *Godspell* and the Teachings of Jesus

There cannot be a question whether these or other rules are the correct ones for the use of "not."
(I mean, whether they accord with its meaning.) For without these rules the word has as
yet no meaning; and if we change the rules, it now has another meaning (or none),
and in that case we may just as well change the word too.[1]

Although the centrality of the kingdom of God in the language, message, and teaching of
Jesus is a commonplace in contemporary scholarship, a debate has raged around the
semantic status of the kingdom of God.[2]

Location, Location, Location

According to the old joke, three things matter in real estate: location, location, and location. Location is equally important to language. Words mean only in a context.[3] Screaming "Fire" on an artillery range, at a firing squad, and in a crowded theater are all different messages. "I'm lost" differs in matters cartographical, in a classroom, and at a revival meeting—as I learned to my dismay when I stopped one Sunday for directions at a Baptist church. Wittgenstein's philosophy deals with the "rules" or the "language games" that constrain linguistic meaning. In particular, Wittgenstein separates the language game of ordinary speech from that of philosophical discourse:

> When philosophers use a word—"knowledge", "being", "object", "I", "proposition", "name"—and try to grasp the *essence* of the thing, one must always ask oneself: is the word ever actually used in this way in the language-game which is its original home?—
> What *we* do is to bring words back from their metaphysical to their everyday use.[4]

Insensitivity to language games causes us to misconstrue meaning, to make (metaphysical) mistakes. Wittgenstein's philosophy, then, is "a battle against the bewitchment of our intelligence by means of language," an attempt "to shew the fly the way out of the fly-bottle."[5]

Foucault deals with another type of context, the "epistemes," a prioris that structure the possibility of knowledge in various historical eras. The episteme, the "positive basis of knowledge," constitutes the era's deep structure for thought and language. Foucault unearths different epistemes by considering three eras' assumptions about the connections between words and things:[6] 1) in the Renaissance, words resemble (or "are") things; 2) in the Enlightenment, words represent things; and 3) in modernity, words reveal the modern subject. The last episteme creates the idea of "man." When that episteme disintegrates, as it already is in Foucault's archaeology, "man" will cease to be.[7]

Historical critics delve into a third type of context, the social provenances that provide contexts for biblical texts. They describe what various biblical texts "meant" in these provenances in order to discover what they might possibly "mean" today. Such worldviews are less Foucault's deep structures and more matters of identifiable subcultures in first-century Roman Palestine or in the broader Hellenistic world.

We could repeat location ad nauseum, because the matter of defining context is as unending as postmodern semiosis. In fact, the very attempt to define context adds yet another contextual layer (as interpretation ultimately begets the history of interpretation). Games, epistemes, and worldviews suffice, however, to raise the question of the context(s) of Jesus' teaching.

According to the scholarly consensus, Jesus proclaimed the kingdom of God but did not define that term.[8] Presumably, that would matter little if we shared Jesus' language game, episteme, and worldview, or if we could unearth them with certainty; however, when the early churches reported Jesus' teaching, they relocated it. In particular, they changed Jesus' language game. What Jesus offered in quotidian Galilean conversations, the churches repeated as canonical pronouncement. The "words of Jesus in red" Bibles of my youth continued this process. In effect, the churches reversed Wittgenstein's process by moving from everyday to metaphysical use. In short, the churches restated Jesus' sayings as, and in, gospel. Q and the Gospel of Thomas, however, provide noncanonical versions of Jesus' teaching[9] because of Q's hypothetical status and Thomas's heretical status. Accordingly, we will focus on those texts here.

Jesus the Teacher at the Movies

Of course, the movies also liberate Jesus' teaching from the canon. Early on, such relocations were minimal. DeMille's visualization of the coffee table Bible, although actually including only a minimal amount of Jesus' teaching,[10] presents that teaching in "scripture" titles amounting to a "red-letter" presentation. DeMille's Jesus speaks canonically, and DeMille (according to the film's titles) offers his film in reverent obedience to Jesus' authoritative command to witness. In fact, that command is Jesus' penultimate speech in the film. Further, Jesus' first words in DeMille's film are "I am come as light," and we hear (actually, we see the title) these Johannine words before we ever see Jesus (through the eyes of the healed blind girl). The disappearing Jesus' last words are also comfortingly divine (as they indicate his conquest of death): "Lo, I am with you always."

Ray and Stevens present far more of Jesus' teaching than DeMille, and they abandon his "red-letter" style. Nonetheless, their Jesus still speaks with an ethereal, authoritative voice. Ray presents Jesus' teaching primarily in one majestic Sermon on the Mount. Clothed dramatically in red, Jesus delivers the sermon (with notable parabolic and Johannine inclusions) authoritatively (although the crowd does ask questions) and ritualistically (concluding the sermon with the Lord's Prayer). Two responses, however, diminish the sermon's effect. Barabbas rebuts it by saying to Judas, "These are only words." Then, Lucius summarizes it for Pilate as a message of "peace, love, brotherhood." That battle scenes dominate this biblical epic make the summary tantamount to a denial of the sermon's significance to first-century Palestinian politics.

Although Stevens abandons "biblical" diction, his Jesus (as introduced through the exotic Byzantine art of a church) remains otherworldly. In particular, Stevens focuses on Jesus' semi-ascetic teaching. Thus, when a man steals Peter's coat, Jesus calms the agitated Peter by offering Peter his own coat (which Peter refuses). In a subsequent scene, Jesus describes wealth as a burden and advises a young man (Lazarus) to give up his wealth. Mary's comment at this point that Jesus "is too good" nicely summarizes Stevens's idealized portrait of Jesus' teaching. He, too, is ethereally "out of touch."

Zeffirelli creates more quotidian and first-century Palestinian settings for Jesus. His Jesus speaks in synagogues—as do other Jews—and in household symposia. In one revealing (also my favorite) scene, he transfers the parable of the prodigal son to Matthew's house in order to heal a rift between Matthew and Peter. In Luke, Jesus tells this parable (and others) in response to the religious leaders' complaints about his associations with sinners (Luke 15:2–3). By contrast, for Zeffirelli, Jesus' parable ceases to become part of a realistic engagement with first-century Jews and becomes a matter of apostolic management. As we have seen, Zeffirelli's whole film operates similarly. Despite Zeffirelli's claim to present Jesus in a Jewish context, he presents a Christianized Judaism and a Jesus who speaks canonically.

Even though Pasolini confines himself rigorously to one gospel, his Jesus speaks less canonically. Pasolini films Jesus less reverently than his precursors.

Instead of a stately Sermon on the Mount, Pasolini presents Matthew 5–7 with rapid cuts attended by changes in lighting, setting, and clothing. By contrast, Matthew's sermon looks artificial. Pasolini erases the gospel and Hollywood calmness. His restless teacher has an angry intensity. He is in, rather than above, the fray. Finally, given Pasolini's omission of Matthew 13 and 24–25 (parables and apocalyptic discourse), his Jesus' teaching is far more worldly than that of his precursors.

Jewison's passion play deals minimally with Jesus' teaching; nonetheless, Jewison de-canonizes Jesus' teaching by placing it in a rock opera. As a result, his Jesus is superstar or celebrity, rather than a messiah or Son of God. Further, various characters—particularly Judas, who has a stronger singing voice—dispute Jesus' identity, teaching, and message. In one amusing scene, dancers offer Jesus various pedagogical (both content and style) suggestions. This interaction and dissent differ from authoritative, canonical pronouncement.

Scorsese also refuses to give Jesus' words a canonical aura. His Jesus is indecisive. He changes his message at least twice. More importantly, he takes no action without coercion or without the assistance of Judas. Scorsese's Jesus never speaks climactically. His teaching is always in dispute. In the most prominent teaching scene, Jesus wonders aloud what will happen if he says the wrong thing. Then he hesitantly offers a parable to an unreceptive, quarrelsome crowd. As he continues to teach, various hecklers criticize his idealistic, childish message. The setting is certainly more ordinary than canonical.

Monty Python and Arcand reduce the canon itself to interpretative dispute. Monty Python does so by hilariously imagining the growth of "gospel" traditions about another messiah, Brian. Attributing (erroneously) miracles and sayings as well as official symbols to the non-savior casts Jesus and his sayings in a burlesque light and leaves us wondering about the credibility of the gospel tradition. When Jesus does teach, the Monty Python troupe leaves us "in the back" with those who misunderstand and quarrel violently over his meaning. In yet another scene, Brian finds himself a prophet among many in the agora. In short, the multitude of prophets and messiahs—as well as a people ever ready to make messiahs to follow—renders Jesus and his teaching common, rather than unique.

Arcand's film also has an embarrassment of Jesuses. More importantly, Arcand's church misrepresents Jesus, and his academy cowardly conspires. While Daniel's modernized passion play liberates Jesus from his ecclesiastical misrepresentation, Daniel's fate warns anyone who would cross such canonical boundaries to be wary.

Godspell anticipates Arcand's trends—a noncanonical language game, a transgression of boundaries, and a passion context. Like *Jesus Christ Superstar*, *Godspell* is a musical version of a passion play that was first a play and only later a movie.

Unlike Jewison's film, however, Greene's *Godspell* gives considerable screen time to Jesus' teaching. In fact, *Godspell* enacts Jesus' parables, locating his teaching: 1) in sacred discontent; 2) in sacred play; and 3) in affective symbol. Although *Godspell* claims to be based on Matthew, its "location" of Jesus' teaching provides more insight into the noncanonical tradition of Jesus' teaching in Q and in Thomas.

Sacred Discontent

The movie opens with a shot of a painted flower on a graffiti-covered fence as an unseen "God" introduces himself as Creator. As the camera pans to the New York City skyline, God says, "And of this pleasant garden that I have mostly goodly planted, I will make him gardener for his own re-creation." Soon, a solitary figure, dressed like a circus ringleader and pulling a circus cart decorated with rainbows and doves, crosses a bridge into the city. Meanwhile, the camera focuses on eight special people in an angry mob in a quarrelsome city. They are distinct from the tumult because they have a fascination with art, music, dance, literature, and so forth (and because of the camera's focus). The ringleader appears mysteriously in their lives (they are often not sure that he is really there) and leads them from the city singing, "Prepare Ye (The Way of the Lord)." The song, of course, identifies the ringmaster as John the Baptist.

Leaving their possessions behind, they gambol in a fountain as John baptizes them. While they play, a surprised John sees a half-naked figure standing on a river's edge. John preaches (only Matthew 3:11) and then baptizes the newcomer. Their conversation (Matthew 3:14–15) introduces the newcomer as Jesus. The baptism clothes Jesus in clown pants, clown shoes, and a Superman shirt. He then leads the troupe in singing "Save the People" as they dance through the park to a junkyard that they re-create with their play and with an abbreviated Sermon on the Mount by Jesus. Thereafter, Jesus leads the motley troupe through an eerily empty city. They dance, play, and enact Jesus' teaching. Other people reappear only at the passion (in the form of police cars) and after the troupe carries the cruciform Jesus through the city and vanishes in the now crowded streets.

Despite the "divine garden" beginning, then, *Godspell* isolates Jesus' teaching from urban modernity with its John the Baptist (that is, wilderness) incursion, with its withdrawal to a junkyard, and with its strikingly empty streets. If the city is a garden, it will be so only as the troupe re-creates the junkyard (and the city?) as a "city of man" through Jesus' teaching of love and forgiveness.

Herbert N. Schneidau claims that the Bible generally has a "sacred discontent" with culture and its cities:

In Genesis, Cain the murderer is the original city-founder, and the Babel story pointedly rejects the great old urban traditions of architectural and astronomical wisdom, which appear to the Hebrews as mere ramifications of the self-deifying pride that is more important to man's buildings than bricks or mortar. A little further in Genesis, Sodom and Gomorrah give a bad name to city-dwelling which continues to resound all through the Bible. . . . This fear and hatred of cities culminates in Revelations [sic], where the "eternal city" Rome becomes Babylon, a symbol of captivity as well as pride. (In apocalyptic writing the New Jerusalem is not an earthly city at all.)[11]

American culture and mythology, of course, also suspects the city because of Romanticism's influence on both American intellectual history and the current American psyche.[12] Thus, in countless American films, the city is bad and corrupt while the frontier and the small town are paradisal. This motif is obvious in Westerns like *Shane*, in the Dirty Harry policeman movies, and also in Capra films like *Mr. Deeds Goes to Town*.[13]

Godspell belongs to this American mythic and cultural tradition. Further, while *Godspell* grew out of the countercultural movements of the 1960s, its success as a film (like that of *Jesus Christ Superstar*) represents the domestication of the countercultural movement. Capitalism effectively consumed both musicals. In fact, rejection of the city and countercultural veneers are big business economically and mythically in America. Despite its surface alienation, then, *Godspell* actually renders Jesus' teaching consumable for post-1970s America by situating it in American Romanticism and in capitalist consumerism. This American location, of course, does liberate the teaching of Jesus from the canon (although that may not be obvious to American Christians). Portraying a clown troupe enacting the parables in an empty city's streets and parks rejects canonical language games.[14]

Historical-critical scholarship has also claimed to liberate Jesus and his teaching from the church. After the formation of the creeds and the canon, the churches presented Jesus as the incarnate Son of God providing eternal life to his believers. While using all four gospels, this neo-Platonic portrait was most dependent on John. Eighteenth- and nineteenth-century scholars turned from John to the Synoptic Gospels to create other images of Jesus. Gradually their focus on the Synoptic Gospels became a focus on the teachings of Jesus. These nineteenth-century scholars created the Synoptic Problem, the question of the literary relationship between the similar yet dissimilar Matthew, Mark, and Luke. Their answer, one that still dominates scholarship, is the two-source hypothesis. Naming Mark the earliest gospel, scholars conclude that both

Matthew and Luke used Mark and that another source (Q) accounts for the non-Markan material common to Matthew and Luke. No copies of Q are extant, but scholars reconstruct (or create) Q from Luke (which most scholars feel preserved Q more faithfully in both order and wording), so citations to chapters and verses in Q actually refer to Luke's text.[15]

In the main, Q is a collection of the sayings of Jesus. While it has a few narrative elements (Q 4:1–13; 7:1–10) and some of John's teaching (Q 3:7–9, 16–17) as well, it has no passion narrative. As traditionally reconstructed, Q's Jesus is an apocalyptic seer proclaiming the advent of the kingdom of God. The Q community understood Jesus himself as the "coming one" of John's preaching and as the apocalyptic Son of Man (for example, Q 11:30; 12:8–9, 40; 17:24, 26, 30).[16] Most scholars despair of a plot in Q,[17] but Kloppenborg detects an important progression(s) in Q:

> The collection opens with John's prediction of the imminent appearance of the Coming One (3:16–17), thereby raising in the audience the expectation of fulfillment. This in fact occurs in 7:18–23 where Jesus is expressly identified with the Coming One. Yet ambiguities persist, since John's Coming One is not obviously consistent with Jesus as he is described in 7:22–23. How is the miracle-worker of 7:22 who points to the presence of the kingdom equivalent to John's coming apocalyptic judge? But this is not the end of it. The title emerges a third time, now in a context (13:25–30, 34–35) which is replete with the motifs of apocalyptic judgment: the Coming One of Q 13:34–35 acquires again the ominous connotations and strongly futuristic orientation of John's figure. Hence this particular logical progression begins and ends in the idiom of apocalypticism, but makes a theological detour in which the motif of the presence of the eschaton in Jesus' activity comes to the fore.[18]

The (narrative) movement identifies Jesus as John's "coming one" and also asserts the fundamental similarity of the missions and messages of John and Jesus. While Jesus' initial teaching (Q 6:20b–49) differs from John, after Q 7:24–28, 31–35, Jesus' message of repentance and judgment sounds increasingly like John (Q 10:12, 13–15; 11:31–32, 49–51; 12:8–9; 13:28–29, 34–35). Finally, according to Kloppenborg, the verse concluding Q identifies Jesus' disciples as those who will dispense the judgment promised by John and Jesus (Q 22:28–30).[19] Intriguingly, this reading of Q has two affinities with *Godspell:* 1) the acculturation of Jesus' teaching; and 2) the enigmatic figure of John the Baptist.

Kloppenborg, like Bultmann before him,[20] isolates two different kinds of sayings of Jesus: 1) announcements of judgment (Q 3:7–9, 16–17; 7:1–10, 18–28, 31–35; 11:14–52; 12:39–59; 17:23–37; 19:12–27; 22:28–30); and 2) sapiential speeches (Q 6:20b–49; 9:57–62; 10:2–24; 11:2–4, 9–13; 12:2–12, 22–34; 13:24–30, 34–35; 14:16–24, 26–27, 33–34; 17:33).[21] Kloppenborg innovates, however, by claiming that this duality represents Q's redactional history and that the wisdom sayings are original. The Q community added the apocalyptic judgments of "this generation" when they became frustrated with the world's rejection of their message.[22] Q's "original" layer, then, is a countercultural wisdom: "Q presents an ethic of radical discipleship which reverses many of the conventions which allow a society to operate, such as principles of retaliation, the orderly borrowing and lending of capital, appropriate treatment of the dead, responsible self-provision, self-defense and honor of parents."[23] In short, Q's Jesus rejects the wisdom of cultural order for the sacred disorder of the kingdom.[24] If Kloppenborg and others are right about Q's redactional history, however, culture consumed this countercultural Jesus just as it has more recently consumed *Godspell*'s clown. In Q's case, however, it was apocalyptic sectarianism, rather than American Romanticism (and capitalism), that did the consuming. In both cases, John the Baptist is the important hermeneutical switching point.

In Q 7:18–28, 31–35, troubled that Jesus does not look like his prophesied, fire-wielding coming one, an apocalyptic John sends disciples to question Jesus (perhaps to remind him of his apocalyptic mission). In response, Jesus reports miracles that imply the arrival of a rather different kind of kingdom (Q 7:22–23) and contrasts his profligate style with John's asceticism (Q 7:31–34). This difference is lost, of course, when Q later presents Jesus' proclamation of a very Baptist-like judgment.[25] With the turn to judgment, Q transforms the subversive sage into the coming one expected by John.

By contrast, *Godspell* rewrites the Baptist in light of a profligate Jesus. Its John comes dancing and singing ("piping") into town. While he calls people to repent, *Godspell*'s John does not bother with invective and threats of judgment. He does not threaten the Pharisees (Matthew 3:7–10), nor does he predict Jesus' apocalyptic judgment (Matthew 3:12). He simply announces Jesus' arrival and superiority (Matthew 3:11). After the baptism, he becomes one of Jesus' disciples.

Thereafter, however, *Godspell*'s John plays an agonistic role. Whenever a teaching's enactment requires conflict, John routinely provides it. Thus, when John objects to Jesus' turn-the-other-cheek teaching, Jesus slaps him to illustrate the teaching. Later, in the Beatitudes' enactment, John starts the only beatitude (Matthew 5:11) that Jesus does not immediately complete. More importantly, in the passion, John plays the role of Judas. In fact, in *Godspell,* John-Judas is the ringmaster (even humming a circus march) who orchestrates the beginning and the end of Jesus' ministry. John-Judas himself affixes Jesus to the cross (or chain-link fence). After the passion, however, John-Judas remains among the disciples and helps carry the dead Jesus through the city.

In both *Godspell* and Q, then, the Baptist consumes Jesus. In Q, an apocalyptic seer overcomes a (temporarily) countercultural sage. By contrast, *Godspell* initially rewrites John in light of a dancing, forgiving Jesus.[26] Once again, however, the countercultural is only temporary. Finally, Greene's John/Judas brings on the passion, after which the clown troupe vanishes into the noisy city. Their sacred discontent is fragile and temporary.

Bring in the Clowns: Sacred Disorder

Countercultural figures necessarily borrow their own identity, at least partly, from the culture they contest. They are not universal. Thus, those depicting the historical Jesus as countercultural situate him against the backdrop of the conventional wisdom and politics of first-century Judaism.[27] *Godspell*'s Jesus is not such a clearly Jewish figure. Instead, *Godspell*'s countercultural figure is a clown, a figure far more common in American film[28] and more in keeping with *Godspell*'s comic message. After his baptism by John, the Afro-coifed, clean-shaven, Caucasian Jesus emerges from the fountain in clown pants, a Superman shirt, and clown makeup. Shortly thereafter, he paints his disciples' faces similarly. This wardrobe, along with the song-and-dance medium and the eerily empty city, depicts Jesus clownishly as "other." He does not belong to the audience's normal reality.

This clown imagery suggests the goodness of the world far more clearly than do images of a countercultural reformer, cynic, or peasant. The clown's credo affirms (natural) life. Thus, in *The Great Dictator,* a Jewish barber (Chaplin) mistaken for Hitler speaks to a Nazi rally:

> I'm sorry, but I don't want to be an emperor. That's not my business. I don't want to rule or conquer anyone. I should like to help everyone— if possible—Jew, Gentile; black men, white.
>
> We all want to help one another. Human beings are like that. We want to live by each other's happiness—not by each other's misery. We don't want to hate and despise one another. In this world there is room for everyone. And the good earth is rich and can provide for everyone.[29]

Bad things do happen in comedy, but they are not final things. Comedy transcends those things.[30] Although Wile E. Coyote fails repeatedly in his increasingly grand technological schemes to trap the Road Runner, he always returns to try again. Tossed and buffeted by society, Chaplin skates blindfolded on the verge of catastrophe in *Modern Times* or does a frantic balancing act on a precipice in *The Gold Rush,* but he is never destroyed. The clown affirms life, and the comic world buoys up clowns. The clown himself/herself, as Chaplin put it, "wears adversity as though it was a bouquet."[31]

Godspell inhabits this same comic world. Thus, the film begins with references to the garden that God has given humans. Later, inside the Cherry Lane Theater, the troupe enacts the parable of the prodigal *to the accompaniment of film clips from classic comedies.* For *Godspell*'s clowns, God's world is the gracious, buoyant world of comedy and Jesus' parables. Accordingly, no one ever really gets left behind. Thus, when the clown troupe enacts the parable of the sheep and the goats (Matthew 25:31–46), Jesus leaves the goats behind only playfully. He quickly returns to restore them to the troupe. It is this same spirit, of course, that finds John-Judas among the disciples at the movie's end. The movie's message is forgiveness for all. Accordingly, at an important juncture, Jesus sings: "Earth shall be fair and all her people one." Only then, for *Godspell,* will God's will be done.

Comedy, however, does also "wear adversity." Thus, if comedy affirms life, it mocks society whose order stifles life. The bumbling of Wile E. Coyote, for example, raises a question mark at the very heart of technological society. Chaplin's *Modern Times* is equally critical of industrial society, because the factory, workers' rallies, and a police state threaten the Little Tramp. In a delightful scene, the factory's machinery consumes the Tramp, but he emerges from the belly of this whale without harm. Society cannot contain him. Within that society, and with no visible means of support, he finds various temporary paradises, including a waterfront shack reconfigured as "Home, Sweet Home" and a profligate festival in a department store. Finally, of course, he simply tramps off down a country road with the girl (at dawn, not sunset).

Godspell, however, finds no happy ending. It climaxes with the passion. That the troupe carries the cruciform Jesus into the city singing "Day by Day" does not resolve the ambiguity. The song-and-dance performances of the Sermon on the Mount and the parables celebrate life, but modern society—in the form of the robot, the police, and the chain-link fence—seemingly has its revenge on the countercultural clown.

Such juxtapositions are central to comedy. Comedy transcends only by dwelling on the human body and its limitations, on sex, bodily wastes, weaknesses, improprieties, and ultimately—like *Godspell*—on death itself. It does not dispense with these limitations. It lives in the incongruities consciousness of limits creates. The gentleman belches, farts, or slips on a banana peel. Or, Chaplin simply dresses as the Little Tramp with pants and shoes too large, with hat and coat too small, and with a flexible cane that provides no support.[32] Similarly, *Godspell's* Jesus wears clown pants and a Superman shirt.

Q, of course, incongruously juxtaposes the kingdom of God with everyday life. Its sayings are remarkably secular.[33] Q's Jesus speaks about shepherds, treasures, sparrows, and the lilies of the field. This language, as well as the content of some parables (for example, Luke's prodigal son or Matthew's vineyard workers),[34] evokes the goodness of reality and the graciousness of God. Q has a fundamental optimism, not a cynicism, about life. Not surprisingly, Q enjoins the hearer/reader to "consider the lilies of the field" (Q 12:22–31) and to remember the sparrows (Q 12:4–7) for the same reason that the Western religious tradition uniformly enjoins gratitude to God the Creator. It trusts life. The effect of Q's sayings is like that of my daughter's favorite story, *Where the Wild Things Are.* Max acts out, is punished, and visits fantastic worlds, but when he arrives home, his dinner is still warm. In Q's non-apocalyptic sayings, the world is like that.

Q's apocalyptic damnations—despite their ostensibly happy ending for the Q community—disturb this comic vision. Comedy does not settle ambiguities so decisively. Thus, while Q's Jesus does not die, *Godspell* ends more comically with the cruciform Jesus. *Godspell* has no resurrection because comedy does not need one.[35] Comedy is neither a happy ending nor a life after death, but an ability to see life differently.[36] It provides a "view askew" (the name of a recent film production company).

In *Iris,* at the funeral of a friend, John Bayley (Jim Broadbent) tells the story of Anna Karenina en route to the train. Although seemingly inappropriate, John's point is that Anna saw something funny on the way and thought that she would tell her lover later only to realize that she could not. She then commits suicide. Bayley comments, "If anything could keep one from suicide, it would be a funny story to tell one's love." For Bayley, his friend was such an audience. Similarly, Crossan observes that after a disastrous loss of comrades in *The Odyssey* (bk. 12), the survivors prepare supper, eat, mourn their lost comrades, and sleep. The order is important because life continues. If tragedy knows death and tears, comedy knows death *and supper:* "If the same life or world or reality can be judged by some as tragic and by others as comic, then the latter has clearly won because it is already comic that the same events could be interpreted in such diametric opposition. Tragedy is swallowed up eventually in comedy."[37] Comedy lives in incongruity, not in its unambiguous resolution. In comedy, we must "stand on the brink of Nonsense and Absurdity and (may) not be dizzy."[38]

Without resurrection and apocalypse, the clown restores the world. In fact, when comedy ends paradisally, "it is with a knowing wink and a mischievous grin" that acknowledges that life is not quite this way.[39] The clown restores the world only as he/she provides an intersection of incongruities. The clown is not apocalyptic hero, but the "lord of ambiguity":

> The clown is lord of that no-man's-land between contending forces, moving back and forth along all those human lines drawn (not without arbitrariness) between law and order, social and antisocial, reason and irrationality, friend and foe, fashionable and unfashionable, important and unimportant. The clown is now on one side, now on the other, and ultimately both and neither. And one of the ritual functions of clowning is to convey a sense of this ambiguity and of the relativity that clings to all finite categories.[40]

Comedy and the clown transgress all our boundaries.[41]

While religious ritual and apocalyptic vision configure the world *sub specie aeternae*, comedy and the clown render the world *sub specie ludi*.[42] Comedy, then, is a secular form of the play that animates ritual, apocalypse, and carnival.[43] It is an epiphany of play (not the sacred). Of course, to the (overly) rational and cynical, play (and *Godspell*'s vaudevillian Jesus' troupe) are simply silly, but comedy delights those who tire of the world (at least, of the socially constructed world).[44]

The Gospels' canonical solemnity and Q's apocalyptic voyeurism obscure the comedy in Jesus' sayings. The Gospel of Thomas, another collection of the (114) sayings of Jesus, differs. Like Q, Thomas contains socially radical sayings and has no passion narrative, but it does not have an apocalyptic worldview. Three themes are prominent in Thomas. First, Jesus is divine wisdom, rather than dying Christ or apocalyptic Son of Man.[45] This secret wisdom, revealed by Thomas and properly interpreted, will deliver from death (Thomas 1). Second, the content of Jesus' wisdom is that the kingdom is within:

> Jesus said, "If those who lead you say to you, 'See, the kingdom is in the sky,' then the birds of the sky will precede you. If they say to you, 'It is in the sea,' then the fish will precede you. Rather, the kingdom is inside of you, and it is outside of you. When you come to know yourselves, then you will become known, and you will realize that it is you who are the sons of the living father. But if you will not know yourselves, you dwell in poverty and it is you who are that poverty." (Thomas 3; cf. 113; Luke 17:21)

Those who know are effectively divine (Thomas 24; 49; 50; 51; 70; 111). They overcome death (1; 11; 18; 19; 85); they are solitary (16; 23; 49; 61; 75); and they make the "two one" (22; 72; 106; 114). These benefits imply Thomas's third theme, that wisdom rejects the world (Thomas 27; 56; 80; 110; 111; 112): "Jesus said, 'Whoever has come to understand the world has found (only) a corpse, and whoever has found a corpse is superior to the world'" (Thomas 56; 112). Accordingly, the Thomistic Jesus' most succinct wisdom is "Become passersby" (Thomas 42).

Clearly, all of this is susceptible to a gnostic interpretation[46] that could deny the world's goodness. At times (for example, Thomas 56), that sense is well nigh inescapable. If so, Thomas is as far from comedy and *Godspell* as Q's apocalyptic voyeurism is, but Thomas's emphasis on the kingdom's presence and its call to become "passersby" could also represent a comic view askew. If so, then "Thomas' Jesus is not really out to change the world. He aims rather to change people's perception of the world and their role in it."[47] If so, of all the collections of Jesus' sayings, Thomas is closest to the clown troupe's comic gamboling in *Godspell.* After all, while the clown troupe struggles to create the "city of man," they are already the "city of God" (in a song based on Matthew 5:14–16).

Interestingly, the Gospel of Thomas figures prominently in a recent film, *Stigmata,* which includes parts of Thomas 3 and 77 in its dialogue. *Stigmata* tells the tale of a young atheist's (Frankie, played by Patricia Arquette) religious possession. When the Vatican learns of Frankie's stigmatic attacks, the hierarchy sends its scientific-debunker-of-miracles priest (Andrew, played by Gabriel Byrne) to investigate. Andrew learns that Frankie's stigmata are genuine— though inspired by the possession of a dead priest who wished to publish Thomas—and that the Vatican has "covered up" Thomas. For *Stigmata,* the institutional church has consumed Jesus because it portrays Thomas not as a Coptic gospel of uncertain date but as a first-century Aramaic gospel likely written by Jesus himself. Andrew, of course, saves the girl, Thomas, and Jesus.

Stigmata's interpretation privileges Thomas's social radicalism by emphasizing its anti-ritual, anti-institutional trends (compare Thomas 6; 14; 89) and its individualistic focus.[48] These same emphases can be read gnostically. Certainly, *Stigmata,* whose storyline is about a possession, privileges the spirit over physicality. Further, *Stigmata* rejects science as an explanatory (and beneficial) system. Andrew twice rejects science, once for the priesthood and then (Vatican science) for Frankie. Thus, except for the nascent romance between Frankie and Andrew, there is little affirmation of the world and even less comedy in *Stigmata.* Of course, religious horror is hardly an ideal genre for comic tone.[49]

Enacting Parables and the Kingdom

Comic "passing-by" is more evident in *Godspell*'s vaudevillian singing-and-dancing clown troupe. They live "in the cracks" of society (mere scenery for their gambols)—without apocalyptic hope, without gnostic revelations, without religious horror, and certainly without canonical authority. By contrast, *Stigmata*'s characters are far too heroic to be so clownish (or childlike; compare Q 10:21; Thomas 21; 22; 37; 46).

Further, where *Stigmata*'s community is Hollywood's typical, besieged romantic duo, *Godspell*'s troupe has the community orientation of Jesus' sayings.[50] In fact, *Godspell*'s vaudevillian reenactment of Jesus' sayings intensifies the communal aura of the sayings, because these disciples—in contrast to those in the canonical Gospels and Thomas—help Jesus tell and enact the parables. They start the Beatitudes that Jesus finishes.

Clint Eastwood's *Bronco Billy* dramatizes a similar community. Bronco Billy McCoy (Eastwood) is the patriarchal head of a flea-bitten, down-on-its-luck traveling Wild West show, a group of cowboys and clowns (according to the introductory song by Ronnie Milsap). The movie opens with Doc's (Scatman Crothers) complaint on behalf of the troupe that they have not been paid in six months. Standing in the rain, an infuriated Billy then berates his "family" as "dirty, lousy ingrates." Repentant, the troupe begs forgiveness, because Billy is their savior, boss, and friend. In the rain, with no money, Billy re-creates his community.

Meanwhile, a rich heiress, Antoinette Lily (Sondra Locke), marries, but her badly treated husband (Geoffrey Lewis) leaves her penniless in a small town. Reluctantly, she joins Bronco Billy's troupe as his female assistant. Thereafter, the movie concerns this heartless shrew's redemption. Gradually, Billy brings her from worldly cynicism to his comic view askew that one can become what one wishes to be. In fact, Billy himself is no cowboy; he is an ex-convict and a one-time New Jersey shoe clerk. Except for Leonard, an army deserter (who Billy saves through self-abasement, not heroism), everyone in the troupe met in prison. In Billy's Wild West show, however, they are who they want to be. Miss Lily's problem, according to Billy's wisdom, is that she does not know who she is. In fact, she is running away from her self (compare Thomas 3). She simply needs to decide what she wants to be and then become it.[51]

After various catastrophes, including a fire that burns their circus tent, they go to an institute for the criminally insane to obtain a new tent. There, Miss Lily's husband, who has been incarcerated for her "murder," exposes her, and the powers-that-be bring her back to New York to resolve matters. Finally, of course, she reunites with Billy through the troupe's manipulations for a climactic Wild West show in Billy's new tent made from American flags sewn by the criminally insane. As the closing credits roll, Ronnie Milsap appropriately sings "Dream on, Bronco Billy," because dreams, re-created selves, and family are what the troupe has. The movie does not end with an apocalyptic finale; the kingdom (the ranch they desire) never arrives. What they have is the road, the show, and their family.

Crossan imagines Jesus and his early followers creating the kingdom similarly:

In the beginning was the performance; not the word alone, not the deed alone, but both, each indelibly marked with the other forever. He comes as yet unknown into a hamlet of Lower Galilee. He is watched by the cold, hard eyes of peasants living long enough at subsistence level to know exactly where the line is drawn between poverty and destitution. He looks like a beggar, yet his eyes lack the proper cringe, his voice the proper whine, his walk the proper shuffle. He speaks about the rule of God, and they listen as much from curiosity as anything else. They know all about rule and power, about kingdom and empire, but they know it in terms of tax and debt, malnutrition and sickness, agrarian oppression and demonic possession. What, they really want to know, can this kingdom of God do for a lame child, a blind parent, a demented soul screaming its tortured isolation among the graves that mark the edges of the village?[52]

According to Crossan, Jesus' answer was to make the rule of God present for the people through a ministry of magic and meal:

That ecstatic vision and social program sought to rebuild a society upward from its grass roots but on principles of religious and economic egalitarianism, with free healing brought directly to the peasant homes and free sharing of whatever they had in return. The deliberate conjunction of magic and meal, miracle and table, free compassion and open commensality, was a challenge launched . . . at civilization's eternal inclination to draw lines, invoke boundaries, establish hierarchies, and maintain discriminations. It did not invite a political revolution but envisaged a social one at the imagination's most dangerous depths.[53]

Further, Jesus invited others to participate in this trickster-like and clownish activity:

To those first followers from the peasant villages of Lower Galilee who asked how to repay his exorcisms and cures, he gave a simple answer, simple, that is, to understand but hard as death itself to undertake. You are healed healers, he said, so take the Kingdom to others, for I am not its patron and you are not its brokers. It is, was, and always will be available to any who want it. Dress as I do, like a beggar, but do not beg. Bring a miracle and request a table. Those you heal must accept you into their homes.[54]

Clearly, this kingdom performance resembles Bronco Billy's Wild West show more closely than it does the imperial church and canonical authority.

It also resembles the antic enactment of Jesus' parables and teachings in the skits and songs in *Godspell*. More importantly, the troupe enacts the film's message of the re-created city of man by "sprucing up" the junkyard in which Jesus' teaching begins and ends. In addition to the painted clown faces and the sunrise painted on a wall, the miracle of the tree epitomizes *Godspell*'s performance. One disciple puts a small sprig in a bucket. In her absence, another disciple replaces it with a much larger tree. When the first disciple returns, she finds herself in the presence of a (comic) miracle.

All of this, of course, is play, pretend, and performance, not reality. *Godspell* and Crossan's Jesus' teachings are art and poetry, a revolution in imagination, not politics. They invite to a view askew like Bronco Billy's. Accordingly, Crossan begins with "*In the beginning* was the performance. . . ." *Godspell*'s language game is similar. It performs the "city of man." If (Crossan's) Jesus performs the kingdom, he does not need to define it. In the context of performance, the kingdom is symbol, not concept. One defines concepts, but not symbols.[55] Symbols evoke:

> The discussion has established the fact that in the proclamation of Jesus "Kingdom of God" was used as a tensive symbol, and that it was used to evoke the myth of God acting as king. The challenge of the message of Jesus was to recognize the reality of the activity of God in the historicality of the hearer's existence in the world, and especially in the experience of a "clash of worlds" as the hearer comes to grips with the reality of everyday existence.[56]

In short, "kingdom" evokes (or enacts) God's rule; it does not define it.

Godspell's enactment of Jesus' teaching provides, like festival, fantasy, and comedy, an alternative reality (of the kingdom of God?). By contrast, reification of Jesus' teaching—whether into cynical philosophy, apocalyptic vision, gnostic revelation, or canonical pronouncement—misses the experience of hearing Jesus' sayings. Of course, *Godspell* is only a movie. The troupe acts and we watch voyeuristically. As such, no one may be (really) performing the kingdom, but the troupe's performance invites us to imagine an alternative city of man:

> It is at the level of the imagination that the fateful issues of our new world-experience must first be mastered. It is here that culture and history are broken, and here that the church is polarized. Old words do not reach across the new gulfs, and it is only in vision and oracle that we can chart the unknown and new-name the creatures.
>
> Before the message there must be a vision, before the sermon the hymn, before the prose the poem.[57]

The troupe performs (dances in) the kingdom.

In short, imagination is more countercultural than concept is.

Godspell's Interpretation of Matthew

I have read back and forth between *Godspell* and the noncanonical sayings of Jesus, Q and the Gospel of Thomas, arguing that both the movie and the sayings share a sacred discontent, live in the creative disorder of play, and enact alternative worlds. *Godspell* itself, however, claims to be based on the Gospel of Matthew. We might think briefly, then, about *Godspell*'s interpretation of Matthew.

On first blush, *Godspell* hardly seems like Matthew. Matthew's Jesus never sings and dances. He hardly seems capable of such. He is an angry rabbi and an apocalyptic prophet (compare Matthew 23–25), not a face-painting clown. Where Matthew's Jesus is angry and authoritative, *Godspell*'s Jesus is whimsical and playful. Here, *Godspell* seems closer to the play and imagination in Q and Thomas than to Matthew.

Matthew's Sermon on the Mount is, however, incredibly important to *Godspell*. In fact, apart from John's baptism and Jesus' passion, the Matthean sermon is the gospel "event" of the film. *Godspell* uses an adapted sermon to structure Jesus' ministry as the clown troupe dances through the park and the city (see figure 4).

Figure 4: *Godspell*'s Sermon

Location	Matthean reference	Synopsis
Junkyard	5:17–20	Fulfill law and prophets
Junkyard	Luke 18:10–14	Pharisee and tax collector
Junkyard	5:24–26	Forgive brother
Junkyard	18:23–35	Unforgiving debtor
Park	5:38–39	Other cheek
Park	25:31–46	Sheep and goats
Park tunnel	7:22–24	Clear eye, one master
Park bench	Luke 10:30–35	Good Samaritan
Park	6:2–4	Secret charity
Park stoa (portico)	Luke 16:19–31	Rich man and Lazarus
Park amphitheater	5:3–12	Beatitudes
Park	7:3–5	Stick in one's eye
Empty streets	5:44	Love your enemy
Park	13:1–9, 18–23	Sower and seed
Park	6:28–30	Lilies of the field
Cherry Lane Theater	Luke 15:11–32	Two sons
River	7:9–12	Prayer, Golden Rule
Ferry	5:14–16	Light of the world

The selections, omissions, and arrangement of the Sermon on the Mount highlight *Godspell*'s message: God forgives, and we should forgive and love our fellow humans. The insertion of various parables unique to Luke augments this message. In fact, the first and last parables in the film—both on forgiveness—are Lukan, not Matthean. The last, the parable of the two sons enacted to the accompaniment of classic film clips in the Cherry Lane Theater (where the play *Godspell* was first performed), nicely epitomizes *Godspell*'s message, because in *Godspell*'s version the brothers are reconciled. No one is left out of the party. Such touches outdo even Luke's concern for gracious inclusions and are rather far from Matthew's Torah concerns.

    Godspell is most like the canonical gospels and least like Q and Thomas when it uses Jesus' sayings to introduce its passion narrative. *Godspell*'s passion is not overwhelmingly Matthean, but two of its touches resemble Matthew.[58] Where

Mark crafts the passion as the death of the divine representative that will usher in the apocalyptic kingdom, and Luke depicts Jesus as the prophet whose rejection brings terrible divine judgments upon Jerusalem, Matthew depicts Jesus' death as the supreme act of obedience of the righteous one. *Godspell* intensifies this element by enlarging its Gethsemane scene with the three temptations from Matthew 4:1–11. *Godspell*'s Jesus triumphantly ends the temptations with "worship him above" (Matthew 4:10, rather than Luke 4:12, "Do not put the Lord your God to the test").

Less obviously, *Godspell* also plays out a variation of Matthew's anti-institutional theme. Where Matthew deliberately arrays Jesus over against the scribes and Pharisees (for example, Matthew 5–6; 23), *Godspell* depicts Jesus' opponents as a huge robot, the police, and John-Judas. The robot is intriguing. It suggests romantic fears about industrial and bureaucratic society. The institution that troubles *Godspell* is modern civilization.[59] Once again, we have arrived at American Romantic aversion to the city and a desire to escape the city for a peaceable garden. The robot is the revenge of industrial society. Although deploying that theme only minimally, *Godspell* is obviously less hopeful than *Modern Times.* Where the Little Tramp enters the machine and escapes, the robot and the fence (a strikingly unique crucifixion) consume Jesus. Unlike the tramp, *Godspell*'s Jesus does not reemerge.

At daybreak, as the disciples sing "Long Live God," the camera focuses on a dead Jesus still affixed to the fence. Removing Jesus, the troupe carries him in cruciform form through the empty city, singing, "Prepare the Way of the Lord" and "Day by Day." Eventually, they vanish into the crowded city as the music continues. If this is a resurrection, it is a very Bultmannian one. If Jesus rises, it is into the songs of his disciples (and Judas-John).[60] It is hardly Matthew's use of the resurrection scene to commission the disciples (Matthew 28:16–20) as the approved, fully trained teachers (or scribes of the kingdom, Matthew 13:52) who succeed Jesus (Matthew 16:18–20; 18:15–20). *Godspell*'s clown troupe may resemble Mark's bumbling, stooge-like disciples or Paul's conception of believers as foolish and weak, but not Matthew's authoritative teachers. Matthew (like Luke) is much closer to the seriousness and polemics of the imperial, canonical church. *Godspell* rejects such order for sacred discontent and dance.

Reading Jesus' Sayings in the Dark: Revisiting Location

Godspell translates Matthew into American culture in the early 1970s, when various powerful forces were domesticating the counterculture. It also translates it into a culture that has long-standing Romantic elements in both its mythology and film. Further, the original playwright is on record as wishing to reanimate the gospel, to rescue it from the deadly clutches of the church, and to set it free in modernity. All of these elements contribute to *Godspell*'s interpretative perspective vis-à-vis Matthew. Interestingly, the resulting translation resembles the non-canonical sayings of Jesus recently recovered by scholars more than it does Matthew.

Location, location, location. Jesus' sayings live in different locations. They operate in quotidian conversations and as canonical pronouncements. They seduce; they proclaim; they demand; and they authorize. They also thrive in different worldviews: in countercultural wisdom; in apocalyptic; in Gnosticism; in canon; and in scholarship. Strikingly, they also transgress various epistemes. In these locations, of course, Jesus' sayings mean differently.

Certainly, Jesus' teaching had a "meaning," or at least a cultural range of meanings in its "original" context, but that context is gone. Now, Jesus' teaching is always "out of place." That alone justifies the sacred discontent and comic eschatology of *Godspell* and scholars, but that also means that no place—not even the clown's troupe—can claim the sayings finally. In this, Jesus himself (in the form of his sayings) has become passerby.[61]

Reading Jesus' sayings in Q and Thomas in the dark with *Godspell*, then, reminds us that the sayings are under-determined. Having a protean quality, they change shape and meaning as they move from culture to culture or from reading to reading. They mean only according to their context or in light of a particular reader's ideology. They mean, that is, only in a particular performance. Of course, this mutability means neither a lost original of these sayings nor an end to their possible meanings (significations) exists. Outside their canonical captivity (where they have a myth and ritual force, certainty, and, therefore, world-foundational quality), the sayings are notably parabolic. Nonetheless, the sayings offer no permanent escape from culture. Our myths and ideologies exert a gravitational pull on us and on them. The sayings do, however, provide imaginative vistas suggesting the boundaries of our world.[62] If they are not (traditional) revelation, they are postcards from the edge.

To read the sayings in the dark, then, is to recognize their potentially parabolic, subversive nature. We easily see and applaud this quality when the sayings subvert an alien order. We academicians happily detail Jesus' subversion of first-century Judaism(s) or Rome's colonizing empire. We are also happy enough—in the academy—when the sayings discomfit the church(es). Whether or not we can handle our own dis-ease if the sayings undermine our own American or academic mythology is another matter and determines whether or not we can stand "on the edge" or in "the dark night of story."

To do so, we must look long and hard at the sayings (or some other parable) in the dark. I have complained that *Godspell* does not liberate Jesus' sayings from American mythology, particularly from American Romanticism. *Godspell*'s dead clown does, however, have certain parabolic potential here. When I watch *Godspell* with religion classes, the dead clown disturbs them. For them, the clown is too burlesque (not serious enough), and the dead clown is too profane. They desire more serious and more triumphant Jesuses. Their reaction is not merely an expression of traditional or conservative Christianity; it also reflects their American sense that Jesus is/should be triumphant and true.[63] *Godspell's* dead clown subverts these mythic certainties.

Godspell also reminds us that Jesus' (death and) resurrection is absent in the sayings. Despite apocalyptic and gnostic interpretations, the Jesuses of Q and Thomas triumph only in their sayings. Of course, these sayings are, as we have seen, at the mercy of later ideologies. The Jesuses of these sayings, then, are closer to a dead—or at least helpless—clown than they are to the triumphant, divine hero of the church and of American mythology. Appropriately, then, *Godspell's* playwright tries to liberate Jesus' sayings from the church with a dead clown carried—not under his own power—by his troupe. We remember, then, that the sayings of Jesus live on—not under their own power, but as they are transported, often in cruciform, by some later (apocalyptic, gnostic, canonical, romantic, and so forth) ideology.

We have not yet, however, arrived at academic discontent. Jesus' sayings challenge us to read them against our own ideology, not against someone else's. Are, then, the sayings—which have been created by the academy—subversive of the academy? To read as I have so far is not necessarily to express a countercultural stance vis-à-vis the modern, often cynical, and certainly individualistic academy. Versus such cynical individualism—which would enact my (Jesus') parables at someone else's expense—perhaps I should return via the dead clown to the *communal* (not individualistic) *performance* of his troupe (and of the communities of Q and Thomas?). In an imaginary conversation, Crossan imagines a traditional Jesus impugning the academy (and his own work):

> "I've read your book, Dominic, and it's quite good. So now you're ready to live by my vision and join me in my program?"
>
> "I don't think I have the courage, Jesus, but I did describe it quite well, didn't I, and the method was especially good, wasn't it?"
>
> "Thank you, Dominic, for not falsifying the message to suit your own incapacity. That at least is something."
>
> "Is it enough, Jesus?"
>
> "No, Dominic, it is not."[64]

Unlike his "Jesus," then, Crossan has not yet arrived at what he depicts as "in the beginning," that is, at "performance." Such humble postcards from the edge are rare in the academy. We arrive there only by losing Jesus, by recognizing a distance between our words and lives and any divine authority.

Notes

1. Ludwig Wittgenstein, *Philosophical Investigations*, trans. G. E. M. Anscombe (Malden, Mass., and Oxford: Blackwell, 1997), 1:547–51 n. (b).

2. Bernard Brandon Scott, *Hear Then the Parable: A Commentary on the Parables of Jesus* (Minneapolis, Minn.: Fortress, 1990), 56.

3. This assertion is by now a semiotic truism. Early structuralists contended that "b" had a meaning only as it differed from "d," or that "hot" had a meaning only as it differed from "cold," "warm," and so forth.

4. Wittgenstein, *Philosophical Investigations*, 1:116.

5. Ibid., 1:109, 309.

6. "Words and Things" is a more literal translation of the French title for the work translated into English as *The Order of Things: An Archaeology of the Human Sciences*, trans. Alan Sheridan-Smith (New York: Vintage, 1994).

7. Ibid., xx–xxiv, 386–87. That Foucault can describe the third episteme likely means that he lives in a fourth (that provided by post-structural analysis).

8. For a classic review, see Norman Perrin, *Jesus and the Language of the Kingdom: Symbol and Metaphor in New Testament Interpretation* (Philadelphia: Fortress, 1976).

9. Sayings of Jesus that appear in Paul and in early Christian writings do not change the canonical language game significantly. By contrast, if sayings in James not attributed to Jesus are actually remembrances of Jesus' words, James de-canonizes in another way not considered here.

10. Jesus' teaching is only minimally important in Griffith and in the biblical epics.

11. *Sacred Discontent: The Bible and Western Tradition* (Berkeley: University of California Press, 1976), 5–6. For Schneidau, the Bible belongs to pastoral societies, history, prophecy, and parable. He also opines that serious literature (largely the novel) continues biblical discontent in modernity.

12. After Puritan and Enlightenment thought, the next notable intellectual influence on American thought was the Romanticism of Emerson, Thoreau, and Whitman.

13. For a discussion of films on this point, see Scott, *Hollywood Dreams and Biblical Stories*, 47–129. On the frontier, see James Oliver Robertson, *American Myth, American Reality* (New York: Hill & Wang, 1980), 92–124; May, *The Cry for Myth*, 91–107; Neale, *Genre and Hollywood*, 133–42; and Chapter 7 below.

14. Reportedly, the original playwright (John-Michael Tebelak) wrote to resurrect the teaching of Jesus from the church's deathly clutches.

15. For lists of Q passages, see John S. Kloppenborg, *The Formation of Q: Trajectories in Ancient Wisdom Collections* (Philadelphia: Fortress, 1987), 92; or Denis C. Duling and Norman Perrin, *The New Testament: Proclamation and Parenesis, Myth and History*, 3rd ed. (Fort Worth, Tex.: Harcourt Brace, 1994), 147–50. From their reconstructions, scholars often print translations of Q. See, e.g., John S. Kloppenborg, Marvin Meyer, Stephen J. Patterson, and Michael G. Steinhauser, *Q-Thomas Reader* (Sonoma, Calif.: Polebridge, 1990), 35–74; and Burton L. Mack, *The Lost Gospel: The Book of Q and Christian Origins* (San Francisco: HarperSanFrancisco, 1993), 71–102.

16. Some scholars attribute the Son of Man title to the Q community, rather than to Jesus. See Hans Eduard Tödt, *The Son of Man in the Synoptic Tradition* (Philadelphia: Westminster, 1965).

17. Thus, John Dominic Crossan, *In Fragments: The Aphorisms of Jesus* (San Francisco: Harper & Row, 1983), 156, 342–45, discusses Q in terms of topical sections: 1) Jesus and John, Q 3:1–7:35; 2) Jesus and disciples, Q 9:57–11:13; 3) Jesus and opponents, Q 11:14–51; and 4) Jesus and the apocalypse, Q 12:2–22:30.

18. Kloppenborg, *The Formation of Q,* 94.

19. Ibid., 95.

20. Rudolf Bultmann, *Jesus and the Word,* trans. Louise Pettibone Smith and Erminie Huntress Lantero (New York: Scribner's, 1958), speaks of Jesus as both eschatological prophet and rabbi.

21. Kloppenborg, *The Formation of Q,* 102–245.

22. Ibid., 317–28. He adds a third redactional level (the temptation narrative) not important for my discussion here. For an expanded social history of the Q community, see Mack, *The Lost Gospel.* For a defense of the (apocalyptic) integrity of Q, see Howard Clark Kee, *Jesus in History: An Approach to the Study of the Gospels,* 3rd ed. (Fort Worth, Tex.: Harcourt Brace, 1996), 74–115. In earlier editions of his work, Kee claimed that only four of Q's fifty-two passages were non-apocalyptic (Q 7:2–3, 6–10; 16:13; 11:34–36; 17:3b–4, 6). In his third edition, he allows more sapiential material, but he still argues for Q's apocalyptic nature.

23. Kloppenborg, *The Formation of Q,* 318.

24. On Jesus' subversive wisdom, see John Dominic Crossan, *In Parables: The Challenge of the Historical Jesus* (San Francisco: Harper & Row, 1973), 53–78; and Marcus Borg, *Jesus: A New Vision* (San Francisco: Harper & Row, 1985), 79–124.

25. Scorsese's *The Last Temptation of Christ* pursues the idea of a very different "development" of Jesus' message: love, axe, and death.

26. *Godspell* interprets Matthew, editing Jesus' (and John's) teaching to emphasize love and forgiveness. The result is very Lukan or, possibly, Q-like. See below.

27. See Borg, *Jesus: A New Vision,* 97–149. Mack's Galilean Cynic Jesus (see his *A Myth of Innocence*) and Crossan's Jewish peasant (see his *The Historical Jesus*) are similar. Many critics, however, argue that these scholars' Jesuses are too universal. For more "Jewish" Jesuses, see the review by Daniel J. Harrington, S.J., "The Jewishness of Jesus," *Bible Review* 3 (1981): 33–41.

28. According to Tatum, *Jesus at the Movies,* 125–26, *Godspell*'s precursor here is Rolf Forsberg's *Parable.* I have not seen this movie. See Harvey Cox, *The Feast of Fools: A Theological Essay on Festivity and Fantasy* (New York: Harper & Row, 1969), 139–42.

29. Cited in Hyers, *The Comic Vision and the Christian Faith,* 8.

30. Ibid., 58–59. See also John Dominic Crossan, *Raid on the Articulate: Comic Eschatology in Jesus and Borges* (San Francisco: Harper & Row, 1976), 17–50.

31. Cited in Hyers, *The Comic Vision and the Christian Faith,* 56.

32. Ibid., 64.

33. Q, like comedy generally, also juxtaposes social radicalism (e.g., Q 6:27–38; 9:57–62; 10:4; 12:22–38, 51–53; 14:26–27) with an affirmation of life. Q's Jesus lives riotously (Q 7:34). For another gamboling Jesus, see Young's *Jesus.*

34. Scholars do not include these parables in Q.

35. In fact, *Godspell* routinely eliminates Matthew's apocalyptic elements. *Jesus Christ Superstar* and *Life of Brian* also abstain from resurrections (at least of Jesus).

36. See Crossan, *Raid on the Articulate*, 146–49. This book provides the best discussion of Jesus' sayings as "comic" known to me.

37. Ibid., 21.

38. Wylie Sypher, cited in ibid., 33.

39. Hyers, *The Comic Vision and the Christian Faith*, 158-59.

40. Ibid., 69–70.

41. The clown, then, is a variant of the mythological trickster who forever transgresses boundaries and lives in the gaps. See William J. Hynes and William G. Doty, *Mythical Trickster Figures: Contours, Contexts, Criticisms* (Tuscaloosa: University of Alabama Press, 1993). Thomas King's *Green Grass, Running Water* (New York: Bantam, 1994) is a delightful novel about the redemptive power of tricksters.

42. Crossan, *Raid on the Articulate*, 32.

43. On play, see Johan Huizinga, *Homo Ludens: A Study of the Play Element in Culture* (Boston: Beacon, 1955). On the importance of festival, see Cox, *The Feast of Fools*; and Hyers, *The Comic Vision and the Christian Faith*, 40–55.

44. Grace presents the same problem for theodicy that evil does. Matthew 20:1–16 (intriguingly, not in *Godspell*) makes this point well. Paul struggles with it throughout Romans and the elder brother simply does not "get it" in Luke 15:11–32.

45. According to Kloppenborg, *The Formation of Q*, 319–20, Q (7:35; 10:22; 11:49–51) also imagines Jesus as divine wisdom. Helmut Koester, *Introduction to the New Testament* (Philadelphia: Fortress, 1982), 2:150–51, agrees, but notes that Q's apocalyptic Son of Man overwhelms this notion.

46. So Helmut Koester, *Ancient Christian Gospels: Their History and Development* (Philadelphia: Trinity Press International, 1990), 124–28; Kloppenborg, et al., *Q-Thomas Reader*, 93–106; and Stephen J. Patterson, *The Gospel of Thomas and Jesus* (Sonoma, Calif.: Polebridge, 1993), 113–214. The main evidence for Thomas's gnostic provenance is its presence in the Nag Hammadi Library, generally considered a gnostic collection of texts. See James M. Robinson, ed., *The Nag Hammadi Library in English*, 3rd ed. (New York: HarperSanFrancisco, 1990), 124–38. I cite this translation of Thomas here.

47. Kloppenborg et al., *Q-Thomas Reader*, 120.

48. *Stigmata* molds Thomas's individualism into a typical Hollywood pattern, that of the good individual versus the corrupt institution. Of course, this pattern also has important religious precursors like St. Francis (whom *Stigmata* often refers to), Dostoevsky's "Grand Inquisitor," and the Protestant Reformation. One wag opined that *Stigmata* apparently did not know that the Reformation had occurred.

49. The configuring of Frankie as a possessed atheist does show, however, some trickster-like qualities. One of the priests in *Stigmata* also recognizes limits poignantly: "Everyone had an

experience of Jesus and wrote different stories. We are all blind men in a cave looking for a candle lit two thousand years ago."

50. Scholars often speak of a Q community (or communities given Q's emphasis on itinerancy) that actualized Jesus' sayings. Even in Thomas's individualistic wisdom, there are traces of community (Thomas 12; 13).

51. Billy's wisdom is rather conventional compared to that of Q and Thomas. It is his practice that is eccentric and, thereby, redemptive for his troupe.

52. Crossan, *The Historical Jesus,* xi. I would prefer to restrict to a particular construct — Q's or Crossan's Jesus —what Crossan says of the historical Jesus. Compare Bultmann, *Jesus and the Word,* 12, 14, who admits that he refers to the earliest collections of sayings as "Jesus's" as a matter of convenience (and faith?).

53. Crossan, *The Historical Jesus,* xii. See further, ibid., 303–53.

54. Ibid., xii.

55. Perrin, *Jesus and the Language of the Kingdom,* 5–6. C. S. Lewis, *Studies in Words* (Cambridge: Cambridge University Press, 1960), 18, says that we define terms "only because we are in some measure departing from their real current-sense."

56. Perrin, *Jesus and the Language of the Kingdom,* 196. Perrin follows Philip Wheelwright's distinction (*Metaphor and Reality* [Bloomington: Indiana University Press, 1968], 92–110) between steno-symbol (logic) and tensive (poetry) symbol.

57. Amos Wilder, *Theopoetic: Theology and the Religious Imagination* (Philadelphia: Fortress, 1976), 1.

58. *Godspell* has notable Johannine tinges in the passion section both in songs (the disciples sing, "Where are you going?" [cf. John 14:5]) and in deeds (Jesus washes their faces and refuses their reciprocity, a reminder of John's foot-washing scene). *Godspell* also abbreviates the passion significantly. It offers three controversies (Matthew 21:23–27; 22:15–22, 34–40), part of Jesus' invective against the scribes and Pharisees (from Matthew 23), Jesus' lament for Jerusalem (Matthew 23:37–39), Judas's plot (Matthew 26:14–16), the supper (Matthew 26:20–29), Gethsemane (Matthew 26:31–42), and arrest (Matthew 26:36–46). Its "cross" departs completely from Matthew.

59. Not incidentally, Bronco Billy refuses to go to New York even for his love, Miss Lily. I am tempted to read *Godspell*'s police in light of the "fascist" fears of 1960s hippies.

60. For Bultmann ("New Testament and Mythology," 38–43), the resurrection was a matter of the disciples' belief in the saving efficacy of the cross.

61. Compare Schweitzer, *The Quest of the Historical Jesus,* 398–403; and Crossan, *Jesus: A Revolutionary Biography,* 193–201. Thomas (42), of course, is precursor here.

62. Their effect, i.e., can resemble that of the letter left in the computer simulation in *The Thirteenth Floor.*

63. Chapter 8 below explores these suggestions in more detail.

64. Crossan, *Jesus: A Revolutionary Biography,* xiv.

Chapter 5

A Hermeneutics of Suspicion: *Il Vangelo secondo Matteo* and Matthew

By midrash the interpreter, either by rewriting the story or explaining it in a more acceptable sense, bridges the gap between an original and a modern audience. The word derives from dārash, to probe or examine; however the work is done, whether by fictive augmentation and change or by commentary, its object is to penetrate the surface and reveal a secret sense; to show what is concealed in what is proclaimed.[1]

Reading Matthew and *Il Vangelo secondo Matteo*

Matthew introduces Jesus elaborately as the eschatological son of David (Matthew 1:1–4:16).[2] Then, Matthew depicts Jesus' attempts to inaugurate the kingdom in Galilee through teaching, miracles, and the enlistment of colleagues (Matthew 4:17–11:1). The kingdom activities quickly embroil Jesus in controversy, and most Galileans and various religious leaders reject the kingdom. Jesus establishes, however, an embryonic, itinerant kingdom community (Matthew 4:17–16:20). Finally, Jesus takes the kingdom activities to Jerusalem. En route, he teaches his embryonic community about his death and their continuing community life in his "absence" (Matthew 16:21–20:34). When Jesus arrives in Jerusalem, he tries to continue the kingdom activities, but the religious leaders kill him (Matthew 21:1–27:66). God resurrects him, however, and he meets his followers in Galilee to send them out on a kingdom mission to the nations (Matthew 28). Within this story, Matthew offers five teaching sections (5–7; 10; 13; 18; 24–25). They provide Jesus' teaching, train the disciples (and the readers), constitute Jesus' legacy, and charter Matthew's kingdom-teaching community.[3]

Pasolini's *Il Vangelo secondo Matteo* so obviously cites and visualizes Matthew that Matthew virtually becomes his screenplay.[4] Of course, visualizing and adding sound to a text, including interpretative music, is a major interpretative move. Further, Pasolini does adapt, revise, and restructure Matthew—particularly in the Galilean ministry section—for his own ends. Pasolini's major interpretation, however, is simply to film *a gospel*. By so doing, Pasolini removes

Matthew from the church(es)'s four-gospel canon.[5] In keeping with his interpretation, Pasolini objected strenuously when his film was released with English subtitles with the title "The Gospel According to St. Matthew." The addition of "saint" does obscure his interpretation of Matthew, so I will refer to the film here by its Italian title, *Il Vangelo secondo Matteo*.

Depending on Matthew, Pasolini's film is consciously late. So, too, is Matthew, because Matthew depends on several precursors: Mark and Q, if the two-source hypothesis is correct, and certainly the Hebrew Bible (in whatever form). Both gospel and film, then, depend on an earlier text, which they reproduce and interpret for their own meaning. Their interpretations find hidden meanings in their precursors that allow them to create a portrait of an angry Jesus protesting an oppressive institution and advocating a worldly Christianity. Their thorough investment in precursors—that is, their intertextuality—renders both gospel and film paradoxical. They are and are not what came before.

Late Texts

Hollywood Jesus films (and the biblical epics) create extravagant backgrounds for Jesus by adding plots and characters to the Gospels. These inventions smooth out literary and cinematic problems in the rather episodic Gospels by placing novelized screenplays and Hollywood conventions between the films (and the audience) and the Gospels. By refusing to novelize Matthew's text, Pasolini mechanically reproduces Matthew.[6] His reactivation, then, nicely reveals Matthew's episodic nature:

> By literally following Matthew's "stylistic accelerations"—the barbaric-practical workings of his narration, the abolition of chronological time, the elliptical jumps within the story which inscribe the "disproportions" of the didactic, static moments such as the stupendous, interminable, discourse on the mountain—the figure of Christ should finally assume the violence inhering in any rebellion which radically contradicts the appearance and shape that life assumes for modern man: a gray orgy of cynicism, irony, brutality, compromise and conformism. . . .[7]

Pasolini also eschews the epic style:

> Using a reverential style for *The Gospel* was gilding the lily: it came out rhetoric. Reverential technique and style in *Accattone* went fine, but applied to a sacred text they were ridiculous; so I got discouraged and was just about to give the whole thing up, and then when I was shooting

the baptism scene near Viterbo I threw over all my technical preconceptions. I started using the zoom, I used new camera movements, new frames which were not reverential, but almost documentary.[8]

To achieve a documentary style, Pasolini shoots the film in black and white, films in the peasant villages of southern Italy, and uses Italian peasants as his actors. The resulting film, then, defamiliarizes Matthew by denying American audiences their two typical interpretative frameworks for Jesus films, Hollywood epic conventions and the canon's four-gospel harmony.

The film, then, forces the viewer to interpret the film consciously, as the opening scenes nicely illustrate. After the opening credits and a dedication to Pope John XXIII, the background music stops and the film proceeds in silence. A pregnant peasant girl looks at an older man, and he walks away. If we know that this is the Virgin Mary and Joseph, we do so only from prior acquaintance with Matthew (or other church traditions). As the man approaches a village, we hear the background noises of village life as the first sounds in the film. The man falls asleep until a young girl in white wakes him to tell him to take Mary as his wife and to inform him that her son is Jesus who will bear his people's sins. If we see this young girl as an angel, we do so on the basis of our prior knowledge of Matthew. Interpretative background music[9] begins again as the man (whom we still know as Joseph only by our prior knowledge) goes back to Mary. Meanwhile, a narrator quotes Isaiah 7:14. When the man comes to Mary, both he and Mary smile, but they remain silent.

Pasolini continues these suggestive silences[10] throughout the infancy section. Mary and her man never speak, but the young girl, the narrator, the wise men, and the religious-political leaders do. Why does Pasolini allow such potent, poignant silences? He may have adopted this style simply for logistical reasons— because he uses amateur actors and he may not want to risk asking for convincing dialogue from them. Alternatively, the combination of peasant silence and the authoritative speech of leaders may be a deliberate Marxist comment on the silencing of peasants by institutional hierarchies. Or, Pasolini may simply be reading and following Matthew,[11] because Matthew's Joseph and Mary never speak. At any rate, as a result, Pasolini does not completely free Matthew from the church. His film does not stand alone. It depends upon Matthew (or other church traditions) for its meaning.

Matthew is also consciously late, and its sense also depends "on the prior existence of another book [the Hebrew Bible], which always tells the sacred truth yet always, despite its apparent completeness, needs completion."[12] Matthew, then, exceeds the Hebrew Bible (or its Greek translation) in a fashion reminiscent of Hebrew poetry:

Although typology is sometimes said to be a Christian invention, it is clearly derived from Jewish habits of thought and reflects Jewish rhetorical modes, some of great antiquity. It has been argued, for example, that the habitual parallelism of Hebrew verse is not so much a way of enforcing a point by repetition as of saying "A, and, what's more, B"; the second colon or verset provides something in excess of the first. And this formula could describe not only the general structure of Matthew's thought ("Israel A, and, what's more, Israel B") but also the texture of his prose. Indeed it is this quality above all others that provides us with a sense of the unity of this Gospel. The "what's more" of his texture reflects the "what's more" of his argument. The excess of B over A is what transforms A and fulfills it.[13]

Matthew revels in this dependency. At every opportunity, some clearly forced, Matthew quotes the Hebrew Bible passage typologically completed by Jesus. Quite often, Matthew introduces the citation with a formulaic "fulfillment" reference most common, although not completely peculiar, to this gospel (compare John 12:38; 19:24, 36): "All this took place to fulfill what had been spoken by the Lord through the prophet . . ." (Matthew 1:22). In fact, Matthew uses this fulfillment formula twelve times.[14] If we add to Matthew's formulaic citations its other less formal references and allusions to the Hebrew Bible (for example, Matthew 2:5–6; 11:10; 15:7–9; 21:13, 16, 42; 26:31), virtually Matthew's whole story becomes a fulfillment of a prior text(s). That Jesus' fulfillment of the law and prophets (Matthew 5:17–20) is ethical, as well as typological, means that the Hebrew Bible remains important for Matthew as guide, *when properly interpreted by Matthew,* for life (Matthew 5:21–6:18).[15] Notably, the Torah fulfillment of Matthew's Jesus exceeds that of the scribes and Pharisees, other notable Torah-keepers (Matthew 5:20; 23).

Matthew highlights its dependence because its precursor confers authority on Matthew's story. The formula citations refer to the precursor to provide warrants rendering Matthew's incidents true and significant. Such typological causation, as we noted in Chapter 3, depends on and creates a notion of divine providence. For many modern readers, of course, Matthew's typological warrants fail to convince. Instead, they call attention to Matthew's interpretative work.[16]

Despite its dependency, Matthew continues its precursor rather freely and willfully. Without Matthew's assistance, we would hardly read Hebrew prophecy (for example, Isaiah 7:14; Hosea 11:1; Jeremiah 31:15) as it does. Further, the Sermon on the Mount's antitheses (5:21–48) also demonstrate a rather cavalier treatment of its precursor. In fact, before long, it is not altogether clear in what sense the Matthean Jesus' "But, I say to you" fulfills Matthew's precursor at all.

This freeness extends throughout Matthew. Matthew's introduction, for example, reduces Israel's history to a forty-two-member genealogy. Arranged in three sets of fourteen, Matthew's genealogy highlights Abraham, David, exile, and the messiah (Matthew 1:1, 17), and it veils the second Temple and the synagogue. In short, Matthew's genealogy devalues Jewish institutions to make way for its own. In Matthew's revisionist story, the messiah follows exile. By contrast, for the Chronicler, the second Temple answers exile. Not surprisingly, Chronicles became the last book in the Hebrew Bible and Matthew the first in the New Testament.

Matthew's version of the infancy and the baptism rewrites as thoroughly. According to Royal David theology, the legitimate king was a literal descendant of David and was adopted as the son of God upon his enthronement (see Psalms 2; 110). Matthew's free use of Isaiah 7:14 to indicate Jesus' miraculous virgin birth creates difficulties for Jesus' legitimacy. Despite the best efforts of the genealogy (Matthew 1:16), Jesus is hardly a literal son of David. In point of fact, Joseph adopts Jesus as his (Davidic) son. Later, at Matthew's baptism, the Matthean God's words echo the ceremonial words by which God adopted the Davidic king at his enthronement. In light of Matthew's virgin-birth story, however, the Matthean Jesus is far more literally son of God than any of his Davidic precursors were. With the virgin birth and baptism, then, Matthew reverses Davidic theology. Where the Davidic king was literally a son of David and an adopted son of God, Matthew's messiah is an adopted son of David and a literal son of God.

While Matthew's reversals are not as drastic as the notion of the new covenant in Hebrews, Matthew has an anxious air of one-upmanship. Aware of its lateness and trying to make the most of dependency, Matthew urgently asserts its value. As a late text, Matthew must exceed, or it has no *raison d'être*. Matthew exceeds as eschatological fulfillment. Given its anxious lateness, it is hardly a surprise that Matthew name-calls (Matthew 6:1–18; 23) and fights so strenuously for ownership of its precursor.[17]

A comic scene in the movie *Snatch* explains Matthew's anxieties quite clearly. As jewel thieves masquerading as orthodox Jewish diamond merchants penetrate a diamond market's security, one of the "Jews" (played by Benicio Del Toro) eschews the literal interpretation of Scripture. Pressed for a reason, he offers a bizarre case, the formation of the Catholic Church because of a mistranslation of the Hebrew word for "young maiden" by the Greek word for "virgin." The error created the prophecy, "Behold, a virgin shall conceive a son." He muses further, "You understand it was the word 'virgin' that got people's attention. It's not every day that a virgin conceives and bears a son. . . . Couple hundred years pass and the next thing you know we have the Holy Catholic Church." When another of

the "Jews" asks him what this means, he replies, "Just because it's written does-
n't make it so." Powerful interpretations (literal or not) do, of course, make it so.
Matthew is in that contentious business of realizing the written, literal text.

Translation as Interpretation

Translations and reproductions are necessary only when we no longer occupy
the time and space of the "original."[18] As Matthew and Pasolini seek to appropriate their precursors' authority, they display the "reproduced," dependent
quality of their work by creating interlinear translations, interweaving their text
and its precursor.[19] While typological hermeneutics is by its very nature interlinear, Matthew's fulfillment citations literally lay the relevant sections of the
Hebrew Bible alongside its Jesus story. Pasolini's reproduction of Matthew is
even more strikingly interlinear. In the subtitled version, in particular, English
viewers have Matthew's words underneath Pasolini's images (and intertwined
with background music and Italian dialogue).[20]

Of course, even an exact reproduction (if such is possible) provides a copy
that stands between the receiver and the "original." More importantly, as the
reproduction inhabits a different episteme than the "original," it means differently.[21] Borges' imaginative creation of "Pierre Menard, Author of Don
Quixote" illustrates the point humorously.[22] Menard aspired to write *Don Quixote*
without translating it and without becoming Miguel de Cervantes. Instead, he
wished to remain Menard and to arrive at *Don Quixote*. From Menard's understandably fragmentary results, Borges' narrator selects this exact reproduction of
chapter nine of *Don Quixote*: ". . . truth, whose mother is history, who is the rival
of time, depository of deeds, witness of the past, example and lesson to the
present, and warning to the future."[23] Borges' narrator, then, observes how
Menard's exact reproduction of Cervantes' eulogy of history fails to mean as the
original did: "History, *mother* of truth; the idea is astounding. Menard, a contemporary of William James, does not define history as an investigation of reality, but as its origin. Historical truth, for him, is not what took place; it is what
we think took place. The final clauses—*example and lesson to the present, and warning
to the future*—are shamelessly pragmatic."[24] Here, then, even the "literal" (reproduction) becomes a trope. Even literal reproductions betray the original.[25] Borges'
narrator provides another example from chapter thirty-eight of Don Quixote,
where Cervantes' *Don Quixote* eulogizes arms and letters before opting for the
superiority of arms. Borges' narrator cannot imagine Menard, the artist, arriving
at a similar position. He attributes Menard's thirty-eighth chapter, then, to his
ironic disposition, his habit of saying the opposite of what he meant. Now, the
same words mean precisely the opposite of what they once meant.

Pasolini's reproduction of Matthew, like Menard's ninth chapter, relocates Matthew in a new episteme. He removes Matthew from tradition and cult and reactivates it in modern politics.[26] No longer the revelation of an institutional church, Matthew becomes a debatable call to social action and belongs potentially to the (peasant?) consumers of Pasolini's film. In short, Pasolini demythologizes and politicizes Matthew.[27]

Matthew similarly politicizes the Hebrew Bible by denying its "natural" meaning, as seen in the synagogue, but Matthew is hardly blatant here. We must read Matthew between the lines or in the dark with Pasolini to see the gospel's politics. What Matthew obviously offers is a remythologizing of the Hebrew Bible (a re-naturalizing of it in the Matthean community).[28] Thus, Matthew reproduces the Hebrew Bible after the fashion of Menard's thirty-eighth chapter. Matthew reads the Hebrew Bible ironically, making it mean the opposite of what it says.

This use of the precursor is even more similar to Cervantes than to Menard. Chapter eight (the end of section one of part one of *Don Quixote*) ends abruptly in mid-battle between Don Quixote and a Biscayan squire. Cervantes (as narrator), then, laments that the historian he was following left the battle in mid-air. Chapter nine (section two) begins with Cervantes' account of his serendipitous discovery in the silk market of Toledo of an Arabic history of Don Quixote written by Cide Hamete Benengeli. Cervantes claims, of course, to follow this fictional historian in order to authorize his work:

> Nevertheless, if any objection can be raised against the truth of this history, it can only be because its author was an Arab, for those of that nation are much inclined to lying; and since they are such bitter enemies of ours, we might more readily suppose him to have fallen short of the truth than to have exaggerated. And this is my personal belief, for when he should and could have let his pen run on in indulgent eulogies of so worthy a knight, he seems to pass over them in silence deliberately, thereby acting badly and with malicious intention. . . .[29]

I can imagine no better exposition of Matthew's rhetoric of excess. For Matthew, too, the Hebrew Bible has fallen just short of the truth, and its other interpreters act maliciously (see Matthew 5:17–6:18; 23).

Creating the Precursor

Unlike Cide Hamete Benengeli and Menard's dependence on their "successors" for "life," the Hebrew Bible exists independently of Matthew. According to T. S. Eliot, however, a new (artistic) work modifies all preceding works of art.[30] With a footnote to Eliot, Jorge Luis Borges goes further, "The fact is that each writer *creates* his precursors. His work modifies our conception of the past, as it will modify the future."[31] Surely, neither the authors of the Hebrew Bible nor the scribes and rabbis who produced the Mishnah read the Hebrew Bible as Matthew does. For those other Jews, Moses gave a complete revelation, passed on in written and oral form by later prophets and scribes. For Matthew, the prophets and Torah—the order is important (see Matthew 11:13)—are no longer primarily Mosaic tradents, they are messianic prophets. In fact, Matthew so thoroughly reconfigures the Hebrew Bible that he prepares the ground for the Christian conception that it is the Old Testament (compare Hebrews 8–10). Rethinking Matthew in light of Borges, Eliot, and Cervantes, we might aver, then, that Jews did not create the Old Testament. Matthew did.[32]

Because of Matthew's institutional and cultural success, we may not notice what Matthew has done to its precursor. Pasolini's interpretation of Matthew is less canonical and, therefore, more obvious, so he reinvigorates the reading of Matthew. We can substitute "Pasolini" for "Menard" in the following quote:

> Menard (perhaps without wishing to) has enriched, by means of a new technique, the hesitant and rudimentary art of reading: the technique is one of deliberate anachronism and erroneous attributions. This technique, with its infinite applications, urges us to run through the *Odyssey* as if it were written after the *Aeneid*. . . . This technique would fill the dullest books with adventure. Would not the attributing of *The Imitation of Christ* to Louis Ferdinand Céline or James Joyce be a sufficient renovation of its tenuous spiritual counsels?[33]

Pasolini has remained Pasolini and arrived at Matthew. We may attribute Matthew to Pasolini. Of course, if we attribute Matthew to an atheist, homosexual Marxist, Matthew becomes political, rather than mythical.

Read with Pasolini, Matthew also takes on, then, Kafkaesque hints of "gloomy myths and terrifying institutions."[34] Despite Matthew's attacks on its predecessors for closed doors (Matthew 23:13), Matthew installs new locked doors to which its community has the "the keys" (Matthew 16:18–19; 18:15–20). For those outside, Matthew's community becomes another threatening doorkeeper. Pasolini's re-creation of Matthew, however, potentially reapplies Matthew's critique to Matthew's own descendants, a powerful, bureaucratic, imperial church (or the film opens and closes new doors).

The Genesis of Secrecy: Deciphering Politics

Contemporary interpreters see texts as doorkeepers hiding their own secrets;

therefore, they create suspicious hermeneutics removing the obvious locked doors in favor of some latent meaning.[35] For them, then, interpretation is less epistemological and more ethical or political. Truth becomes ideology. The matter is less what is communicated and more what is done and who is empowered. For the suspicious, texts reveal/conceal in order to empower, and, of course, interpretative acts ultimately empower interpreters.[36]

As a Marxist (and reportedly fascinated by Freud), Pasolini interprets Matthew suspiciously. Within the canon of the church, Pasolini discovers a secret, and his film "releases a revolutionary gospel, a materialistic Matthew."[37] In Matthew, Pasolini finds class conflict, not divine revelation, and a social, not a spiritual, message. For Pasolini, Christ's demands to leave work, follow him, and love your neighbor are revolutionary calls to political reform:

> For a Frenchman [*Il Vangelo*] may be a religious film. For an Italian pro-
> letarian, there is no ambiguity. Christ is a member of the sub-proletariat
> and is involved with others of this class. An historical relationship exists
> between Christ and the proletariat; he would not have done anything if
> he had not been followed by proletarians. The Pharisees would not have
> killed him. And the proletariat would have remained immersed in an
> unhearing darkness without the revolutionary teachings of Christ.[38]

Accordingly, his staging and camera situate John the Baptist and Jesus between the people and the powers-that-be. At the baptism, John calls the people to repentance (Matthew 3:2–3). When the religious leaders walk by on a path, John harangues them viciously (Matthew 3:7b–10). The abrupt change in tone and Pasolini's decisive cuts highlight the different audiences. Underlining the point, Pasolini turns the camera back to John and the people for words of "hope" (Matthew 3:11–12). While reproducing Matthew, then, Pasolini places the Baptist visually in the midst of class conflict.

Pasolini treats Jesus' entry into Jerusalem similarly. Once again, the social critic is with the people while the religious leaders are isolated and above. Jesus and the happy people, mostly children, enter in joy. The happiness (Jesus smiles) contrasts starkly with Jesus' alternation between impassivity and explosive anger in the rest of the film. In the Temple, as the leaders watch from above, Jesus' anger returns, and the camera focuses on the religious leaders as the object of Jesus' ire (Matthew 21:13). Only when Jesus' gaze returns to the children (and their hosannas) do the smiles return. When the leaders object, Jesus reviles them, cursing them with scripture (Matthew 21:16).

Overlooking the city thereafter, Jesus also curses an unproductive fig tree. In Pasolini (but not Matthew), Judas remarks on the tree's subsequent withering (see Matthew 21:18–22). The tree appears again between the leaders' murderous plot (Matthew 26:3–5) and Judas's defection (Matthew 26:6–16). Again, Pasolini amplifies and (now) vilifies Judas's role by attributing the querulous words of Matthew 26:8–9 to him.[39] At Jesus' response, he immediately and smilingly—to maximize the perfidy—strikes his deal with the religious leaders. Finally, we see another barren tree (though not the fig tree) when Judas hangs himself. By juxtaposing withered trees and Judas, Pasolini offers yet another judgment of the elite. Not only are they unproductive, they also belong with Judas as shedders of innocent blood (compare Matthew 23:29–36; 27:3–10, 18–26).

Intensifying the aura of conflict, Pasolini films each of the controversy stories in Matthew 21–22, but only one of the parables. Once again, the camera isolates the rulers above. When the controversies begin, the leaders ask questions from an elevated window. Suddenly, without transition, as Jesus responds, they are reduced to Jesus' level. Jesus' words, then, dethrone the leaders.

After a fade to black, Pasolini presents Jesus' lengthy denunciation of the religious leaders (Matthew 23). Pasolini privileges this speech in several ways. First, he films only this speech in its entirety. Elsewhere, even in the Sermon on the Mount, Pasolini abbreviates and rearranges (or omits altogether). Second, it is the only speech where Pasolini includes the crowd's presence. In particular, the crowds are not present for the Sermon on the Mount. There, Pasolini shows only Jesus (against various backdrops and in different clothing). For most of Matthew 23, however, Pasolini films Jesus "from afar," as if the camera (and the audience) is in or beyond the crowd. Once again, Jesus separates the people and the audience from the leaders. Pasolini only cuts away to show the ominous arrival of soldiers, to focus on the crowds during the words on "righteous blood" (Matthew 23:35), to show the city during the words of desolation (Matthew 23:37–38), and to film Jesus in close-up during the final beatitude (Matthew 23:39).

Not surprisingly, the powers-that-be callously do away with this social critic. The leaders' plot, Judas's defection, and the supper follow immediately upon Matthew 23. As a result, Jesus' indictment of the leaders before the crowds, rather than the Temple act or the raising of Lazarus, becomes the reason for Jesus' death. Interestingly, Pasolini succeeds here where scholars have largely failed. Doing away with a social revolutionary is far more understandable than dispatching the Son of God, an ethicist, an apocalyptic seer, or a cynic sage.

Pasolini visualizes the establishment's callousness even more clearly with the Baptist's fate at the hands of a jack-playing girl. Most of the scene proceeds in silence. The only words are Salome's request and Herod's immediate capitulation. The jacks, the silences, and the haste emphasize the callousness of John's subsequent decapitation, which we see allusively. Neither Salome nor Herod cares.

Pasolini's early films (for example, *Accattone, Mamma Roma*) depict similar fates (employing religious iconography) for the Roman sub-proletariat, but the

Christian mythologizing of the proletariat's fate reaches its height in *La ricotta.*[40] In that short film, produced with three other shorts by important European directors and released together as *RoGoPaG* (or *Laviamoci il cervello*), Pasolini films the filming of a passion play (with Orson Welles as the director). Pasolini's film climaxes with the death of an unnoticed proletariat, Stracci, playing a thief on a cross. As the chronically hungry man dies because he has gorged himself on ricotta cheese, everyone else discusses matters related to the ongoing filming. Their indifference overwhelms. He has to die to be noticed.

We might say the same thing about Jesus, but Pasolini does not. He is less interested in Jesus' afterlife than in his peasant fate, so the dominant visuals of the passion are Jesus' consumption. During the trial, for the first time since the ministry began, the camera loses Jesus.[41] In a striking departure from the frequent close-ups of the isolated Jesus (and even from the camera work for Matthew 23), Pasolini shoots Jesus' trial from the crowd with Peter. We can hear Jesus (he has very little to say), but we cannot make him out. He is too far away, and heads and buildings obscure our view. The camera focuses instead on Peter's denial and on Judas's fate (Matthew 26:69–27:10). Jesus is lost here and subsequently in the workings of bureaucratic machinery. Visually, then, Pasolini's man of the people suffers the people's fate. He has not delivered them, as *La ricotta* makes hauntingly clear. Jesus' successors are the victims of bourgeois society.

Clearly, Pasolini reads Matthew profanely. Matters differ with Matthew, but Matthew exceeds Pasolini as a suspicious reader. Matthew creates not one, but two books, a gospel and a "previously nonexistent book called the Old Testament."[42] In the Hebrew Bible, Matthew finds not class, but prophecy; but the glut of fulfillment that Matthew establishes sates its eschatological drive. Matthew's community is the end. That community simply needs to reproduce Matthew in its teaching and practice.[43]

Thereby, Matthew's suspicion arrives at more institutional succession than Pasolini's film. I think again of Matthew's keys (Matthew 16:18–20), which Matthew cloaks not only with humility and forgiveness, but also with the presence of Jesus (Matthew 18:20). That cloak empowers and hallows in the most literal of senses, because Matthew's Jesus is no less than Emmanuel (Matthew 1:23–25). For Matthew, that divine authority ultimately devolves upon the disciples (Matthew 16:17–20; 28:16–20), who are, of course, the Matthean church, teaching nothing less than Matthew.[44]

Here, Matthew's teaching sections are crucial, because they complete Matthew's transubstantiation. The community member who internalizes the Matthean "Jesus' speeches is to be conformed to the shape of his life."[45] At least, that community member internalizes Matthew's Jesus and ideology (and accepts Matthew's authority). The line of replacement (the preferred religious term is "succession") is clear. First, Matthew replaces God with Jesus (Emmanuel). Then, Matthew replaces Jesus with authorized Matthean disciples. In sum, Matthew itself replaces (or becomes) Jesus.

Accordingly, Matthew claims that Jesus is present (as Matthew) in its community, and it also imagines that God will ultimately judge the world according to the Matthean Jesus' words (Matthew 7:21–27; 25:31–46). Here, of course, is a remnant of eschatology, though postponed, to reckon with (the point of Matthew 24–25). Here, Matthew is far more doctrinaire than Pasolini. Matthew's assertions finally forgo politics, ideology, and interpretation for truth. In fact, its assertions sound like institution (empire) building.

Worldly Christianity

Institutions and empires belong to this world, so Matthew founds a worldly Christianity. Accordingly, Matthew's eschatological discourse (Matthew 24–25) mutes Mark's apocalyptic discourse (Mark 13). As we have seen, Mark uses Jesus' apocalyptic forecast to elide the time between crucifixion, destruction of the Temple, and gospel. Thus, Mark's readers, as well as its disciples, await the returning (not the resurrected) Jesus in Galilee (Mark 16:7–8; compare 13:14). Mark has no need, then, to found a lasting institution or to articulate a livable ethic. In fact, its ethic is "unto death" (Mark 8:34–9:1).[46] By contrast, Matthew disassociates Jesus' prophecy about the destruction of the Temple (Matthew 24:1–2) from the end simply by having the disciples ask separate questions about the fate of the Temple and the end (Matthew 24:3).[47] Further, Matthew conceives, by extension and placement, the mission to the nations as an interim between Jesus and the end (Matthew 24:14; compare Mark 13:10). Thus, while Mark ends in Galilee awaiting Jesus, Matthew ends with the disciples' commission to the nations.

Matthew also adds a number of eschatological parables depicting the ethic of work and watchfulness necessary to the interim between Jesus and the end (Matthew 24:45–25:46). One does not assume that the master's delay means he will not return (Matthew 24:45–51); one does not minimize the wait by carelessly failing to provide oil for one's lamp (Matthew 25:1–13); and one does not fail to steward the master's goods (Matthew 25:14–30). Further, these parables imagine a final judgment that reckons the deeds of an entire life (Matthew 25:14–46), not an apocalyptic crisis demanding faithful martyrdom. As a result, Matthew's eschatological judgment resembles that of the Qur'an more than that of Mark.

Further, the emphases in Matthew 25:31–46 remind us of Matthew's continued focus on following the teachings of Jesus (for example, Matthew 5:17–20;

7:21–27). Living according to Jesus' words—however revolutionary, messianic, or eschatological we take them to be—is rather different than bearing Mark's martyr-cross. Matthew does not expect its followers to die, although some may.[48] It expects them to live according to Jesus' Torah, to live in the kingdom *in the world* (see Matthew 5–7; as well as the missionary injunctions in Matthew 10; 28:16–20).[49] Compared to Mark's martyr ethic, Matthew is well on the way to Luke's understanding of "cross-bearing" as a call to daily self-abnegation (Luke 9:23). By taking Mark's kingdom secrets into the world, Matthew does to apocalyptic what the scribes and Pharisees had done to the priests' Torah. It profanes and democratizes the revelation.[50]

In one sense, Pasolini's gospel is more worldly than Matthew. He follows Marx's political critique of bourgeois society by dramatizing the fates of the sub-proletariat and peasants with his protagonists as well as by transforming the church's spiritual gospel into social critique. His Jesus is a violent social critic,[51] intensifying our awareness of Matthew's own angry and confrontational Jesus. Neither Pasolini nor Matthew's Jesus is ever conversational. Both Jesuses are absolute (not dialogic) speakers.[52] In addition to rendering Jesus as social critic, Pasolini also omits altogether the esoteric parables (Matthew 13) and the eschatological discourse (Matthew 24–25).[53] In short, Pasolini's Jesus belongs to this world.

Pasolini is not, however, a doctrinaire Marxist. Unlike Marx, Pasolini does not altogether reject religion. In fact, Pasolini made *Il Vangelo secondo Matteo* in part because he felt that Catholicism—in the new form aborning in Pope John XXIII to whom Pasolini dedicated his film—might reinvigorate Marxism. For Pasolini, Marxism and Catholicism share a common enemy in bourgeois materialism (later the enemy was consumerism), and they can reinforce one other:

> Catholicism must be capable . . . of taking into account the problems of the society in which we live; and so too must Marxism face the religious moment of humanity. There will always be an irrational, religious moment. Improving the social sphere will place the moment of the religious problem in a different perspective; once class oppression is over, man will confront only his own human nature—death.[54]

In short, Pasolini is using both Marxism and Catholicism critically. To an orthodox Marxist, Pasolini's notion of a this-worldly Jesus and of religion's practicality is ethereal nonsense. Luis Buñuel's *Nazarín* seems more orthodox. It portrays a simple priest, Nazarío, whose attempt to follow the simple teachings of Jesus leads to the destruction of others and himself. Nazarío is a "spiritual fool" in the vein of, but more mockingly critical than, Cervantes' Don Quixote.[55]

Pasolini's Jesus is no such fool. Pasolini's Jesus is more Gramscian than Marxist. For Gramsci, artists and intellectuals foster a "national-popular" mythology as a basis for social reform. If the political goal is Marxist, Pasolini's "national-popular" mythology in *Il Vangelo secondo Matteo* is Catholic (Matthean).[56] When Pasolini politicizes Matthew, then, he is also remythologizing it as a peasant gospel. As we shall see below, this mythologizing ultimately renders Pasolini's film somewhat otherworldly.

As importantly, while Matthew's Jesus prepares scribes for the kingdom of heaven (Matthew 13:52), Pasolini's Jesus stands alone. The fact, for example, that Pasolini films the Sermon on the Mount as a monologue by Jesus—with no visible audience—is, in a sense, typical of his isolated Jesus. The people, and his followers for the most part, are a silent mass:

> Totally dominated and overwhelmed by Christ, his followers, as critics also observed, are fatally removed from him. . . . Christ appears, in fact, as a kind of Biblical intellectual who, despite an immense desire to be "organically" linked to the people, cannot breach the immeasurable gap between them. One is left to wonder how his mute and passive followers will be able to further his teachings once he himself is gone.[57]

In short, Pasolini's Jesus provides for no institutional successor. In fact, Pasolini has omitted most of the elements that provide Matthew's succession, the five teaching sections. He does use parts of three of them (Matthew 5–7; 10; 18), but his omission of Matthew 13 and Matthew 24–25 is telling. While these omissions make Jesus less esoteric and less eschatological and, thus, more worldly, they also destroy Matthew's training of the disciples as Jesus' worldly replacement.

Although Pasolini's Jesus prepares for no successor, he does find successors in the oppressed poor and in an unending sequence of peasant/proletariat martyrs. In this sense, Jesus is fatefully similar to Stracci (the "hero" of *La ricotta*) and Accattone. Not incidentally, Jesus' first speech in Pasolini's film already says this. Omitting the missionary instructions to do what Jesus has done (Matthew 10:5–15), Pasolini's Jesus predicts his followers' sufferings (Matthew 10:16–39, with some omissions). In particular, Jesus comes not "to bring peace, but a sword." Unfortunately, for Pasolini's heroes and his beloved peasants, the sword still belongs to the elite.

Perhaps, then, Pasolini is not so far from Buñuel after all. The difference, of course, is that Pasolini identifies with his Jesus far more than Buñuel identifies with Nazarío. Pasolini's Jesus does find, then, one other successor in Pasolini, the alienated intellectual who stands between the elite and the people and is for the people. Like many other Westerners, including Matthew's author, scholars, and film directors, Pasolini identifies with Jesus and, consciously or unconsciously, re-creates him after his own image.[58]

Paradoxical Texts

Our discussion of *Il Vangelo secondo Matteo*'s ambiguous "worldliness" reveals certain paradoxes. In particular, the film juxtaposes Marxism and Catholicism, Jesus and Italian peasants, and social critics and their institutional acceptance. Interestingly, Matthew contains quite similar paradoxes.

Whether or not Pasolini's film reinvigorates either Marx or Jesus, it does imagine an ambiguous, worldly Christianity that criticizes oppressive institutions. Like the prophets of old, however, it is only critique. Pasolini has no program for arriving at the socially just or classless society. His film simply mythologizes (idealizes or romanticizes) the oppressed and the social critics of all ages.[59] Such idealism can have no more than an uncertain relationship to the world.

While not juxtaposing Marxism and Catholicism, Matthew creates similar tensions by juxtaposing an intense sense of eschatological fulfillment with a preparation for an institution/community in the continuing world. After Matthew's typologically constructed Jesus story, what is left to happen? What remains is, of course, the Matthean Jesus' words (Matthew 24:34–35). Unlike the Markan Jesus' apocalyptic words, the Matthean Jesus' words demand "fulfillment" in the continuing world (Matthew 5:17–20; 7:21–27). Accordingly, Matthew's Jesus predicts not only the crisis of the end (Matthew 24:4–31), but also the sufferings associated with kingdom missions (Matthew 10:16–42).

As Matthew continues Mark's intimations of imminence, its ethical demand has the sense of an inserted interim. How long does that interim last? The end does not come with the destruction of the Temple or the death of the first generation.[60] For Matthew, the matter is a divine mystery, but only the wicked and unfaithful act as if the end will not come (Matthew 24:45–25:30). To deal with the interim, Matthew imagines its continuing-kingdom community fulfilling—that is, living—Jesus' words.

As a result, Matthew is a "late" text not only with regard to the Hebrew Bible, but also with regard to Jesus. Matthew consciously inhabits the world after Jesus. The text protests the continuing presence of Jesus (Matthew 18:20; 28:20) because the text has replaced (effaced) Jesus. Matthew portrays both Jesus (Matthew 4:17) and the disciples (Matthew 10:7) proclaiming the gospel of the kingdom, but now someone else—Matthew's commissioned disciples—has that task (Matthew 24:14; 26:13; 28:16–20). What they preach and teach is nothing other than Matthew itself, for Matthew is the gospel of the kingdom.[61]

The resurrection scene commissions Jesus' replacements, Matthew and its community of disciples. The resurrection also provides, however, a "proleptic parousia."[62] As such, the resurrection (and Matthew) replaces—quite weakly—the apocalyptic end.[63] If the kingdom arrives in Matthew's Jesus, it is not the apocalyptic finale, but the institution of the "mixed" body of the church (compare Matthew 13:36–43). Of course, saying that Matthew and its community is the kingdom come is about as satisfying as saying that the classless society arrives in *Il Vangelo secondo Matteo.*[64]

For Matthew, Jesus' continuing presence apparently means that history has two stages: before Jesus and during Jesus. Jesus is first present personally and then through Matthew (and its community).[65] Here, of course, Matthew engages in mythology (or ideology), not history. When it claims that Jesus remains present, Matthew has set Jesus free from history.

Pasolini's *Il Vangelo secondo Matteo* also mythologizes, but by juxtaposing Jesus and Italian peasants. This combination de-historicizes both Jesus and the peasants. Jesus is no longer all that Jewish. He symbolizes an angry, intellectual social critic translatable from place to place. He can even be a Marxist. Similarly, his peasant audience becomes the symbol of the oppressed of all ages. Finally, his opponents, although envisioned as the Jewish religious leadership, also become symbolic of the "bosses" of all ages. All of this, of course, is to engage in national-popular mythology.

This mythological tact somewhat defuses Matthew's anti-Semitism. Matthew deliberately sets Jesus in opposition to the Jewish religious leaders. They deem him a blasphemer (Matthew 9:3, 34; 10:25; 12:24; 26:63–65) and plot his murder (Matthew 12:14; 26:3–5; 27:1–2, 20). As Matthew's Jesus is Emmanuel, the religious leaders thereby align themselves with the kingdom of evil (Matthew 12:33–42; 13:37–43) and become the models of Matthean vice. They are hypocrites (Matthew 6:1–18; 23). For Matthew, they are delusional and self-destructive, because their opposition to Jesus suicidally brings innocent blood upon themselves (Matthew 23:29–39; 27:24–26).[66] In all this, the Matthean Judas (who like the religious leaders always addresses Jesus as "rabbi," while the other disciples call him "Lord") symbolizes the Jews (Matthew 27:3–10).

The crowds are long ambivalent, but they, too, ultimately side with their leaders against Jesus (Matthew 26:47, 55; 27:20–25, but contrast 26:4–5). In a sense, the crowds are not unlike a Greek chorus, because they serve as foils and backdrops for the action. In particular, in the passion, their portrayal helps to depict Jesus' isolation. Nonetheless, the "his blood be on us and on our children" of Matthew 27:25 leaves a lasting impression. For Matthew, leaders, Judas, and the crowds—not Pilate—are responsible for Jesus' death.

Not surprisingly, this portrayal justifies a move toward the Gentiles as the kingdom audience. There are, however, tensions in Matthew on this point. For example, it is rather clear that Gentiles are a "late" and decidedly "secondary" audience (Matthew 10:5–6; 15:21–28). Further, some point out that Matthew never really ends the mission to the Jews imagined in Matthew 10. In fact, Jesus asserts that the mission will be ongoing at the end (Matthew 10:23). For Matthew, then, the story on the Jews is hardly over.

More importantly, Matthew imagines the Torah—as interpreted by Matthew—to be still in effect.[67] Scholars generally see Matthew as the most "Jewish" of the four canonical Gospels.[68] If anti-Semitism lurks in Matthew, then, it is self-hatred or self-denial. There is, then, a deep tension in Matthew between its affection for Torah and its embryonic anti-Semitism. This tension is not unrelated to the fact that Matthew's community is engaged in a project far too similar to that of the Pharisees and rabbis for comfort, but Matthew's subsequent cultural importance renders its "narcissism of small differences" rather unfortunate. Forgetting Matthew's historical location, subsequent readers have taken Matthew's interpretations and ideology as truth. Accepting Matthew's ethical dualism has led many in the West to consider "Pharisee" a synonym for hypocrite.[69] Further, the cultural domination of Matthew's mythology has regrettable consequences in terms of disenfranchisement and dehumanization. All in all, we have reproduced Matthew's mythology of "innocent blood" far too literally.

In some respects, *Il Vangelo secondo Matteo* simply raises the ante. No Jesus film puts more responsibility on the Jewish leaders for the death of Jesus[70] or renders a more confrontational Jesus. Pasolini even keeps the "blood on our hands" speech. As Pasolini uses an off-stage speaker, however, it is not clear who speaks and, thus, not clear that the "whole" people (compare Matthew 27:25) has sided with the leaders. Even more unfortunately, Pasolini uses a moment of black screen at the cross to allow a narrator to intone Isaiah 6:9–10. Once again, however, the identity of the speaker is ambiguous. Does the narrator indict ancient Jews for rejecting Jesus or does Pasolini indict the elite for the continuing fate of peasants?

These ambiguities are a part of Pasolini's mythologizing, his removal of the story from its historical context and reproduction of it in another medium and culture. This mythologizing, particularly as it is a Gramscian remythologizing of Matthew, has the potential to liberate Matthew from anti-Semitism. For Pasolini, Jesus' antagonist is bourgeois modernity with its bureaucratic society and consumer capitalism, not an ethnic group. The result is altogether more palatable to contemporary ideologies and mythologies (like the American mythic pattern of the lone, righteous hero versus the corrupt group).

Read with Pasolini, Matthew becomes less anti-Semitic and more anti-institutional and anti-bureaucratic. In fact, on this point, Pasolini's reading is similar to that of Arcand. The modernized passion play of *Jesus of Montreal* is disturbingly anti-Semitic, because the actor playing the Jewish leader motivates Pilate's decision to crucify Jesus. Arcand, however, has "boxed" this play within his film's indictment of modern society. In the film's larger story, Christian church leaders, the police, advertisers, lawyers, and intellectuals are the oppressors martyring Daniel. If Jewish leaders were influential in Jesus' death, Arcand nicely reminds us of subsequent history, when Christian church(es) (and societies) have been responsible for far more religious persecutions. In fact, with the carefully nuanced Le Clerc, Arcand humanizes both the victims and the oppressors. While Pasolini also contains the gospel's anti-Semitism in a larger indictment of modern society, he is less interested in personalities. Pasolini obscures the personalities and mythologizes the whole in order to create a darker vision in which various institutional forces collide.

Pasolini's mythologizing rescues the "peasant" Jesus by using the church's favorite gospel against itself. Ironically, Catholicism embraced his film. Pasolini dedicated his film to Pope John XXIII. The film was shown to cardinals during Vatican II. Both the International Catholic Film Office and the National Council of Churches gave it awards. It was first shown in America at a benefit for a Catholic school.[71] Recently, it was named to a "best all time" list of films by the Vatican. Notably, it was the only Jesus film on the list. If Pasolini criticized the church, the church did not notice.

According to Pasolini, the good Marxist is not orthodox. A good Marxist breaks all the rules.[72] Similarly, Matthew's Jewish Jesus challenges and critiques Judaism and its institutions—particularly the Temple and the Torah—but then presents himself as the fulfillment of the law and the prophets. Matthew, then, is even less orthodox than Pasolini. After criticism, it establishes new rules. If it is ironic that the church consumed Pasolini, it is not ironic that the church consumed Matthew. While Matthew has a tense if not paradoxical relationship to apocalypse and Judaism, it evidences less tensions vis-à-vis institution, as long as that institution is Matthean. When Matthew grew up, it became part of an empire's mythology. Read with Pasolini, the growing pains there become less opaque. Read in the dark, Matthew exists in tension with its imperial progeny.

Reading Matthew in the Dark: This is That[73]

Pasolini's *Il Vangelo secondo Matteo* has an anxious this is that relationship with Matthew. It both is and is not Matthew. No film is more faithful to a gospel, yet Pasolini also liberates Matthew from its ancient and its canonical confines.

Pasolini interprets Matthew with the camera, with music, and with selections and alterations of the text. As a result, Pasolini's film operates within a Gramscian rather than an ancient Jewish worldview. Pasolini sees class and bourgeois society, not the Pharisees and scribes, as the antagonists of peasants of all times. Finally, Pasolini's film rejects all institutions, even Matthew's.

Matthew has less anxious relationships with its precursors because it has consumed them more completely; nonetheless, it, too, is and is not those originals. Matthew claims to fulfill the Hebrew Bible. It replaces Moses' Torah with the Matthean Jesus' teaching and the Temple/synagogue with the Matthean community. The Christian canon's retention of the Hebrew Bible as the Old Testament (that is, as created precursor) means, however, that Matthew did not completely efface the Hebrew Bible.

Mark did not survive as well. In the Christian canon, Matthew precedes Mark and connects Mark to the Old Testament. Matthew also provides background for Mark's mysterious Jesus. Luke succeeds Mark and connects Mark to the apostolic church. Luke, then, replaces Mark's absent Jesus with a present apostolic church. As we have seen, Matthew acts similarly to the scribe who thoughtfully provided Mark with a very Matthean ending (Mark 16:9–20). Fixed between Matthew and Luke, Mark languished in its canonical captivity until the nineteenth century, when scholars began to read it independently.

It is Jesus, however, that Matthew has consumed most completely. Jesus continues and speaks only as Matthew says he does—in Matthew and Matthew's community. Despite its claims to enthusiasm (a god [with]in), then, Matthew veils Jesus as much as it reveals him, because Matthew stands between Jesus and its community. Matthew has replaced Jesus.

When we read Matthew in the dark with Pasolini, this process becomes quite obvious. As Pasolini's precursor, Matthew's Jesus is a peasant resisting oppressive institutions and is consumed by those same institutions. What Pasolini omits in his reproduction of Matthew, and which is, thereby, highlighted by reading Matthew with his film, is Matthew's use of Jesus to create a new institution. Matthew's Jesus, the Jewish peasant, founds Matthew's all-consuming institution, an institution that disowns and defames its own precursors (including Jesus).

Pasolini's "literal" (but partial) reproduction of Matthew "outs," then, Matthew's own political and mythological acts. Denuded of its mythic brocade, neither Matthew's interpretation of the Hebrew Bible nor its Jesus is "natural." They only appear to be because of the mythic power of Matthew and its institutions (both church and academy). They are, instead, Matthew's ideological acts of enfranchisement and disenfranchisement. Read in the dark, Matthew's gospel becomes (again) a debated (political) and debatable interpretation of Jesus and Judaism.

The move from myth to politics destructs the mythic/sacred authority of Matthew's excluding institution. More pointedly, it calls a halt to sacred violence, because it highlights the fact that Matthew elevates Jesus and the disciples at the expense of Judas and the Pharisees.[74] Typically, interpreters obscure this political act by claiming, for example, that the Romans, not the Jews, were responsible for the death of Jesus, or by effacing Matthew's key players—Judas and the Jews—from the story altogether.[75]

Does this "cover-up" also account for the striking, scholarly omission of Matthew 23 (the calumny versus the Pharisees) from Matthew's "so-called" five blocks of teaching material? Refreshingly, Pasolini will have no part of such sanitizing. As a result, he forces us to see Matthew's defamation of Judas and the Jews. In fact, he even raises the ante on that process, filming only Matthew 23 in toto, increasing Judas's role and perfidy, leaving the statement about "his blood on us," and having a narrator intone Isaiah 6:9–10 to the accompaniment of a black screen at the cross. By not erasing the Jews from the story, Pasolini enables us to see both them and Matthew's exclusionary myth at work. We cannot look away. Pasolini illumines, then, the blood that Matthew is spilling at the cross.

Reading Matthew in the dark, we also notice, in a quite different (non-mythic) light, that Judas dies.[76] As Pasolini's precursor, we also see Matthew's Jesus as another peasant trodden underfoot. In Pasolini's light, then, we cannot look at Matthew's cross without thinking of Judas hung and of poor, unnoticed Stracci (the dying peasant thief in *La ricotta*) as well. Such askew views, of course, deconstruct Christian mythology. They forgo the redemptive cross; they consider Judas the Jew; they deify Judas as well as (or rather than) Jesus;[77] or, in Pasolini's case, they render Jesus as another (but articulate) Stracci. Reading Matthew's Jesus as Stracci (or as inseparably bound up with Judas and Judaism) sheds light on our own institutions and ideologies. Whom do we exclude from the kingdom? What peasants and past do we willingly sacrifice? Whose innocent blood do our mythologies shed? In our increasingly contentious world, Muslims come immediately to mind. Not only politically, but cinematically as well, Muslims (and Arabs) have become the vilified other, the scapegoats that justify our violent empire maintenance.[78] Perhaps, in light of recent events, we should revisit Matthew through DeMille[79] as well as Pasolini, and find the blood of Muslims at the cross as well.

Notes

    I. Kermode, *The Genesis of Secrecy*, x. Compare Paul Ricoeur, *Freud and Philosophy: An Essay on Interpretation*, trans. Denis Savage (New Haven, Conn.: Yale University Press, 1970), 26.

2. For discussions of Matthew's structure, see Donald Senior, *What Are They Saying about Matthew?* (New York: Paulist, 1983); Jack Dean Kingsbury, *Matthew: Structure, Christology, Kingdom* (Philadelphia: Fortress, 1975), 1–41; and David L. Barr, "The Drama of Matthew's Gospel: A Reconsideration of Its Structure and Purpose," *Theology Digest* 24 (1976): 349–59. Matthew is an intensely "ordered" gospel, segmented by various formula markers: e.g., 1) "Now when Jesus had finished . . ." (Matthew 7:28; 11:1; 13:53; 19:1; 26:1); and 2) "From that time Jesus began . . ." (Matthew 4:17; 16:21).

3. According to Benjamin W. Bacon, *Studies in Saint Matthew* (London: Constable, 1930), 81–82, 265–335, these five blocks of material are Jesus' Torah, so Matthew presents Jesus as the new Moses. The idea of five teaching sections ignores teaching "blocks" like Matthew 23.

4. The narrator's asides frequently become the directions for the set and the camera.

5. See George Aichele, "Translation as De-Canonization: Matthew's Gospel According to Pasolini," *Cross Currents* 51, no. 4 (Winter 2002): 524–34; and Zygmunt G. Barański, "The Texts of *Il Vangelo secondo Matteo*," *The Italianist* 5 (1985): 85, 88–90, 101.

6. Walter Benjamin, "The Work of Art in the Age of Mechanical Reproduction," in Walter Benjamin, *Illuminations*, ed. Hannah Arendt; trans. Harry Zohn (New York: Harcourt, Brace, & World, 1968), 223. I follow Aichele's lead ("Translation as De-Canonization") in reading Pasolini in light of Benjamin. In light of *Il Vangelo secondo Matteo's* conscious lateness, it is interesting that "secondo" can mean "following, subsequent, secondary" as well as "according to."

7. Pasolini, cited in Naomi Greene, *Pier Paolo Pasolini: Cinema as Heresy* (Princeton, N.J.: Princeton University Press, 1990), 73. Oswald Stack, *Pasolini on Pasolini: Interviews with Oswald Stack* (Bloomington: Indiana University Press, 1969), 9, claims that Pasolini superimposes a traditional Christology drawn from Christian music and art on the brusque, literal text of Matthew.

8. Cited in Stack, *Pasolini on Pasolini*, 83–84. Bart Testa, "To Film a Gospel . . . and Advent of the Theoretical Stranger," in Patrick Rumble and Bart Testa, eds., *Pier Paolo Pasolini: Contemporary Perspectives* (Toronto: University of Toronto Press, 1994), 180–87, asserts that the Gospels are only "pretexts" for the Hollywood epic. Notably, before filming *Il Vangelo*, Pasolini had mocked the biblical spectacle in *La ricotta*. Geoffrey Nowell-Smith, "Pasolini's Originality," in Paul Willemen, ed., *Pier Paolo Pasolini* (London: British Film Institute, 1977), 9–11, contrasts Pasolini's editing with that of Hollywood film. Pasolini's film was released in America after Stevens's film, but their proximity contrasts Pasolini's style with that of Hollywood epic (and its cast of stars) nicely.

9. On Pasolini's interpretative music, see Greene, *Pier Paolo Pasolini*, 76; and Aichele, "Translation as De-Canonization," 530.

10. Pasolini's "silences" differ dramatically from Matthew's extensive teaching sections. See Barański, "The Texts of *Il Vangel secondo Matteo*," 88.

11. In fact, the film follows Matthew's text rigorously through 4:11. At 4:12, Pasolini invents a scene showing John in prison and treats the ministry thereafter more freely.

12. Frank Kermode, "Matthew," in Robert Alter and Frank Kermode, eds., *The Literary Guide to the Bible* (Cambridge, Mass.: Belknap Press of Harvard University, 1987), 398.

13. Ibid., 388. On typology, see Chapter 3 above. On the form, function, and ideology of Hebrew parallelism in poetry and prose, see Robert Alter, *The Art of Biblical Poetry* (New York: Basic, 1985); and James Kugel, *The Idea of Biblical Poetry* (New Haven, Conn.: Yale University Press, 1981).

14. See Matthew 1:22–23; 2:15, 17–18, 23; 3:3; 4:14–16; 8:17; 12:17–21; 13:14–15, 35; 21:4–5; 27:9–10. Matthew 3:3 does not use the word "fulfill" (cf. Matthew 2:5–6). These fulfillment citations are all from the narrator except for Matthew 13:14–15, which the text places in the mouth of Jesus (cf. Luke 22:37). The precursor of Matthew 2:23 is unknown. The narrator misattributes Matthew 13:35 and 27:9–10. Compared to known Hebrew, Aramaic, and Greek manuscripts, Matthew is quite "creative." See Krister Stendahl, *The School of St. Matthew and Its Use of the Old Testament* (Philadelphia: Fortress, 1968), 97–127; and Richard Longenecker, *Biblical Exegesis in the Apostolic Period* (Grand Rapids, Mich.: Eerdmans, 1975), 133–37, 140–52.

15. On Matthew's view of the law, see Senior, *What Are They Saying about Matthew?* 47–55. According to John P. Meier, *Law and History in Matthew's Gospel: A Redactional Study of Matthew 5:17–48* (Rome: Biblical Institute Press, 1976), 25–40, 162–67; and *idem, The Vision of Matthew: Christ, Church, and Morality in the First Gospel* (New York: Paulist, 1979), Matthew's view of the death-resurrection as a "proleptic parousia" means that the law is no longer in force as it was during Jesus' own life. The end of the age has come (Matthew 5:18), so now Christian (Matthean) morality is in force. In addition to the sermon's antitheses, Meier makes much of the fact that circumcision does not appear in the commission in Matthew 28:16–20.

16. In particular, the citations render Matthew's "history" suspect. Is Matthew offering a history or a commentary (a fiction) based on a prior text? For discussion with reference to the passion narrative, see Kermode, *The Genesis of Secrecy,* 75–123; and, more recently, Crossan, *The Cross That Spoke.*

17. On name-calling in early Christianity and Judaism, see Morton Smith, *Jesus the Magician* (San Francisco: Harper & Row, 1978). While an anxiety of lateness dominates early Christianity, early Christians do not admit their lateness. They claim that the Johannine Jesus is before Abraham (John 8:39–59) and that Pauline faith is that of Abraham (Galatians 3:6–4:31). Islam also anxiously claims to be the true Abrahamic religion. In traditional societies, the "old" has more cachet than the "new."

18. See Benjamin, "The Work of Art in the Age of Mechanical Reproduction," and *idem,* "The Task of the Translator," in Benjamin, *Illuminations,* 71–72. The word "original" is hardly fortuitous in our case, because no original "Matthew" exists. When we read Matthew, we read fragmentary copies, recently reconstructed critical texts, or some late-arriving translation. Furthermore, even if the "original Matthew" were available, as we have seen, it would already be commentary.

19. Benjamin, "The Task of the Translator," 82.

20. Aichele, "Translation as De-Canonization," 525–26.

21. Pasolini's interpretations are obvious if one compares his interlinear words and visuals with DeMille's visual Bible. Where Pasolini reproduces Matthew's words (and silences) quite

literally, DeMille lays an eclectic selection of words from the four canonical gospels (and his own novelizing additions) alongside his visualized Bible.

22. In Borges, *Ficciones,* 45–55.

23. Ibid., 53.

24. Ibid.

25. On Pasolini's "literalness" as a failed interpretation (in another film), see Roland Barthes, "Pasolini's *Salò:* Sade to the Letter," in Willemen, ed. *Pier Paolo Pasolini,* 64–66. By the way, Pasolini claims that he offers Matthew by analogy, not exactly. See Stack, *Pasolini on Pasolini,* 82.

26. Compare Benjamin, "The Work of Art in the Age of Mechanical Reproduction," 222–27.

27. I use "myth" here in Barthes' sense, not Bultmann's. For Roland Barthes, *Mythologies,* trans. Annette Lavers (New York: Hill & Wang, 1972), 142–48, a culture's mythological apparati render its history and social construction as "natural" and "given." Barthes, then, endeavors to "politicize" myth. For Bultmann, "New Testament and Mythology," myth is: 1) antiquated cosmology (to be dismissed); and 2) reflections of primitive (nonphilosophical), existential anthropology (to be reinterpreted).

28. Of course, Pasolini remythologizes (in a Gramscian sense) just as much as Matthew does. See below.

29. Miguel de Cervantes, *Don Quixote of La Mancha,* trans. Walter Starkie (New York: New American Library, 1979), 109.

30. "Tradition and the Individual Talent," in T. S. Eliot, *The Sacred Wood: Essays on Poetry and Criticism* (London: Meuthen, 1960), 49–50.

31. "Kafka and His Precursors," in Jorge Luis Borges, *Selected Non-Fictions,* ed. Eliot Weinberger; trans. Esther Allen, Susanne Jill Levine, and Eliot Weinberger (New York: Penguin, 1999), 365.

32. Compare Kermode, *The Genesis of Secrecy,* 18. On the creation of the Old Testament by the church, see Hans von Campenhausen, *The Formation of the Christian Bible,* trans. J. A. Baker (Philadelphia: Fortress, 1972), 1–102; and Aichele, *The Control of Biblical Meaning,* 15–37.

33. Borges, *Ficciones,* 54–55.

34. In Kafka's haunting "Before the Law" (which appears in various forms from a brief parable to the last chapter in the unfinished novel, *The Trial*), a threatening doorkeeper denies a countryman admittance to the Law. The denials go on throughout the countryman's life until at death's door the doorkeeper tells him that the (now closing) door was, in fact, intended just for him.

35. Thus, e.g., Marx, Nietzsche, and Freud decipher the "ciphering guile" respectively of social being, the will to power, and the unconscious through "the double guile" of their suspicious hermeneutics. See Ricoeur, *Freud and Philosophy,* 33–34.

36. See Kermode, *The Genesis of Secrecy,* 2.

37. Aichele, "Translation as De-Canonization," 533.

38. Pasolini cited in Greene, *Pier Paolo Pasolini,* 77.

39. On Pasolini's amplification of the roles and characters of Judas and Mary, see Barański, "The Texts of *Il Vangelo secondo Matteo*," 85, 91, 97–98.

40. See Greene, *Pier Paolo Pasolini*, 21–28, 62–66.

41. See Barański, "The Texts of *Il Vangelo secondo Matteo*," 91.

42. Kermode, *The Genesis of Secrecy*, 18.

43. Even the Gentiles, the "new" target of the teaching in Matthew 28:19, are not really new. Matthew prefigures them in the wise men, in the Syro-Phoenician woman, and in frequent threats of a replacement people.

44. In their earlier mission, the disciples did not teach (Matthew 10:5–8). They could not, because they had not yet been completely trained by the Matthean Jesus' teaching (cf. Matthew 13:52). Only when they have learned their Matthean lessons (the teaching sections, Matthew 5–7; 10; 13; 18; 24–25) are they commissioned to teach; i.e., at the end of Matthew.

45. Jack Dean Kingsbury, *Matthew as Story*, 2nd ed. (Philadelphia: Fortress, 1988), 111.

46. See, however, Dan O. Via Jr., *The Ethics of Mark's Gospel in the Middle of Time* (Philadelphia: Fortress, 1985).

47. As Pasolini's Jesus ends the invective of Matthew 23, he comments (aside) the words of Matthew 24:1. While omitting the apocalyptic discourse altogether, Pasolini photographs falling buildings during the earthquake at the cross (Matthew 27:51). As a result, Pasolini connects Jerusalem's destruction with the cross even more closely than the Gospels do. This fall is, of course, no apocalyptic end.

48. Matthew does have the words about taking up the cross (Matthew 16:24–28) as well as the prospect of suffering in mission (Matthew 10:16–42) and in apocalyptic crisis (Matthew 24:9–31); however, these teachings do not dominate Matthew as the martyr-cross does Mark.

49. For surveys of diverse interpretations of the sermon, see Harvey K. McArthur, *Understanding the Sermon on the Mount* (New York: Harper & Row, 1960), 105–27; R. A. Guelich, "Interpreting the Sermon on the Mount," *Interpretation* 41 (1987): 117–30; and W. D. Davies and Dale C. Allison Jr., "Reflections on the Sermon on the Mount," *Scottish Journal of Theology* 44 (1991): 283–309.

50. According to W. D. Davies, *The Setting of the Sermon on the Mount* (Cambridge: Cambridge University Press, 1965), 305–7, the sermon's concerns are those of the rabbis in Pirke Aboth 1.2. Various scholars have imagined the historical occasion for Matthew as a Christian community's Torah-wrangling with a synagogue "across the street." See Davies, *The Setting of the Sermon on the Mount*; and Duling and Perrin, *The New Testament*, 333–39. For other possibilities, see Senior, *What Are They Saying about Matthew?* 5–15.

51. Pasolini claims that the Matthean Jesus' "I have not come to bring peace but a sword" led him to make his film (Testa, "To Film a Gospel," 208 n. 39).

52. Testa points out that Pasolini's isolation of Jesus, as well as his frequent use of frontal close-ups during Jesus' preaching/teaching, visually renders the Matthean Jesus' "absolute" confrontational style (ibid., 197). That the Matthean Jesus begins with "I say" (throughout Matthew 5) and ends with "You say" in the passion (Matthew 26:25, 64; 27:11) dramatizes this confrontational style.

53. He did shoot the eschatological discourse. See Stack, *Pasolini on Pasolini,* 96–97.

54. Pasolini, cited in Greene, *Pier Paolo Pasolini,* 71–72. On the "Italian" quality of this combination, see Stack, *Pasolini on Pasolini,* 7. For Pasolini's criticisms of Catholicism, see ibid., 14.

55. Some critics read the end of the film—an old woman gives Nazarío a pineapple as he trudges down a road to prison—as a moment of grace. If so, it is a grace that rescues a man victimized and degraded by the otherworldly teachings of Jesus. Compare Buñuel's *Viridiana. La Última Cena (The Last Supper)* also portrays religion's negative influences. A slave owner hosts a "last supper" for twelve slaves during Holy Week. He lectures them on the benefits of slavery during the feast. When he leaves, the manager demands that they work on the holiday. The resulting revolt has predictably bloody consequences.

56. On Gramsci's influence on Pasolini, see Greene, *Pier Paolo Pasolini,* 27–35, 54–60; and Stack, *Pasolini on Pasolini,* 8, 22–25. "National-popular" is a Gramscian phrase. Pasolini felt *Il Vangelo* to be his most Gramscian or "national-popular" work, but his poem, *Le ceneri di Gramsci (The Ashes of Gramsci,* 1957) antedates this film (see Greene, *Pier Paolo Pasolini,* 56–57, 79).

57. Greene, *Pier Paolo Pasolini,* 79.

58. See ibid., 67–80, 218–23; Barański, "The Texts of *Il Vangelo secondo Matteo,*" 87, 98–101; and Baugh, *Imaging the Divine,* 100–101. Notably, Pasolini, a poet, also thought of Jesus as a poet. See Stack, *Pasolini on Pasolini,* 77–78.

59. On Pasolini's romantic mythology of the peasants, see Stack, *Pasolini on Pasolini,* 7–9, 21–22; and Nowell-Smith, "Pasolini's Originality." It is unfair to call this *no program.* Pasolini believes that the restoration of myth and epic, lost by the bourgeoisie, will reanimate life and culture. Compare Borges, "The Telling of the Tale."

60. Apocalyptic sects have an amazing ability to deal with the cognitive dissonance of failed predictions by recalculating the time of the end and by pronouncing terrible judgments on doubters (for example, 2 Peter 3). Matthew follows the same pattern.

61. See Kingsbury, *Matthew: Structure, Christology, Kingdom,* 129–37. As Matthew is for an ongoing community, Matthew presents the disciples more "respectfully" than Mark. Matthew's disciples are people "of little faith" (Matthew 6:30; 8:26; 14:31; 16:8; 17:20).

62. Meier, *Law and History in Matthew's Gospel,* 35–40.

63. Signs of the end also attend Jesus' death (Matthew 27:51–54).

64. For a discussion of Pasolini's "disenchantment" with the results of Marxism, illustrated by interpretation of both his creative and theoretical work, see Greene, *Pier Paolo Pasolini.* Her discussion of *Uccellacci e uccellini* is particularly relevant (ibid., 80–91).

65. See Kingsbury, *Matthew: Structure, Christology, Kingdom,* 25–36. For a different view, see Meier, *Law and History in Matthew,* 25–40.

66. See Kingsbury, *Matthew as Story,* 115–27; and David Rhoads, "The Gospel of Matthew. The Two Ways: Hypocrisy or Righteousness," *Currents in Theology and Mission* 19 (1992): 453–61.

67. The tension between law and grace typical of Protestantism is alien to Matthew (cf. Matthew 20:1–16). Matthew's world is like that of Judaism and Islam. The giving of revelation—by which one then lives—is grace.

68. If we were to place Matthew in a spectrum of "Jewish" Christianity, I would consider James less ambiguously Jewish than Matthew, and Hebrews and John more uncertain about their continuing relationship with Judaism than Matthew. Meier's observation that circumcision does not appear in the commission (Matthew 28:16–20) is certainly worth remembering, however (*Law and History in Matthew's Gospel*, 28–30).

69. Walsh, *Reading the Bible*, 388–92.

70. Tatum, *Jesus at the Movies*, 110–12.

71. On the film's reception among Catholics and others, see Tatum, *Jesus at the Movies*, 112–15. The Catholic Baugh, *Imaging the Divine*, 94, calls it "the masterpiece."

72. Cited as the epigraph to Greene, *Pier Paolo Pasolini*.

73. For Longenecker, *Biblical Exegesis in the Apostolic Period*, 38–45, typological exegesis asserts, "this is that." Compare Stendahl, *The School of St. Matthew*, 183–206.

74. Matthew read in the dark with Pasolini does what Girard says the Gospel does. Without a conversation partner like Pasolini, Matthew does what Girard says that myth does. See René Girard, *The Scapegoat*, trans. Yvonne Freccero (Baltimore: Johns Hopkins University Press, 1986).

75. For a typical scholarly erasure, see Crossan, *Who Killed Jesus? Exposing the Roots of Anti-Semitism in the Gospel Story of the Death of Jesus* (New York: HarperSanFrancisco, 1995). Given American pluralism, Hollywood Jesus films, unlike Pasolini and Arcand, are more and more sensitive to anti-Semitism and also efface the Jews. This pattern reaches an extreme in the Italian/American Zeffirelli. See Chapter 2 above.

76. Given Matthew's Emmanuel theology, he also dies God-forsaken.

77. I allude respectively to the attempts of Hyam Maccoby, *Judas Iscariot and the Myth of Jewish Evil* (New York: Free Press, 1992), 4–8, 17, 166–68; Klassen, *Judas*, 28–40, 96–115, 160–76; and Borges, *Ficciones*, 151–57, to rehabilitate Judas. Each author must displace, if not deconstruct, Christian mythology. Maccoby rehabilitates Judas by rejecting the Christian (Pauline) myth of the redemptive cross. Klassen reads Matthew's Judas the Jew in light of Jewish rituals of repentance and with assumptions about the nobility of suicide. Borges creates a gnostic Judas. See Chapter 2 above.

78. See Miles, *Seeing and Believing*, 68–93.

79. We would converse with *The Ten Commandments*, not *The King of Kings*. As we have already seen, DeMille uses the former film to hallow Christian America during the Cold War. Accordingly, he elides differences between Jews and Americans. In Jethro, he also provides a precursor for the Muslims. Jethro describes himself to Moses as one of the descendants of Ishmael, one of the obedient. He then instructs his daughter to teach Moses "their ways." Thus, DeMille locates and unites Americans, Jews, and Muslims at Sinai (in the 1950s). The Christians are the notable absentees. While I do not think we should elide differences between religious groups, I suggest that we endeavor to find those victimized by our institutions and myths at the cross, given its (and Jesus') mythic significance in our culture, even if that is anachronistic.

Chapter 6
The Alien and Alienating Past:
King of Kings and Luke

The problem was not, as so many theologians then believed, that the Biblical critics
[i.e., historical critics] emerged from their libraries with results disturbing to believers,
but that the method itself, which led to those results, was based on assumptions quite irreconcilable
with traditional belief. If the theologian regards the Scriptures as supernaturally inspired,
the historian must assume that the Bible is intelligible only in terms of its historical context and
is subject to the same principles of interpretation and criticism that are applied to other ancient
literature. If the theologian believes that the events of the Bible are the results of the supernatural
intervention of God, the historian regards such an explanation as a hindrance to true historical
understanding. If the theologian believes that the events upon which Christendom rests are unique,
the historian assumes that those events, like all events, are analogous to those in the present
and that it is only on this assumption that statements about them can be assessed at all.
If the theologian believes on faith that certain events occurred, the historian regards
all historical claims as having only a greater or lesser degree of probability,
and he regards the attachment of faith to these claims as a corruption of historical judgment.[1]

Religious developments originating in the Biblical tradition may be seen as causal factors
in the formation of the modern secularized world. . . . We would contend that here lies the great
historical irony in the relation between religion and secularization, an irony that can be
graphically put by saying that, historically speaking, Christianity has been its own gravedigger.[2]

Reading Luke and *King of Kings*

Luke begins with priests, prophets, and people worshipfully acclaiming the arrival of divine salvation.[3] This auspicious start continues beyond Luke's introduction (Luke 1:1–4:13) into Luke's very brief, but miraculous Galilean ministry (Luke 4:14–9:50). The sermon that opens that ministry, however, better portends the rest of Luke's story, a tale of Jewish rejection and Gentile salvation (Luke 4:16–30). The Galilean ministry also ends ominously, when Jesus "sets his face" to go to Jerusalem to die as a rejected prophet. The lengthy approach (or travel narrative) to Jerusalem depicts Jesus' ministry as a time of crisis demanding decision (Luke 9:51–19:40).⁴ Jesus' lament and Temple act (Luke 19:41–48), which begin the Jerusalem ministry (Luke 19:41–24:53), are paradigmatic of that hostile time. The leaders and people reject Jesus, and Jesus predicts the city's destruction. For Luke, Israel rejects her salvation, and its narrative ends with an impetus to the nations.

Nicholas Ray's *King of Kings* has a similar fourfold structure: 1) an elaborate introduction; 2) a time of miracles; 3) a training of the disciples; and 4) a hostile Jerusalem ministry. Ray's introduction, however, differs strikingly from Luke's. *King of Kings* begins with the tragedy of Rome's imperial oppression of the Jews, not with divine salvation. Despite various maleficent rulers and false messiahs, the people survive through their hope of a messiah. After its lengthy introduction (including Jesus' infancy as well as tales of Jewish woe), *King of Kings* juxtaposes Barabbas's successful raid on the arriving Pilate's army with John's baptism of Jesus in the Jordan. Intertwining these stories, *King of Kings* begins its tale of two messiahs, one of war and one of peace. Judas, one of Barabbas's guerrilla warriors, bridges the two stories. While Barabbas plots against Rome, Jesus ministers "miraculously" to the people and delivers a majestic Sermon (on the Mount) of peace, love, and the brotherhood of man. Even Jesus' disciples do not take to this message quickly, so Jesus retires with them for extended training. Eventually, Jesus preaches peace in the Jerusalem Temple as the Romans crush Barabbas's failed revolt in the courts outside. An anguished Judas, then, tries to force Jesus to use miracles against Rome by betraying him to the powers-that-be. Refusing to test God, Jesus falls victim to Pontius Pilate despite Lucius's efforts to defend him. While Judas and the people choose Barabbas as their messiah, Lucius confesses that Jesus is the Christ (messiah) at the cross. The result is a Luke-like move from Jews to (modern) Gentile believers. Thereafter, the resurrection is anticlimactic.

In addition to similar structures, then, both Luke and *King of Kings* locate Jesus in the politics and history of first-century Palestine. This historical move secularizes Jesus and creates the problem of his "pastness," but the histories—both gospel and film—connect us with this past. In the process, they also universalize Jesus. Not surprisingly, the past and universal Jesus lacks specificity and presence. He becomes an archetypal pattern authorizing a triumphal Christianity. The continuing presence of "elder brothers," however, renders the triumph somewhat ambiguous.

In the Midst of Empire

Of the gospels, only Luke mentions a Roman emperor (Luke 2:1; 3:1). The first reference dates Jesus' birth to the time of Augustus:

> In those days a decree went out from Emperor Augustus that all the world should be registered. This was the first registration and was taken while Quirinius was governor of Syria. All went to their own towns to be registered. Joseph also went from the town of Nazareth in Galilee to Judea, to the city of David called Bethlehem, because he was descended from the house and family of David. (Luke 2:1–4)

The passage also connects Jesus with another king, the Davidic dynasty and the messianic expectations associated with it (see Luke 1:32, 69–71; 2:11, 26). Like Matthew, however, Luke has difficulty combining the notion of Jesus' Davidic ancestry with the story of his virgin birth, because the latter means that Joseph, the son of David, is not Jesus' father (Luke 1:26–38; 2:5–7; 2:48–49; 3:23). To deal with the problem, Luke simply shifts attention to Jesus' birth in Bethlehem, David's city. While Matthew uses Torah (Micah 5:2) to locate Jesus there, Luke uses Augustus's decree. Luke's focus suggests that this God manipulates imperial decrees as easily as Matthew's God orchestrates Torah.

The registration is for taxation, and taxation is for empire maintenance, but Luke's decree contains the seeds of the empire's destruction. The connection of taxation and David recalls 2 Samuel 24, the story of God's punishment of David for his misguided registration of the people. For some strands of the Hebrew Bible, registration falsely claims that God's people belong to the king. For Luke, too, the people belong to God, not to king or emperor (see Luke 20:20–26).[5]

Luke's second reference to imperial rulers reinforces its focus on God's direction of events, that is, on its *"salvation* history" nature.[6] After cataloguing the levels of imperial administration ruling Palestine (who resemble closely Ray's triumvirate of power), Luke states, "the word of God came to John" (Luke 3:2). Grammatically, the rulers are adverbial. The subject of Luke 3:1–2 is God's word, which "comes" into a history rendered thereby mere setting for the divine salvation (compare John 1:14).

Luke ends similarly. The Judean triumvirate—the high priest, Pilate, and Herod Antipas—crucify the innocent Jesus (Luke 22:47–23:49), but this "crime" is merely the stage for the trumping divine word/act, the resurrection that enthrones Jesus as messiah.[7] Only after the resurrection does the Lukan Jesus refer to himself as messiah (Luke 24:26, 46). The sermons in Acts reiterate this point repeatedly: the powers/people crucified Jesus and God raised him (for example, Acts 2:23–24). Acts confirms the resurrection's triumph.[8] It also locates Jesus even more thoroughly in the empire as the apostles and Paul recapitulate Jesus' innocent lifestyle and message before new powers: for example, Roman administration (Acts 16; 18; 24–25; 28); Greek philosophy (Acts 17); and Hellenistic religion (Acts 16; 19).

King of Kings also places the Jesus story firmly in the midst of imperial politics. In fact, the focus on the "times" overwhelms the movie's Jesus. After showing "most irreverent" Pompey's profanation of the Temple, the opening
narration, written by Ray Bradbury and narrated by Orson Welles, continues:

> Thus, for more than 50 years after Pompey's invasion, the history of
> Judea could be read by the light of burning towns. If gold was not the
> harvest, there was a richness of people to be gathered; the battalions of
> Caesar Augustus brought in the crop. Like sheep from their own green
> fields, the Jews went to the slaughter; they went from the stone quarries
> to build Rome's triumphal arches. But Caesar could find no Jew to press
> Rome's laws on this fallen land, so Caesar named one Herod the Great,
> an Arab of the Bedouin tribe, as the new, false and maleficent King of
> the Jews. But from the dust of Herod's feet, rebellions of Jews rose up,
> and Herod, in reply, planted evil seeds from which forests of Roman
> crosses grew high on Jerusalem's hills. And Herod, passing pleased,
> bade the forest multiply.[9]

For the details of this oppressive colonization, *King of Kings* relies heavily on
Josephus.[10] For Josephus, the Roman destruction of Jerusalem is a divine punishment of the people (for example, *Jewish War* 1.1–30; 2.345–401;
5.362–419). This sin-theodicy approach agrees formally with that of the
Former Prophets (see 2 Kings 17:7–18; 21:10–15) and Luke (see Luke
19:41–44; 23:26–31), both of which assert that God destroyed Jerusalem
because the people did not heed the prophets who called them to repentance.
By contrast, Josephus's point is that the Jews should have cooperated with Rome
as he did. In the aftermath of the Shoah,[11] Ray departs from this sin-theodicy
approach to present Rome's colonization as a crime against humanity. Thus Ray
shifts the onus for the destruction from the Jews to the Romans.[12]

Ray still uses, however, a salvation-history style. His "politics" are also mere
setting for a "divine word." Thus, after depicting the tumultuous, oppressive
times, *King of Kings* privileges an extended version of Jesus' Sermon on the
Mount. The sermon responds ethically or religiously to oppression, not politically. Ray emphasizes the importance of this sermon by tracing thereafter the
tragic failures of Barabbas's and Judas's more political-military solutions.

Despite the movie's historical dramatization, Ray's interpretation of the sermon universalizes the Jesus story. Ray abstracts and generalizes Jesus' message.
In fact, Lucius's summary of the sermon as a message of peace, love, and the
brotherhood of man sounds remarkably like the message of modern, liberal
Christianity. As a result, then, *King of Kings* has a rather Eurocentric "heart," a

tendency to state the Christian message in terms of modern liberalism, rather than in terms more likely in first-century Judaism.

In presenting the Jesus story as a universal (and liberal) ethic, Griffith's *Intolerance* is Ray's most obvious cinematic precursor. As we have seen, while Griffith tells four stories set in four different times, the four stories are actually repetitions of one story, the story of the fate of innocents at the hands of interventionists and do-gooders. While the result nicely dramatizes Griffith's message of pacifistic nonintervention, the universal message becomes rather nonhistorical.

Luke's Jesus is equally universal. Only Luke continues the quote from Isaiah 40:3–5 explaining the Baptist's activity, far enough to include the phrase "for all flesh" (Luke 3:6). Only Luke has Jesus authorize a "Gentile" mission during his own ministry (Luke 10:1–20).[13] Further, throughout his ministry, the Lukan Jesus includes the outcasts of his society, incorporating women, tax collectors, and Samaritans in his mission. The expansion to the nations predicted by the risen Jesus (Luke 24:45–49) and realized (somewhat grudgingly) by the apostles and Paul in Acts confirms this "universal" portrait of Jesus. Acts itself is even stylistically like Griffith's film, for its apostles repeat the pattern of the Lukan Jesus' life wherever they go—Jewish opposition and Gentile acceptance. As in Griffith, we have a narrative pattern transporting a universal message (all the characters in Luke-Acts also have the same message)—not history.[14]

Their universalizing tendencies give Luke, Ray, and Griffith a curious relationship to empire. In the midst of oppressive empires, their universalizing message is itself a form of empire building. Luke-Acts simply replaces the Roman Empire (and Hellenistic culture) with the triumphant Lukan message. Ray and Griffith imagine wistfully the triumph of peace over politics. Such empires, even if they begin with the lowly and the oppressed, inevitably lead to their own violent exclusions: of Jews and heretics in Luke-Acts; of the Pharisees (as symbol of hypocritical do-gooders) in Griffith; and of both freedom fighters and quislings in Ray.[15]

Despite their universalizing, Luke and Ray do "historicize" Jesus vis-à-vis their precursors. Luke forgoes apocalypse and rabbinic schools to narrate the fate of the Lukan Jesus and his followers in the Roman Empire. Similarly, *King of Kings* forgoes *Intolerance*'s fourfold, "same old" story for a dramatization of Jesus' (or Ray's) message in its oppressive "times." *King of Kings* treats DeMille's *The King of Kings* in a similar way.[16] Thus, Ray's Jesus is a far less transcendent figure than DeMille's omnipresent, personal savior. Ray's Jesus is a victim of his times. Despite the nonpolitical nature of his message, he is a political plaything and ultimately disposable. With Ray's Jesus, only his message—not his person—is universal. By contrast, DeMille's Jesus himself transcends history, as his resurrection appearance over a modern city demonstrates. In sum, Ray's Jesus is more human and, thus, more historical than DeMille's.[17]

The Problem of the Past

DeMille's silent film, juxtaposing images from Christian paintings and illustrated bibles with scriptural titles, offers an illusion of immediacy. His film's images and words replicate a Bible familiar to its audience.[18] By contrast, Ray's historical presentation distances Jesus. Accordingly, Jesus' presence needs mediating, and *King of Kings* employs an omniscient, ubiquitous narrator (Orson Welles) to that end. Quite simply, Jesus is available to the viewer only as the narrator offers him.

The narrator introduces the film, setting the historical context of oppression and the people's hope for a messiah. In fact, no character speaks until Joseph asks for a room for his pregnant wife. The narrator intrudes frequently thereafter to set the scene, to note the passage of time, and to explain ancient customs. The film also uses the narrator (or Lucius) to report the scientifically troubling miracles of Jesus. More importantly, the narrator provides crucial "inside views." Thus, he instructs the audience that Judas must decide whether to follow a messiah of war or a messiah of peace. Later, the narrator confides that Jesus called the Twelve and taught them his way of peace, but they, like the crowd, wanted revolution. In two crucial, intertwined scenes, the narrator explains Judas's betrayal as his "testing" of God by contrasting the scene with Jesus' preparation for trial and death in the garden. Finally, the narrator ends the story by reporting Jesus' burial and his resurrection appearances. We see the risen Jesus only in his appearance to Mary Magdalene. Otherwise, we have only the narrator's words, Jesus' voice, and the shadow of the cross on the beach. All in all, then, the hardworking narrator of *King of Kings* packages and presents Jesus.

Luke's narrator is equally important[19] and provides even more information than does Orson Welles about staging, customs, and motivations. The Lukan narrator's packaging of Jesus is most obvious at the beginning and end of Luke. In the preface (Luke 1:1–4), the Lukan narrator admits his distance from Jesus. He is not an eyewitness,[20] and others have already written about Jesus, but the narrator claims to have "investigated" matters thoroughly and to present them in an "orderly" fashion. The Lukan narrator, then, unabashedly offers his Jesus as his own historical reconstruction.[21]

Further, the narrator dismisses Jesus at the end of Luke (Luke 24:50–53) by depicting Jesus' ascension (repeated in Acts 1:6–11) and reporting the disciples' continued worship of Jesus and God. Apart from that worship, Jesus is no longer a part of "normal" life. In fact, Jesus' last words predict his replacement by inspired witnesses (Luke 24:46–49; compare Luke 3:16; Acts 1:4–5). By ending with a departed, replaced Jesus, Luke differs markedly from Matthew's continually present Jesus (Matthew 28:16–20; 18:20) and Mark's expected Jesus (Mark 16:7).

Luke's narrator obviously and obtrusively stands between his absent Jesus and his implied audience. Further, the Lukan narrator creates intervening "witnesses" as his sources (Luke 1:2; 24:48).[22] These witnesses are crucial to Luke's narrative rhetoric. They witness the entire career of Jesus, including the cross (Luke 23:49), and ultimately replace Jesus (Acts 1:15–26). Thereafter, Acts tells the tale of these witnesses (and Paul). By this story, Luke-Acts itself also becomes a witness "connecting" Luke's readers with the absent Jesus. The result is a subtle upgrade in the authority of the Lukan narrator and text. That admittedly not-a-witness (Luke 1:2) becomes the only one offering testimony.

Lucius, Ray's most creative addition to the Jesus story, is his comparable "witness." He connects (by witnessing) the entire Jesus story of *King of Kings.* He supervises Herod's slaughter of the innocents, arrests John the Baptist for Herod Antipas, spies on Jesus' peace ministry for the Judean triumvirate, and defends Jesus as the court-appointed advocate at Pilate's trial. More importantly, he is the crucifixion's most crucial witness. He is, however, notably absent during the resurrection scenes.

As the primary antagonist of Barabbas, Lucius is also the representative of Roman colonial order. At one point, Pilate remarks that there would be no empire without men like Lucius. Despite Ray's distaste for colonization, he presents Lucius as a noble Roman, a man of personal integrity struggling with tyrannical rulers. Thus, Lucius initially refuses Herod's order to slaughter the innocents. Although forced into the reprehensible act, he later redeems himself by covering up Jesus' origins. When the holy family returns to Nazareth, instead of exposing Jesus, he merely tells the family to include him in the census. Later, when Antipas wishes to arrest John, Lucius demands to know the grounds. When John is arrested, Lucius ameliorates his situation as he can. When Jesus is arrested and tried, Lucius becomes his court-appointed advocate.

The characterization entices the audience to identify with this noble Roman. In fact, he provides the audience a vehicle into the story. Obviously, the imperial American Cold War audience of *King of Kings* has more in common with Lucius than they do with the pacifist Jesus. Further, by employing Lucius to report various troublesome miracles (nature miracles) rather than dramatizing them, *King of Kings* minimizes potential tensions between the prescientific Jesus story and the highly technological America of the 1960s.[23] Lucius, then, instructs postwar American secularists on the care and handling of the Jesus story. Lucius, despite his disbelief in God (he opines that he has seen too much violence to believe), is open to reports of Jesus' miracles and listens carefully to Jesus' teaching. Finally, forced to defend Jesus, he apparently comes to believe in Jesus' innocence. Thus, in his last interview with Barabbas, Lucius holds Barabbas, formerly a respected enemy, in contempt. Experienced in and sickened by violence, Lucius has been moved by Jesus' peace message and resolute character. At the cross, then, he declares that Jesus is the Christ (messiah).

Lucius also serves as a foil for Judas. Attracted to Jesus, Judas defects from Barabbas (we first see Judas in the film with Barabbas in the opening raid on the Romans); however, when his former friend's revolution fails, Judas tries to force Jesus to take action versus the Romans. The narrator comments ominously that his betrayal was a decision to "test" Jesus' divine power. That this "test" is wrong is obvious from the scene with which Judas's betrayal is paired, the garden. In fact, the camera cuts back and forth between the praying Jesus and the arriving soldiers and Judas as Jesus prays, "not as I will." This depiction also resonates with an earlier scene, the wilderness, which ends with Jesus saying, "I won't test God" (compare Luke 4:12–13).[24]

As Judas moves away from Jesus, Lucius moves toward Jesus; however, that he "converts" to Jesus is not altogether clear. While a likely interpretation, Lucius does not appear in the film after the cross. In particular, he is not present with the disciples during the resurrection sequence. I am not sure, then, that he necessarily represents commitment to the cause of Christ then or now. He may remain, then, "unchurched," a representative of the honest, modern "religious" seculars of the film's audience.

As he packages the Jesus story for later consumption, Lucius is also the film's foil for Luke. Like Luke, which charters a Gentile Christianity, he also provides a way in for those later and other than the original audience of Jesus. Like Luke, Lucius also stands between secularity and religion. Only their trajectories differ. While Lucius represents a move from secular modernity toward the religious past of the Jesus story, Luke represents a move from religion toward secularity, a move that its salvation-history reputation obscures.

By locating Christianity in the empire, Luke secularizes the movement. Thus, Luke intertwines Jesus' death and the fate of Jerusalem (Luke 13:31–35; 19:41–44; 20:9–19; 23:28–31; compare 7:30; 10:1–16; 11:29–32, 45–52; 13:1–5), but it does not see Jerusalem's fall as the divine, apocalyptic end. Instead, Luke depicts Jerusalem's fate as a typical military event (but still indirectly a divine vengeance) (Luke 21:20–24). Further, on four separate occasions, Luke-Acts displaces or defers the time of the end (Luke 17:20–21; 19:11–27; 21:7–8; Acts 1:6–9). In the Lukan apocalypse, in particular (Luke 21), Luke repeatedly postpones the end. What are in Mark "signs of the end"—false messiahs, wars, natural disasters, persecutions, and Jerusalem's destruction—are, for Luke, part of "the time of the Gentiles." For Luke, the fulfillment of that time (Luke 21:24) separates "historical" matters (Luke 21:7–24) from the Lukan apocalypse (only Luke 21:25–28, with ethical injunctions in 21:29–36).[25] Instead of this age and the next, then, Luke-Acts imagines a time before Jesus, the time of Jesus, and the time of the witnesses to the nations. Jesus becomes *der Mitte die Zeit.*[26] Obviously, this historical periodization distances Jesus from subsequent times.

By acting as a historian, the narrator of Luke-Acts starts down a path leading to modern secularity and to nineteenth-century historical criticism, liberal Protestantism's response to secularity. To make the point as graphically as possible, we might say that Luke's narrator is as much the first historical critic as he is a salvation-history theologian. As this chapter's first epigraph indicates, Luke's historical approach has three heretical principles: 1) criticism; 2) analogy; and 3) correlation. The first means that judgments about the past are not certain, but probable and revisable. Instead of divine absolutes, history dwells in relativity. The second means that the past and the present are not radically dissimilar. As a result, Christian origins are no longer unique. The last means that all events are to be explained in terms of a historical nexus of causation. Consequently, miracle and supernatural causation are not legitimate explanatory devices.[27]

Of course, Luke's narrator (and later historians and theologians) does not always follow these three principles rigorously. Thus, while the Lukan narrator implies an adherence to critical investigation in Luke 1:3, he retreats to Christian catechism in Luke 1:4.[28] Whatever his critical claims, then, the narrator is a fairly credulous tradent, striving to strengthen the catechetical faith of his audience (see Acts 20:25–35).[29] By contrast, the Lukan narrator is quite faithful to the second principle. Luke's Jesus is hardly unique. His successors live lives like his. As Luke-Acts offers a salvation history, its narrator never considers the third principle. God is the cause of Luke-Acts' history.

My point, however, is not to give the Lukan narrator a grade using nineteenth-century criteria.[30] Rather, my point is that he begins the secularization process at the end of which stands historical criticism. Despite his analogical efforts, the past has become alien and alienating.[31] No wonder, then, that in *King of Kings,* Lucius stands outside and looks in (even after his "conversion"). History has left us all outside the past. The narrator of Luke-Acts is the first (extant) to deal with the alien, alienating Christian past. To do so, he falls into an oxymoronic dualism—a myth—that unites (with considerable tension) history's relativity with a universal (salvific) message. The result is an apology, masquerading as history, in defense of Christian truth. Biblical historical criticism still uses similar tactics.

Writing History: Generic Conventions

History is not merely the past or its investigation. It is also a genre(s) of narrative(s). After researching the past, Luke's narrator and Ray couch their results in existing genres. Ray operates within the Hollywood genre of the biblical epic while Luke-Acts resembles ancient histories. As we have already seen, however, Luke's focus on divine causation is inconsistent with history.[32] Those discussing Luke as a history, then, categorize it as a particular kind of history. Thus, Aune describes Luke-Acts as one of the Hellenistic "general histories," histories narrating "the important historical experiences of a single national group from their origin to the recent past." Later, Aune restates the definition and replaces "origin" with "mythical beginnings."[33] Accordingly, Luke-Acts describes the origins of the people called Christian by combining myth and history. General histories, however, usually unite a dim mythic past with a more recent historical past. In Luke-Acts, the recent past is mythical. As a result, Aune ultimately decides that Luke's closer generic connections are with Hebrew history (or Hellenistic epic or prose mythography). In content and form, Luke has at least three important precursors in Hebrew narrative: 1) 1 and 2 Samuel; 2) 1 and 2 Kings; and 3) Jonah.

The story of the establishment of the Davidic monarchy, 1 and 2 Samuel, is the important precursor for Luke's announcement of its messianic king. Luke's infancy narrative borrows elements from the story of Samuel's miraculous birth to Elkanah and Hannah (1 Samuel 1).[34] Other elements of Luke combine his presentation of Jesus more clearly with Samuel's David. Thus, Jesus is born in the city of Bethlehem, and Luke 1:32–33 recalls God's promise to David of an everlasting dynasty (see 2 Samuel 7:8–16; 23:1–7). While Jesus is messiah at important junctures (for example, Luke 2:11, 26; 3:22; 9:20, 35), the resurrection enthrones him as messiah most decisively (Luke 24:46).

The question of the legitimacy of the king dominates 1 and 2 Samuel, but not Luke.[35] Instead, Luke's conflict details Israel's rejection of the prophet Jesus who offered her salvation. That rejection, of course, condemns Israel to destruction (Luke 6:22–23; 11:47–51; 13:34–35; 19:41–44; 20:9–19; 23:28–31; Acts 3:23; 7:51–53). This pattern, as we have seen, follows 1 and 2 Kings (particularly 2 Kings 17:7–23), which also blames Israel's destruction on the people's failure to heed repentance prophets.

For Luke, the rejection of Jesus also explains the inclusion of the Gentiles.[36] Here, Luke does not follow 1 and 2 Kings or (most of) the prophets, because the latter generally assume that the judgment of the nations will bring Israel's salvation, not that the judgment of Israel will bring the salvation of the Gentiles.[37] Jonah's story of the salvation of hated Nineveh (contrast Nahum), however, is precursor. While Luke anticipates the salvation of the nations quite early (Luke 3:6; 4:16–30), the narrative of Acts increasingly leaves the Jews behind after the martyrdom of Stephen (see Acts 13:46–47; 18:6; 28:28). The last passage, which effectively ends Acts, is a decisive moment, and leaves the impression that Luke-Acts is more concerned with Gentile than with Jewish salvation. Here, of course, Luke-Acts has gone beyond Jonah.

The salvation of the nations does not obviously concern Ray's *King of Kings.* The movie owes more to the stories of the coming of the king (1 and 2 Samuel) and of Israel's tragedy (1 and 2 Kings). In fact, Ray weaves these themes together in the story of Judas, who chooses Barabbas, the messiah of war, rather than Jesus, the messiah of peace. The implication, an ominous one in Cold War America, is that by so choosing, the Jews (and Americans?) have failed to escape the "spiral of violence" begun by Pompey's colonization. While Ray does minimize the anti-Semitic elements in Luke, the slain bodies lying in the Temple court after Barabbas's failed revolution imply the future consequences of the "wrong" choice of Judas and the religious leaders.

This violent battle scene identifies the main generic precursor of *King of Kings* as the biblical epics of Hollywood.[38] The trailer advertising the film (which opens my video copy) presents the film in the epic style. It trumpets the cast of thousands—seven thousand assembled for the Sermon on the Mount—the huge expense of the film, the cast of well-known international actors, the dramatic setting of the story, and the story's historic significance. The trailer accurately describes the film by saying that the story is set in the midst of barbaric tyranny and that Jesus' story comes "out of the shadows" of ruthless power and idolatry. With a dash of Dickens, the trailer's closing titles set the story even more firmly on an epic stage: "It was a time of fear. It was a time of love. It was the time of *King of Kings.*" In fact, *King of Kings* is the epic Jesus film and offers the audience more action—two epic battles—than any other Jesus film.[39]

Ray does, however, add his own distinctive touches to the epic format.[40] In particular, despite the wide-screen action, he strives for intimacy. Thus, *King of Kings* has several "family structures" reminiscent of those in *Rebel without a Cause,* Ray's most famous film. Herod Antipas's incestuous desires for Salome seem a darker version of the tension between Judy (Natalie Wood) and her father. By contrast, Jesus' easygoing relationship with his mother and his heavenly father is something not available to any of the troubled teenagers in *Rebel without a Cause.* For this reason, Babbington and Evans assert that *King of Kings* is Ray's answer to the problems of the families that he depicted in *Rebel without a Cause.*[41]

Actually, both films provide their alienated heroes with a surrogate family (respectively, Jesus' followers and Judy and Plato). Further, both films have characters who struggle to find "the father." Jesus does not so struggle, but Judas and

Plato (Sal Mineo in *Rebel without a Cause*) do. Both Judas and Plato struggle with their identity, seek a model to follow, and find themselves situated between violent and peaceful friends. On various occasions, Plato tries to make Jim Stark (James Dean) into his surrogate father. Although more successful than Judas, who is riven between two surrogate fathers (Barabbas and Jesus), Plato also comes to a tragic end.

Of course, Ray's Jesus is no Jim Stark (James Dean). Jesus is not a typical Ray teenager enacting adolescent rebellion.[42] *King of Kings* would be an altogether different film if he were. It might have some similarity to Scorsese's *The Last Temptation of Christ*, but it would not be very much like Luke, because Luke's Jesus (like John's) has a far less tumultuous relationship with God than do those of Matthew and Mark. Luke, for example, does not have the cry of dereliction and has Jesus accept God's will in Gethsemane after only one prayer.[43] Nevertheless, Ray's Jesus does recall Ray's fascination with youth and idealism. Thus, Jeffrey Hunter, who played Ray's Jesus (in his thirties), is notably younger than his precursor, H. B. Warner, who played Jesus in *The King of Kings* (in his fifties). Babbington and Evans opine, then, that Ray's film executes "a double act of transgressive oedipal intertexuality"; that is, Ray's young Jesus replaces DeMille's fatherly Jesus, and his secular (that is, historical) vision replaces DeMille's devout one.[44]

Ray's focus on Jesus also moves the film away from the indirect Christ of the biblical epics. Instead, *King of Kings* follows the standard Hollywood "biopic" depiction of a hero's self-recognition, ordeal, and triumph/tragedy.[45] It is notably weak, however, in the self-recognition segment, and it sets Jesus' career in its times so fully that the life often seems an afterthought. Thus, we arrive at Jesus' baptism by John only after a lengthy introduction to the "times" and after Barabbas's dramatic guerrilla raid. Further, the baptismal recognition belongs to John, not Jesus. Thus, in the next scene, John arrives at Mary's house for a discussion about her son's career, a matter already decided (down to the ominous mission to Jerusalem) before Jesus' temptation. Further, Ray emphasizes the physical struggles of Jesus in the wilderness. Although the narrator comments that Jesus brought forth his soul to be seen of himself, it hardly seems a genuine struggle for self-recognition. Jesus' career is fated.

Jesus' struggles are external, not internal.[46] Like other biopic characters, Jesus is a reforming, innovative individual in conflict with established institutions and traditions.[47] Not surprisingly, then, Ray characterizes Jesus by juxtaposition. Most obviously, he contrasts Barabbas and Jesus, the messiahs of war and peace. Ray also juxtaposes Jesus with the Roman conquerors. Thus, Pompey, clad in scarlet, profanes the Temple. The Romans are routinely in red thereafter. Jesus appears at first in white, but he dons a red robe for the Sermon on the Mount. Later, Herod Antipas mockingly clothes Jesus in a red robe, which he wears for most of his suffering. The color serves to contrast Jesus' message and character with those of the Romans.[48]

The supporting cast essentially provides a variety of possible responses to Jesus and to Roman oppression. Like the Gospels, then, Ray also tends toward characterization by binary opposition. People are either for the messiah of war or the messiah of peace. As a result, dramatic interest focuses not on Jesus, but on those characters—like Judas and Lucius—who are moving from one pole to the other. As a result, *King of Kings* does not quite succeed as a Jesus biopic.

Jesus is too passive. Thus, one of the lasting images of *King of Kings* is the silent Jesus, with head bowed, waiting for Pilate to decide his fate.[49] As in Luke, and in contrast to the movie supposedly based on Luke by Krish and Sykes, the death of Ray's Jesus is not salvific. He is simply a victim of historical forces beyond his control.[50] In fact, given the forest of crosses that climax the narrator's introduction to the film (as well as the pyre of burning bodies), Ray's Jesus is simply another Jewish victim of Roman oppression.

Not surprisingly, then, we are left finally with Jesus' shadow. In one healing sequence—although we finally see Hunter's eyes in wide screen—we generally see Jesus' shadow on the wall as people are healed. Further, except for an appearance to Mary Magdalene, Jesus' shadow dominates the resurrection scenes. In the film's last scene, we hear Jesus' words as he sends the disciples to the nations. As they leave, in the movie's last shot, we see a shadow form a cross with their abandoned fishing net on the beach. That shadow is what remains.

Only a shadow remains.

Losing a Grip on Jesus: The End of Uniqueness

Further, the passive (touchstone) Jesus "gets lost" in the subplots featuring John the Baptist, Mary, Barabbas, Judas, Lucius, and others. Here, the crux of this "loss" lies in history, not in Hollywood novelization. When Ray, like Luke, places Jesus in history, Jesus loses his uniqueness because of the principle of analogy.[51] In short, Ray's Jesus is hardly unique.[52] First, he is a Ray character.[53] He is one lone innocent and one victim among a "forest of crosses." Second, Ray's two-messiah story means that Jesus is only one messiah among others. At one point, Herod Antipas wonders why the Jews never tire of "inventing" these figures. Third, Ray's Jesus is a prophet like John the Baptist. In fact, *King of Kings* imagines John as Jesus' forerunner in a quite literal way. Thus, John preaches in Jerusalem,[54] falls afoul of the authorities, and comes to a bad end. Of course, Ray's John defers to Jesus, as do the gospel Johns, but Jesus remains a figure very much like John. That Herod Antipas repeatedly asks if Jesus is John is entirely understandable in Ray's film.

Luke's Jesus also lacks uniqueness, because he too is one prophet among many. Again, Luke's John and Jesus are so similar that Luke more carefully and more artificially separates John from Jesus than does any other gospel. Thus, Luke's John defers to Jesus even in the womb (Luke 1:41–44). Further, only Luke notes that Herod imprisoned John before embarking on its narration of Jesus' (temptation and) ministry (Luke 3:19–20). Further, only the Lukan Jesus separates his era from John's (Luke 16:16). The Lukan separating of Jesus and John continues in Acts when an important pericope reiterates that the Holy Spirit comes only through Jesus' baptism, not John's (Acts 19:1–7; compare Luke 3:16–17; Acts 1:5). Obviously, if the Lukan John and Jesus were not very similar, it would not be so important to work so hard to distinguish them.

Further, Luke's Jesus lacks uniqueness because Luke reduces (elevates?) Jesus to apostolic status. As we have suggested before, the Lukan Jesus, Peter, and Paul have lives following a similar pattern: empowerment with the Spirit; opening sermon; miracles; opposition from the Jews; travels preaching the gospel; arrest and imprisonment; Jewish trial for blasphemy; and Roman trial for sedition (the last applies to Jesus and Paul alone).[55] Such parallels illustrate the nature of Lukan discipleship (see Luke 6:40; 9:23) and provide a sense of an apostolic tradition that guarantees the reliable continuance of the Lukan gospel. But an unintended—and unremarked—consequence of these parallels is that the Lukan Jesus becomes merely the first in a series of Christians (or Christian leaders). Accordingly, in Luke's resurrection appearances, disciples know Jesus in the breaking of bread and the interpretation of Scriptures (Luke 24:30–32, 45–49), or as he acts as the first Christian priest.

That Jesus is the first in a series of Christians differs remarkably from Matthew's mythically present Jesus (Matthew 18:20; 28:18–20). Luke simply does not need this ongoing presence, because the Lukan Jesus is only part of the ongoing action of God. Luke can afford an ascension ending Jesus' "real" presence, then, for spirit-led activity continues (and went on before Jesus in Luke 1–2).[56] Luke's story is ultimately about (a universal) God, not Jesus (for example, Luke 1:47, 77; 2:30; Acts 2:22–24, 32–36; 10:38–40; 13:23, 30). God's story precedes (Luke 1–2) and succeeds Jesus (Acts). Perhaps we should not forget that for Luke, Jesus is not even God's only son (see Luke 3:38; and the various references to God as "our" or "your" Father).[57]

Triumphal and Prophetic Christianity:
Does the Empire Strike Back?

Apart from the resurrection, Luke's Jesus would be so non-unique that he would look like very much like an "acceptable loss" (along with John the Baptist, previous prophets, and ultimately the Jews) in the drama of God's triumphal salvation. Such a view would be eerily like the view that Ray's Romans take of the forest of crosses in Palestine. All these Jews are acceptable losses in the course of the triumphal Pax Romana. For Luke, however, the resurrection redeems Jesus, so Luke makes much more of the resurrection than either Mark or Matthew. Luke's resurrection is a death-undoing, public triumph.

Compared to Mark and Matthew, Luke's resurrection appearances are semi-public. They include Mary Magdalene and two disciples (other than the Twelve) on the road to Emmaus, as well as the eleven. Further, Luke's resurrected Jesus engages in mundane social activities: eating, breaking bread, interpreting Scripture, and worshiping. Further, Luke's resurrected Jesus ascends to heaven in the presence of his disciples, an event that Luke-Acts twice reports (Luke 24:51; Acts 1:9–11). Finally, and most importantly, Jesus' witnesses—Peter, John, Stephen, and Paul—publicize the message of Jesus' resurrection before Jesus' enemies, the Jewish religious leaders and various Roman administrators.

In Acts, the innocence-vindicated pattern continues with a vengeance. As Pervo has noted, *the repeated story* (thirty-three times by his count) in Acts is a miraculous near-escape from death by one of Jesus' witnesses.[58] Further, Acts, like Luke, repeatedly presents these witnesses as "innocent" before various Roman tribunals. Of course, to continue this fantasy, Acts ends before the outcome of Paul's Roman imprisonment. Ending as it does, however, Luke-Acts demonstrates Jesus' (and Christianity's) triumph before the world by taking the message to Rome, the center of the world, where Paul preaches the gospel "without hindrance." The adverb (*akôlutôs*) translated by this phrase is literally the last word in Acts.[59] It follows the phrase "with all boldness," the characteristic attitude of the post-resurrection witnesses of Jesus before the authorities (see Acts 4) in contrast to their pre-resurrection fears and denial (Luke 22:54–65).

The result is a triumphal vision of Christianity. In Luke-Acts, Christianity expands miraculously throughout the Roman Empire despite, if not because of, various persecutions and trials. This expansion portends the imperial triumph of Christianity. Ultimately, Luke-Acts (and other texts) belongs to the Constantinian church and supplies that imperial institution's chartering apostolic myth. Of course, Luke-Acts only suggests that later triumph, because, at the time of the writing of Luke-Acts, the Roman Empire continues in full sway. The triumphalism of Luke-Acts, then, is metaphor, myth, prophecy, or fantasy, not history; and Christianity's triumph is immaterial (spiritual). This "triumph," like the kingdom of Ray's Jesus (or the freedom Jesus provides the Baptist in his cell), does not obviously challenge Rome; nonetheless, Luke-Acts views Rome with some disdain. Although it does not predict the empire's immediate apocalyptic comeuppance, it rejects the empire's finality (see Luke 20:20–26). Thus, as we have seen, the empire is mere setting for God's salvation (Luke 2:1–7) and judgment (Luke 19:41–44; 20:16; Acts 3:23).

At the same time, Luke-Acts also has a rather realistic view of the witnesses' fate before the empire. Although God often delivers miraculously, the powers beat, imprison, and, on occasion, martyr the witnesses.[60] Further, while the trial scenes in Acts may demonstrate the innocence of the witnesses, they also extend the conflict between the witnesses and the world beyond Jerusalem into the empire. Finally, the witnesses' message about the resurrection not only challenges the Jewish religious leaders, but also Roman administration (Acts 16; 18; 24–25; 28), Greek philosophy (Acts 17), and Hellenistic religion (Acts 16; 19). In whatever way Luke-Acts is triumphal, then, it is also prophetic vis-à-vis the world/empire. If it advocates living within that world (rather than divine or human revolt), it also supports a discontent with that world. That discontent does not, however, extend to Christian empire.[61]

In *King of Kings*, Christianity's triumph is even more mercurial (or shadowy). Ray's prophetic witnesses—the Baptist and Jesus—are far less successful than those of Luke-Acts. John dies without issue; Jesus' apostolic succession is not storied; and the Roman Empire continues. The biblical epics (for example, *Quo Vadis? The Robe, Demetrius and the Gladiators*) make the empire's conversion to Christianity clearer.

The Robe, for example, also tells the story of a centurion at the cross, named Marcellus (Richard Burton), but its Marcellus differs dramatically from Lucius. First, Marcellus is the protagonist of *The Robe*, while Lucius is a (major) supporting character. Second, Lucius's appearance at the cross and "conversion" happen near the end of *King of Kings*. That the "conversion" happens so late makes it difficult to determine its effect and consequences. By contrast, Marcellus's appearance at the cross happens relatively early in *The Robe*, and thereafter the movie follows Marcellus's tormented path to Christianity. In the grand finale, Marcellus—like Jesus and his Lukan witnesses—stands trial for treason before evil Caligula. When Marcellus contends that he can be both a good Christian and a good Roman, Caligula sentences him to death. Marcellus and Diana, converted by his example, march out to martyrdom to the accompaniment of the "Hallelujah Chorus." The result is a portrait of a Roman centurion indistinguishable from the Stephen of Luke-Acts. The martyrs have triumphed over Rome, or, better, Marcellus represents proleptically the Christianization of Rome and the arrival of a Christian empire.

Ray's Lucius does not represent the triumph of Christianity over Rome. While Lucius represents the best of Rome, Ray's colonizing Roman Empire is hardly good. Further, most of the Roman officials in the film are dangerously ambitious, and their hirelings are unctuous and deadly. Lucius himself is repeatedly a party to suspect events. In short, while Marcellus makes it clear that one can be a good Roman and a good Christian, Lucius leaves us in doubt. In fact, as Lucius moves toward Christianity, he becomes less comfortably Roman. He subverts orders (not reporting the twelve-year-old Jesus to Herod Antipas), cares for Roman prisoners (taking away John's chains), and kneels before Rome's victims (at the cross). In sum, Lucius, like the Lukan witnesses, ultimately stands in tension between Jesus and empire.

This portrayal succeeds earlier biblical epics that routinely portray the United States as a Christian empire or Christian Rome in order to justify its role in the Cold War.[62] Thus, *The Robe* plays out the theme not only of Marcellus's conversion, but also of the question of good and bad Romans/leaders. Marcellus and his father represent the good rule of republican government while Caligula represents tyranny. The contemporary allegory for Cold War audiences is patent. DeMille's *The Ten Commandments*, with his introductory homily on freedom and democracy, is even more blatant. For these movies, the rise of Christianity and the exodus from Egypt are important because they justify a contemporary Christian empire of freedom and democracy.[63]

Critics have castigated Ray severely for playing this same game. Moira Walsh, for example, ends a scathing review of *King of Kings* by claiming that the film does not present Christ as "an irresistible challenge to man's conscience," but instead supplies "a tranquilizing drug" equating Christianity with the American way of life. For Walsh, it does not bid us take up our cross and follow Jesus; it bids us "take up our credit card" and follow.[64]

To me, this interpretation completely misses *King of Kings* and fails particularly to see its deformation of the biblical epic genre. Ray's story of two messiahs does raise the issue of proper rule, but it does not resolve it in a way palatable to Cold War America. Like Griffith during World War I, Ray highlights Jesus' pacifism. This focus hardly justifies Cold War America. It either points to that empire's impossible ideal (we often idealize that which we cannot have), or it challenges the empire even more radically. In *King of Kings*, the empire—Roman or Christian—is coming apart and maintains itself only by violence. If we are going to draw analogies between the film and Cold War America, they would be unsettling ones for patriots unless they (or we) can still manage to see ourselves as a peaceable kingdom. Ray lives after the Christian empire. Jesus and Christianity have become part of the alien past. It is Jesus' shadow that remains, and that shadow haunts, rather than justifies, empire.[65]

To summarize, Luke-Acts and *King of Kings* imagine Christianity's triumph, but neither writes when Christianity is triumphant. Thus, their stance vis-à-vis Christian (or Roman) empire is somewhat ambiguous. Perhaps, we could best express their respective views by describing them as prophetic realism and as secular faith.[66] Or perhaps we could switch the terms and they would still apply equally well. After all, they both stand at different ends of the same historicizing and secularizing trajectory. Discontented with the world, both live in it and try to live well. If Lucius reduces the Jesus story to what a modern secularist can appropriate, Luke-Acts reduces the Jesus story to what an apostolic witness can proclaim. Where Luke reaches to the future through an apostolic church, Ray reaches to the past through a secular humanism.

Reading Luke in the Dark: Remembering Our Elder Brothers

The apostolic witnesses of Luke-Acts are quite memorable, but Luke-Acts connects the story of Jesus through John the Baptist to the "previous" people of God as well (see Luke 16:16). When Christianity became an empire, it easily forgot these elder brothers. As a result, Luke 15:11–32 is an emblem of Luke-Acts' afterlife, because interpretation has almost uniformly remembered this story as the parable of the prodigal son. Its opening line, however, describes it differently: "There was a man who had two sons" (Luke 15:11).[67]

To live comfortably with Luke-Acts' vision of Christian triumph and (Constantine's subsequent) Christian empire, we must forget that other elder brother. In fact, to live comfortably in any empire, we must forget those who are violently excluded, or if we think of them, we must think of them as the barbaric enemy who deserve to be excluded.

Ray's *King of Kings*, however, reminds us of that elder brother. When he sets Jesus in the midst of Rome's oppressive colonization of Judea, he remembers other victimized Jews. His story of Jesus' death redeems their suffering and memory because Jesus, the remembered, is only one among many Jewish victims.

Ironically, then, while *King of Kings* does not bother to include the parable, it does a better job of recalling the elder brother than does the traditional "prodigal son" interpretation.[68] Ray, then, is more redemptive than most of Luke's interpreters. In this, his film resembles *Godspell,* as that film's version of the parable redeems both brothers. Ray, however, does not Christianize the elder brother. He cannot, because Christianity has become part of the past for him. In fact, we might say that Jesus has become the elder brother—the shadow from the past—for Ray's film and for many modern Americans. While this approach cannot satisfy the orthodox, Ray does redeem Jesus for new prodigals.

Ray's discontent with empire—Roman, Christian, and American—may also help us to remember those excluded. With Ray's help, we can return to Luke-Acts and remember Luke's concentration on the elder brother, instead of the exclusionary words of Acts 28:28. Luke's parable, after all, ends not with the return of the prodigal or the feast, but with the father going out again (Luke 15:28) to speak with the elder brother whom he describes as "always with me" (Luke 15:31–32).

Further, we should remember Ray's Lucius one last time. Compared to this parable, Lucius becomes a multifaceted signifier. He signifies—quite dimly compared to Marcellus and Luke-Acts—the conversion of the Gentiles. He, thus, seems a late arriving prodigal. In the dramatic action of the film, however, Lucius is Jesus' elder brother. He cares for Jesus, and he stands and watches without participating in the festivities until the very end. Perhaps, just perhaps, he comes in at the cross. Finally, Lucius also signifies more recent modern secularists for whom Jesus has become the alien past and who have trouble appropriating that past. Here, too, Ray is hopeful and redemptive. He provides us all a way to remember the elder brother—even if he is Jesus, a Jew.[69]

Reading Luke in the dark with Ray, we see that the tension between the elder brother, the Jews, and (Gentile) Christians haunts Luke far more than it does Mark or Matthew.[70] While Luke has notable anti-Semitic and pro-Gentile elements, as we have seen, Jesus the Jew; the "prophetic" nature of John, Jesus, and the (Jewish) apostles; and the incorporating words of Luke 15:31–32 highlight unresolved tensions between Jews and Christians in Luke's narrative (and mythic) world. Luke simply cannot let the Jews go, even as it tries to disown them. They are in the text's last gasp (Acts 28:28).

In fact, reading Luke in the dark, we notice various tensions suspended mythically. Ray makes it terribly clear that Luke (or the Jesus story) creates such a tension for him, because his film is a post-Christian (empire) epic. What Ray deals with as an uncomfortable tradition (as he is disturbed by empire) is for Luke an immaterial fantasy of a glorious, imperial future in tension with a far less glorious present. Further, Ray's depiction of empire, with its forest of crosses and funeral pyres, helps us reconsider the healthiness of Luke's fantasy. Of course, as we live in post-Christian America, perhaps, we should not work ourselves into a liberal dither (or guilt). After all, Luke's fantasy became a material reality only temporarily. Only its material remains (its corpse) remain.[71]

Finally, as we have noted, Ray's historical dramatization of the Jesus story reveals the hopeless tensions in Luke's salvation-history worldview, that is, the incongruity between its myth and history. That Luke finds a universal salvific message in a particular past makes its mythic status unmistakable. While its narrator claims to engage in historical research, Luke is covertly mything. A particular (Jesus) becomes a universal (God). A (Jewish) prophet becomes Lord and Christ. And most covertly, a non-witness (the narrator) pronounces the lasting testimony (Luke-Acts) to these matters.[72] As Luke creates, thereby, *in nuce*, the (myth of the) apostolic church, Luke is the elder brother of orthodoxy.

But Luke is also historical. We may disdain this "history's" credulity, honesty, or facts, but it remains our precursor in the awareness of Jesus as alien past. As history, then, Luke is the elder brother of heresy as well. Reading Luke in the dark, we find in Luke, in the linchpin of the imperial canon, heresy.[73] Of course, in some quarters, it is well known that heresy precedes orthodoxy.

Notes

1. Van A. Harvey, *The Historian and the Believer: The Morality of Historical Knowledge and Christian Belief* (Philadelphia: Westminster, 1966), 5.

2. Berger, *The Sacred Canopy*, 128–29.

3. For introductions to reading Luke, see Robert Tannehill, *The Narrative Unity of Luke-Acts: A Literary Interpretation*, 2 vols. (Minneapolis, Minn.: Fortress, 1990); and Charles H. Talbert, *Reading Luke: A Literary and Theological Commentary on the Third Gospel* (New York: Crossroads, 1982).

4. A repeated Lukan pattern—"life running into crisis, crisis, life on a new course" (see John Drury, "Luke," in Alter and Kermode, eds., *The Literary Guide to the Bible*, 435)—demonstrates how different Lukan crisis is from that of apocalyptic.

5. Taxation figures prominently in Luke in its stories of redeemed tax collectors (Luke 5:27–32; 19:1–10) and in the charge of tax evasion (peculiar to Luke) at Jesus' Roman trial (Luke 23:2). Except for the Zacchaeus incident, Ray utilizes these Lukan elements. At the trial, in particular, Ray's Pilate wonders what would become of the empire if people followed Jesus' teaching on taxes.

6. See Hans Conzelmann, *The Theology of St. Luke*, trans. Geoffrey Buswell (Philadelphia: Fortress, 1961). The original German title, *Der Mitte die Zeit*, is more expressive of Conzelmann's position. See also Charles H. Talbert, "Luke-Acts," in Eldon Jay Epp and George W. MacRae, S.J., eds., *The New Testament and Its Modern Interpreters* (Philadelphia: Fortress, 1989), 297–320.

7. Despite its claim to be based entirely on Luke, Krish and Sykes' *Jesus* (1979) presents Jesus' death as "sacrificial." The movie opens with a title taken from John 3:16–17, retains the questionable Luke 22:19b–20, and, in striking contrast to Luke's spare passion narrative, concentrates visually on the agony of Jesus en route to and on the cross. Even the movie's title segment emphasizes the cross, because the "J" in "Jesus" starts as a brilliant light that forms the shape of a cross before mutating into the "J."

8. Compare W. C. Van Unnik, "'The Book of Acts,' the Confirmation of the Gospel," *Novum Testamentum* 4 (1960): 26–59. That Acts is the second volume of Luke is the scholarly consensus. For a recent critique, see Mikeal C. Parsons and Richard L. Pervo, *Rethinking the Unity of Luke and Acts* (Minneapolis, Minn.: Fortress, 1993).

9. From film narration, cited in Geoff Andrew, *The Films of Nicholas Ray: The Poet of Nightfall* (London: Charles Letts, 1991), 181–82, who claims that the narration was added after Ray lost control of the film.

10. See Stern, Jefford, and DeBona, *Savior on the Silver Screen,* 68. After the disastrous Jewish revolt of 66–73 C.E. in which he fought on both sides, Josephus wrote to advance himself, to defend the Romans to the Jews *(Jewish War)*, and to extol Jewish religion to the Romans *(Antiquities of the Jews)*. See Crossan, *The Historical Jesus,* 91–102; and Shayne J. D. Cohen, *Josephus in Galilee and Rome: His Vita and Development as a Historian* (Leiden: Brill, 1979).

11. In the opening sequence, Jewish bodies are piled on a burning pyre before a smiling Herod whom the narrator identifies as an Arab. This scene suggests both the Shoah and Arab-Israeli conflicts.

12. Ray claims he wanted to avoid anti-Semitism. See John Francis Kreidl, *Nicholas Ray* (Boston: Twayne, 1977), 190. The film does avoid various anti-Semitic sections of the Jesus story: the antitheses of the (Matthean) Sermon on the Mount; most of the controversy pericopes; the cleansing of the Temple; the trial before the Sanhedrin; and the oracles about Jerusalem's destruction.

13. The mission of the seventy (or seventy-two) may symbolize a mission to the Gentiles, as Jewish legend considered there to be seventy/seventy-two nations. In addition, Luke does not restrict the disciples' mission to the Jews as Matthew specifically does (cf. Luke 9:1–6; Matthew 10:1–15).

14. Compare Norman Petersen, *Literary Criticism for New Testament Critics* (Philadelphia: Fortress, 1978), 82–83.

15. Luke-Acts became the key document in the canon of the imperial (and apostolic) church; cf. Mack, *Who Wrote the New Testament?* 225–39.

16. On the similar titles, see Tatum, *Jesus at the Movies,* 75; Stern, Jefford, and DeBona, *Savior on the Silver Screen,* 62–64; and Andrew, *The Films of Nicholas Ray,* 180.

17. Ray's concern for realism is obvious in the following remark: "Well, if he is walking down a dirt road with his disciples, and he has to take a piss, dust will rise from the road." Cited in Kreidl, *Nicholas Ray,* 189. As he offers historical drama, Ray necessarily humanizes Jesus, as compared to DeMille's divine Christ. That Ray focuses on Jesus' teaching, downplays the miracles and resurrection, and does not render Jesus' death as notably salvific, also contributes to the

humanizing (or profanation) of Jesus. Except for the minimization of the resurrection, these points are also characteristic of Luke's Jesus. Ray does, however, offer a scene where Lucius informs Barabbas that the man Jesus dies for him. Ray concludes this scene with Lucius telling Barabbas to go and look at the one who is dying for you. From Barabbas's cell, in a subjective camera shot, we see Jesus pass by with his cross. This shot suggests a wider sacrificial significance to Jesus' death than the film as a whole. Once again, like Luke, Ray's movie is not a cohesive whole, but holds salvation (theology) and history in mythic tension.

18. That DeMille minimizes Jesus' radical sayings and presents a popular, Protestant image of Jesus furthers the illusion of presence. The heavy-handed narration also distinguishes *King of Kings* from the silences of Pasolini's *Il Vangelo secondo Matteo*.

19. For James M. Dawsey, *The Lukan Voice: Confusion and Irony in the Gospel of Luke* (Macon, Ga.: Mercer University Press, 1986), 103–24, 152, the author and Jesus advocate a path of humiliation, while the narrator languishes in cultic adoration of Jesus.

20. The word for "eyewitness" in Luke 1:2 is *autoptai*. A descendant of the word appears in English as "autopsy." That linguistic connection intensifies Jesus' distance.

21. The rhetoric suggests a presentation of a "true history" of Jesus. According to Kreidl, *Nicholas Ray,* 194, Ray's films, including *King of Kings,* often have this same rhetoric.

22. Compare Cervantes' fortuitous discovery of the work of Cide Hamete Benengeli. See Chapter 5 above.

23. *King of Kings* visualizes only those miracles that can be explained psychosomatically and those important to the plot/theme, like Jesus' intimate stilling of a violent demoniac. This "calming" contrasts powerfully with the violent anger of Barabbas, whom the narrator describes as the sea that would not be stilled.

24. The "test" theme is prominent in Luke in the temptation and at the passion, where mocking leaders and a dying thief challenge Jesus to save himself miraculously (23:35–39). The Pharisees also tempt and test Jesus repeatedly (in the absence of Satan after Luke 4:13). Testing is a major theme in Ray's movie as well, but Ray displaces the motif from the Pharisees to Judas.

25. Perhaps, we should read Acts as the fulfillment of the time of the Gentiles. Acts 28:28–32 is certainly triumphal, but Acts 20:25–35 suggests an ongoing history beyond Acts.

26. Conzelmann, *The Theology of St. Luke,* 16, 20–24, 170, who first identified this pattern, bases it on Luke 16:16, on John's exclusion from the kingdom (cf. Luke 3:18–20; Acts 1:5; 11:16; 18:24–19:7), and on Satan's exclusion from Jesus' ministry (Luke 4:13; 22:3). Charles H. Talbert, *Literary Patterns, Theological Themes, and the Genre of Luke-Acts* (Missoula, Mont.: Scholars, 1974), 15–26, 96–103, identifies four stages, adding a sub-apostolic era in light of Acts 20:25–35.

27. These are Troeltsch's three principles. See Harvey, *The Historian and the Believer,* 3–37. On the method's secularity, see also Walter Wink, *The Bible in Human Transformation* (Philadelphia: Fortress, 1973), 4, 38–41; and Edgar Krentz, *The Historical-Critical Method* (Philadelphia: Fortress, 1975), 6–32, 56–61.

28. The Greek verb that the NRSV translates "you have been instructed" is *katêchêthês.*

29. Talbert, *Literary Patterns, Theological Themes, and the Genre of Luke-Acts*, 15–26, 96–103; and *idem, Luke and the Gnostics* (Nashville, Tenn.: Abingdon, 1966), 83–92, argues that Luke-Acts creates an apostolic tradition to ward off heresy. On the myth of a fall from a golden age of truth into diversity and heresy, see also Walsh, *Reading the Bible*, 24–27, 411–17, 474–85; and Wilken, *The Myth of Christian Beginnings*.

30. Nineteenth-century and more recent historiography do differ. For recent discussions of historiography, see Norman J. Wilson, *History in Crisis? Recent Directions in Historiography* (Upper Saddle River, N.J.: Prentice Hall, 1999); and Georg G. Iggers, *Historiography in the Twentieth Century: From Scientific Objectivity to the Postmodern Challenge* (Hanover, N.H.: Wesleyan University Press, 1997). Harvey's work nicely demonstrates, however, that Troeltsch's problems remain unresolved theologically.

31. See Walter Wink, *The Bible in Human Transformation*, 65–67; and Wilson, *History in Crisis*, 6–15, 24–41. Wilson (ibid.) discusses various possible relationships between the present and the past in modern historical theory.

32. On Luke as, by turns or in tandem, theologian and historian, see Talbert, "Luke-Acts," 297–300, 310–12.

33. David Aune, *The New Testament in Its Literary Environment* (Philadelphia: Westminster, 1989), 88, 139–40.

34. Luke divides elements of this story between the dual births that open its story. Luke uses the conference with the priest (significantly altered), the miraculous birth to a barren woman, and the Nazarite vow in John's birth and story. Luke reprises Hannah's praise (1 Samuel 2:1–10) for Mary rather than for Elizabeth (Luke 1:46–55). The young Samuel's closeness to God (1 Samuel 2:11–3:18) may provide a deep background for Luke 2:41–52.

35. Ray's story of two messiahs resembles this Luken precursor more closely. Incidentally, as his messiahs are of decidedly different character—one of war and one of peace—his film reflects not only on the identity but also on the nature of the true messiah.

36. The opening sermon in Nazareth foreshadows Luke's narrative pattern: 1) Jesus arrives in Nazareth and announces the arrival of God's salvation for the oppressed (Luke 4:16–21); 2) Jesus declares himself a rejected prophet (before such rejection occurs) (Luke 4:23–24); 3) Jesus reminds the people that the prophets Elijah and Elisha miraculously delivered Gentile sufferers while Israelites suffered (Luke 4:25–27; 1 Kings 17:8–24; 2 Kings 5:1–24); 4) enraged, the people try to kill Jesus, but he temporarily escapes (Luke 4:28–30).

37. See Walsh, *Reading the Bible*, 258–60.

38. Its producer was Samuel Bronston, who set up an independent company in Spain to produce epic films (including *El Cid, 55 Days at Peking*, and *The Fall of the Roman Empire*). On biblical epics, see Chapter 2 above.

39. *King of Kings* is less generous with sex. Ray's Mary Magdalene is rather demure compared to DeMille's version. She is the woman saved from stoning by Jesus in an important scene, but she becomes a follower of Jesus through a conversation with Mary, not Jesus. Except for the resurrection appearance, then, Ray keeps her at a distance from Jesus throughout the film. Ray is

not nearly as interested in her "domestication" as DeMille is. Ray restricts the titillation to the salacious Salome, who pursues, at length, the head of John the Baptist. For Ray, the important female character—and her role is greatly amplified—is Mary, the mother of Jesus. Several characters (a camel driver, Lucius, John the Baptist, Mary Magdalene, and Jesus) come to Mary's home for counsel. In fact, in a homely scene, it's Mary who knows when Jesus must go to Jerusalem and that he will not return (to fix her chair).

40. On the distinctive features of Ray's cinema, see Andrew, *The Films of Nicholas Ray*, 11–25, 179–84. Critics generally consider *Johnny Guitar* and *Rebel without a Cause* Ray's distinctive films. According to Kreidl, *Nicholas Ray*, 28, 43–59, Ray's cinema is "off-center." It does not nicely fit generic expectations.

41. Babbington and Evans, *Biblical Epics*, 133. Ray is polarizing tensions in *King of Kings* that he presents less mythically in *Rebel without a Cause*.

42. The teenagers of *Rebel without a Cause* are not unique in Ray's oeuvre. See the hero (Nick Romano) in *Knock on Any Door* ("And You'll Find a Nick Romano").

43. Luke 22:43–44 is generally thought to be a late addition. See Metzger, *A Textual Commentary on the Greek New Testament*, 177.

44. Babbington and Evans, *Biblical Epics*, 138. Critics nicknamed *King of Kings* "I was a teenage Jesus."

45. Ibid., 128; cf. Neale, *Genre and Hollywood*, 60–65.

46. In other scenes—like Gethsemane and the passion—Ray maintains this external (epic?) perspective with a focus on physical suffering and a tendency to provide heavy-handed narration. The "inside views" come from Jesus' speech and from inferences based on his endurance at his trials. For Ray, Jesus is the Sermon on the Mount and this (physical) suffering.

47. Neale, *Genre and Hollywood*, 63. According to Andrew, *The Films of Nicholas Ray*, 181, this pattern, in a tragic form, is typical of Ray's cinema.

48. On Ray's interpretative use of color, see ibid., 22; and Kreidl, *Nicholas Ray*, 55–56, 197–200. Notably, after his conflict with his father, Jim Stark dons a famous red coat.

49. Gerald E. Forshey, *American Religious and Biblical Spectaculars* (Westport, Conn.: Praeger, 1992), 94. The "times" and the epic battle scenes overwhelm Jesus. Thus, while Jesus supposedly preaches in the Temple (which we do not see even though we have been waiting, since John the Baptist announced its necessity, for this to happen), we are outside with Barrabas's revolt. Like the crowds, we pay to see Barabbas, not Jesus.

50. Stern, Jefford, and DeBona, *Savior on the Silver Screen*, 72.

51. The notion of Jesus' uniqueness and of a "lost original" Jesus is also impossible in the unending semiotics of postmodernism. Accordingly, Arcand's *Jesus of Montreal* and *Monty Python's Life of Brian* struggle with an embarrassment of Jesuses and messiahs. On losing Jesus, see Chapters 2, 4, and 8.

52. Once again, divergent elements occur, because Ray allows several characters—Caiaphas, Pilate, and Lucius—to protest Jesus' "difference."

53. His characterization resembles Ray himself; cf. Kreidl, *Nicholas Ray*, 88–90, 193–94; Andrew, *The Films of Nicholas Ray*, 1–3; and the discussion in n. 47 above.

54. Notably, Ray's John, not Jesus, performs a Temple act that leads to his death.

55. For investigations of the parallels between Luke and Acts, see A. J. Mattill, "The Jesus-Paul Parallels and the Purpose of Luke-Acts: H. H. Evans Reconsidered," *Novum Testamentum* 17 (1975): 15–46; and Talbert, *Literary Patterns, Theological Themes, and the Genre of Luke-Acts.*

56. Luke's action effectively begins with and ends looking forward to "acts" of the Holy Spirit (Luke 1:35; 3:16, 22; 4:1, 14; 24:49; Acts 1:5, 8). The spirit motivates most important narrative actions in Acts (e.g., Acts 2; 8:15–17, 29, 39; 9:17; 10:19–20, 44–47; 11:1–18; 13:4, 9; 16:6–10; 19:1–7, 21). This list is not inclusive.

57. For Luke, Jesus is born of the Spirit in a dissimilar way from the disciples (Luke 1:30–38), although how different from that implied by 3:38 is not clear.

58. Richard I. Pervo, *Profit with Delight: The Literary Genre of the Acts of the Apostles* (Philadelphia: Fortress, 1987), 13–18.

59. Frank Stagg, *The Book of Acts: The Early Struggle for an Unhindered Gospel* (Nashville, Tenn.: Broadman, 1955), 1–12, calls this conclusion an "epitome in an adverb."

60. If, as many critics have thought, Luke-Acts is an apology for Christianity to the empire, it is a very clumsy one, as it depicts Roman administrators as so weak (or greedy) that they routinely oppress innocent people. See Tannehill, *The Narrative Unity of Luke-Acts*, 2:297–329.

61. James D. G. Dunn, *Unity and Diversity in the New Testament: An Inquiry into the Character of Early Christianity* (Philadelphia: Westminster, 1977), 180–84, 351–59, reads the emphasis on the Spirit in Luke-Acts as an implicit rejection of imperial notions of succession, office, and institution. Somewhat ironically, given Luke-Acts' place in later myths about apostolic tradition, Luke-Acts also depicts tradition as a critical canon for later churches (see Acts 20:25–35). Institutional empires, however, easily subsume tradition for their own devices, typically making it a weapon versus opponents (heresies). Further, the Spirit is, in one sense, simply another name for Luke's colonizing (read "universal") God.

62. See Babbington and Evans, *Biblical Epics*; Forshey, *American Religious and Biblical Spectaculars*; and Wood, *America in the Movies*. Lucas' *Star Wars: Episode II: Attack of the Clones* reprises the same drama. It will be interesting to see if "Christian nation" rhetoric returns to the movies in the aftermath of recent conflicts with Islamic nations.

63. Horror and science fiction films from the era also deal with Cold War fears, particularly with the fear that the war would be lost and invaders would transform Americans into zombies (people living under tyrannical regimes).

64. Moira Walsh, "Christ or Credit Card?" *America* (21 October 1961): 74.

65. Incidentally, Ray presents Jesus as a challenge not only to a military but also to a capitalistic nation. Thus, at Jesus' trial, Pilate remarks tellingly that if people followed Jesus' teaching about taxation, the empire could not stand. On this point, Ray's Jesus is more challenging than DeMille's Jesus, but less challenging than Stevens's Jesus.

66. Like salvation history, these terms are oxymoronic dualisms (myths).

67. Scott, *Hear Then the Parable*, 99–125, points to other exclusions by titling his discussion "I Remember Mama." Incidentally, while the mother is missing from this parable, the father (Joseph) is missing in the surrounding gospel.

68. Ray's Mary tells the parable of the lost sheep to Mary Magdalene. Perplexingly, Krish and Sykes do not include the "two sons" parable in their Jesus film either.

69. Reportedly, the working title of Ray's film was *The Man from Nazareth*. While that might suggest a Western, it also reminds us of Jesus' Jewishness.

70. In the gospel's parable, both sons are Jewish. The Lukan "time of the Gentiles" has not yet arrived. Obviously, then, I am resignifying the elder brother within the larger narrative mechanics of Luke-Acts (i.e., the move toward the Gentiles).

71. It also continues as a reactionary fantasy.

72. As we have already seen, Luke is historical criticism's elder brother here.

73. We might say that Luke (or its narrator or even orthodoxy itself) is "of the Devil's party without knowing it."

Chapter 7

Romancing the Past:
The Greatest Story Ever Told and John

Everything was predetermined from the moment when, unable any longer to endure the idea of waiting until the morning to press a kiss upon my mother's face, I made up my mind, jumped out of bed and, in my nightshirt, went and sat by the window through which the moonlight came, until I heard M. Swann leave. . . . I heard the door open, the bell tinkle and the door shut again. . . . I heard these sounds again, the very identical sounds themselves, although situated so far back in the past. . . . I was startled at the thought that it was, indeed, this bell which was still tinkling within me. . . . To endeavour to listen to it from nearby, I had to descend again into my own consciousness. It must be, then, that this tinkling was still there and also, between it and the present moment, all the infinitely unrolling past which I had been unconsciously carrying within me. When the bell tinkled, I was already in existence and, since that night, for me to have been able to hear the sound again, there must have been no break of continuity . . . since this distant moment still clung to me and I could recapture it, go back to it, merely by descending more deeply within myself. It was this conception of time as incarnate . . . which I was now determined to bring out into such bold relief in my book.[1]

Reading John and *The Greatest Story Ever Told*

Scholars often divide John into two parts, a book of signs (John 1–12) and a book of glory (John 13–21).[2] In the book of signs, various characters misunderstand Jesus' signs (John's word for miracle) and sayings, so Jesus eventually discourses at length on Johannine semiotics.[3] The book of signs builds (somewhat) to two decisive signs disclosing that Jesus, rather than Jewish institutions, provides light (John 9) and life (John 11) from above. While some believe, two Sabbath healings (John 5; 9) and Jesus' claims about his identity provoke murderous opposition. After the resurrection of Lazarus, the resulting murderous plans of the Jews, and the sudden interest of Greeks, Jesus announces that the "hour" of his glorification has arrived (John 12:23; 13:1). Jesus then describes his passion as his exalted, glorified return to the father and enjoins his disciples to abide in him (John 13–17). The passion—an action of the Johannine Jesus (John 18–19)—and cameo-like resurrection appearances (John 20–21) confirm the teachings of the farewell discourse.

A narrator reciting part of John's prologue (John 1:1–5) opens *The Greatest Story Ever Told* while the camera pans a Byzantine church to focus on a priestly Christ. The screen fades to black; the narrator speaks of light in the darkness; and a star transforms into the flame of an oil lamp in a stable. The baby arrives in a dark, hostile world that will ineffectually try to overcome it. The film segues to the time of the adult Jesus, and various officials maintain place and position murderously. The Baptist raises his voice in protest. After rejecting the Dark Hermit's temptation of an "easy life" in the wilderness, Jesus follows John's prophetic lead in an itinerant, Galilean ministry in which he emphasizes a semi-ascetic trust in a merciful God. Taking a dim view of these confrontational prophets, the authorities arrest John and watch Jesus closely. After Antipas kills John, Jesus narrowly escapes, retreating first to Nazareth (where his hometown rejects him), and then to the Jordan. Learning of Lazarus's illness, Jesus returns, and his resurrection of Lazarus leads to his acclamation as messiah at the walls of Jerusalem.

In the second act, Jesus enters Jerusalem in triumph, cleanses the Temple, and preaches there about God's desire for mercy and his own identity as the divine light. Arrested and tried, Jesus seals his own fate before the Sanhedrin by blatantly admitting that he is the son of God. Convinced that Jesus' kingdom is ethereal, Pilate tries to release Jesus, but ultimately orders Jesus' crucifixion to maintain order. After Jesus dies outside the city (uttering all seven words from the cross), Peter kneels before an empty chair and Mary Magdalene visits an empty tomb. After reports reach the disciples of Jesus' resurrection, they see a larger-than-life Christ in the sky. This commissioning Christ, then, becomes the Christ of the Byzantine church art with which the movie began.

Both John and *The Greatest Story Ever Told* reveal fantastic, alternate worlds to which the audience belongs only tangentially, but to which the gospel and film provide material connections. Gospel and movie naturalize these alternative realities by depicting them in terms of cultural myths familiar to the audience. Gospel and film, then, simultaneously imagine Jesus as an ethereal, elusive stranger and clothe him with familiar meaning.

Revelations

Neither John nor *The Greatest Story Ever Told* centers on a conflict, problem, or lack that must be resolved. Instead, they unveil character.[4] John reveals Jesus as the one from above. As the prologue announces Jesus' identity, narrative interest arises from plumbing the significance of this identity, from watching other characters struggle with it, and in exploring what it means to be part of the community of the one from above (see John 1:10–13).[5]

John uses characters, then, to explore Johannine sight (insight) and disciple-ship (commitment) (John 20:24–31).[6] Some cannot see because they seek self-ish advancement (John 9; 12:36–43). Some come for the bread (John 6:26). Some see the signs and come to faith (John 2:11, 23; 20:30–31). Beyond "sign faith" is a faith that does not need to "see" (John 4:48; 20:29). John begins with sign faith (John 20:30–31), but extols the post-Jesus, mystic faith of the enlightened sectarian community more highly (John 14:20–26; 16:4, 12–15). John's characters, then, are caricatures expressing and providing lessons in Johannine ideology. They induce Johannine faith (insight).[7]

The characters in *The Greatest Story Ever Told,* particularly Stevens's special creations, like the Dark Hermit and Lazarus, are similar caricatures. The Dark Hermit is Stevens's Satan figure. Like Luke's Satan, the Dark Hermit appears primarily in the wilderness temptation, where he vainly tempts Jesus to an "easy life."[8] The Dark Hermit returns during the passion (he—and the religious authorities led by Sorak—also appears at Capernaum to monitor Jesus' activi-ties) to motivate Jesus' opposition. He is there as catalyst when Judas betrays, when Peter denies, and when the crowd shouts for Jesus' crucifixion. The pri-mary purpose of Stevens's Dark Hermit, then, is to reveal the demonic charac-ter of Jesus' opponents and of the road not taken by Jesus.

Lazarus is a far more human character. Stevens combines the Johannine Lazarus with the Synoptics' rich young man to create a melancholy God-fearer who cannot give up his wealth and follow Jesus. Lazarus is Jesus' friend, not his disciple. In Stevens's rhetoric, Lazarus creates a livable human space between Jesus (the ideal) and the opposition inspired by the Dark Hermit. Far more clearly than the Jesuses of DeMille and Ray, Stevens's Jesus articulates a semi-ascetic ethic in conflict with the American Dream (or at least the good life as portrayed by Hollywood and commercial TV). That Jesus does not disown Lazarus, even though Lazarus cannot follow Jesus' ethic, reconciles the Jesus tra-dition with a capitalist empire and audience.[9] Lazarus, then, provides the audi-ence a way into the film (and the Jesus tradition) without sacrificing their comfortable American lives. Attitude, not wealth, matters. With Lazarus, one can be a wealthy Christian (or at least an American God-fearer).[10]

Both gospel and film also use characters to explore the rejection of the reve-lation. John's explanation is a three-stage process. First, roughly in John 1–4, John presents the revelation from above as so completely beyond human ken that it mystifies all and sundry. In John 3, it mystifies Nicodemus, a noted Jewish intellectual. No one from below quite understands the world above, because those from below try to assimilate the world above to this-worldly patterns.

Nicodemus's humorous attempt to understand *anôthen*, either "again" or "from above," as born "again" from his mother's womb is typical (John 3:3–4). Second, beginning with John 5, John depicts a murderous opposition to Jesus. The opposition arises because the religious authorities consider Jesus a Sabbath-breaker and a blasphemer (John 5:16–18; 10:33). The prologue's description of Jesus, of course, belies this erroneous identification. Third, John traces their error to their "sinful" blindness. Claiming to see—in particular, claiming to know Jesus' origins—they become blind because they situate Jesus in this world (John 6:41–42; 7:27, 41–42, 52; 9:29–34). They lack Johannine insight.[11]

The narrator's final condemnation, followed ironically by Jesus' claim to bring salvation, not judgment (John 12:44–50), is John 12:37–43. Citing Isaiah 6:9–10, the narrator attributes their blindness to divine determination (John 12:37–40), but the comment that even Isaiah saw "his" (Jesus') glory confirms their wickedness (John 12:41). They are fearful and ambitious (John 12:42–43). That their condemnation occurs between the affirming divine voice from heaven (John 12:28) and Jesus' final offer of mercy, not judgment (John 12:44–50), simply drives the final Johannine nail into their coffin.

John's Judas provides a personal and more troublesome version of this same story. He incarnates those ethically unfit for and divinely rejected by the revelation. He is a devil (John 6:70–71). He is a thief (John 12:6). He is possessed by the devil (John 13:2). His betrayal fulfills prophecy (John 13:18). Satan enters him (John 13:27). When he leaves the table, the narrator comments, "And it was night" (John 13:30). Given the Johannine light-dark dualism, that comment—somewhat unnecessary in what appears to be a supper context—is quite suggestive. He has left the light for the dark (compare John 3:19–21). Not surprisingly, then, Judas finally stands with the opposition (John 18:5).

Stevens treats Jesus' opposition similarly. The opposition rejects Jesus in order to maintain their place (and the Roman peace). In a particularly chilling scene, in the aftermath of the people's dispersion from the Temple, Pilate stands on a balcony and remarks on the sweet sound of silence.[12] If anything, Stevens devotes more attention (and more time) to the opposition than John does. He also adds to their nefariousness with the invention of caricatures, like Sorak and the Dark Hermit, who function solely to motivate evil.

Moreover, these inventions indicate that Stevens is less comfortable attributing (evil) matters to God than John, whose use of prophecy ultimately lays matters squarely at God's feet (for example, Isaiah 6:9–10 in John 12:38–40; Psalm 41:9 in John 13:18). Stevens is more comfortable "blaming" the Dark Hermit. This device rationalizes John's explanation of evil dividing the divine weal and woe between different characters. The trajectory from John to Stevens resembles that from 2 Samuel 24:1 to 1 Chronicles 21:1. What the former attributes to

God, the latter attributes to Satan (the Dark Hermit), but Stevens's Dark Hermit is not clearly Satan. As such, he allows Stevens to bathe evil in (psychological) mystery, rather than in supernatural determinism.[13] Stevens also presents Judas's motivation ambiguously. Visually, Stevens often separates (and alienates) Judas from the other disciples and Jesus. Further, in the passion, Stevens cinematically joins Judas and the Dark Hermit. They lurk in the shadowy streets while Jesus and the disciples sit at table (compare John 13:30). Visually, Judas belongs with the Dark Hermit, but Judas's action is not otherwise explained. In fact, his conversation with Caiaphas and Sorak suggests that he is trying to save Jesus from himself.[14] As a result, Stevens's Judas is less a supernatural dupe and more a psychologically riven character.

Matters of the Heart

The revelations of John and *The Greatest Story Ever Told* are about "life." Thus, resurrection scenes climax both halves (respectively, those of Lazarus and Jesus) of their narratives. The gospel and the movie, however, differ noticeably on the "life" they offer. John reveals a life from a God above, suggesting a metaphysical dualism similar to Plato, Philo, or the gnostics. By contrast, for *The Greatest Story Ever Told,* the revelation is the God who dwells within each of us.

Thus, in his opening sermon in *The Greatest Story Ever Told,* sitting under a bridge with his disciples (with various people, including Roman soldiers, tromping overhead),[15] Jesus demands that his disciples live semi-ascetic lives based on a trust in God (see Matthew 6:19–21, 25–33; 7:1–2); however, he prefaces that demand with the Johannine claim to be the bread from God that satisfies human hunger. We have here, then, an ethic that depends on prior divine provision. The disciples can live semi-ascetically because God has given them what they need.

That provision does not arrive ritually, so Jesus' first sermon does not include the sacramental and ritual allusions in its precursors (see John 6; Matthew 6:1–18). In fact, as the repeated citations of Hosea 6:6 indicate, Stevens's Jesus has an animus toward ritual.[16] Sans ritual, God's provision comes either through the person of Jesus or simply from within the disciple. Stevens focuses on the latter possibility. Thus, in the midst of this first sermon, when a disciple asks when the kingdom will come, Jesus replies that it is within (compare Luke 17:21; Thomas 1).

Later, entering Capernaum, Jesus rephrases this point when he calls Matthew, the tax collector, to follow him. In the midst of an amusing exchange about what Jesus has that can be taxed, Jesus claims that he has only his father to declare. When Matthew asks where this father is, Jesus replies that he lives in the heart. Stevens's Jesus, then, deals with "internal" matters, with the care of the soul. Accordingly, in his initial meeting with Lazarus, Jesus condemns a neglect of God, an attitudinal matter, not material issues like wealth.[17]

The internal struggle that this teaching precipitates is obvious in Jesus' own wilderness temptation,[18] in Lazarus's sorrow, and in the healing miracles. Stevens interprets the latter psychosomatically, so Jesus cures a lame man (Sal Mineo) in the Capernaum synagogue simply by talking to him. Jesus leads the lame man from hostility, cynicism, and skepticism to trust by convincing him that he is crippled only in his soul and that his faith is weaker than his legs.

At his trial before Pilate, Jesus reaffirms this internal focus by asserting Johanninely that his kingdom is not of this world.[19] Of course, a "kingdom not of this world," like the kingdom within, may mean several things, and John and *The Greatest Story Ever Told* employ similar language to mean differently. For John, the care of the soul requires a mystical connection to Jesus. For Stevens, it requires a struggle with psychological gods and demons. Thus, Stevens's Jesus engages in his own struggle to trust God semi-ascetically and calls others to that same struggle, a struggle for psychological maturity and a subsequent, semi-ascetic lifestyle.[20]

Stevens's inwardness is clearly at home in a modern Romanticism that "replaces traditional notions of transcendence—a beyond or an above—with the depths of the human psyche."[21] The American precursor of Stevens's ethical version of this modern Romantic religion is Emerson, whose "The Divinity School Address" attributes the divinity-within teaching to Jesus and then draws an ethical conclusion: "That is always best which gives me to myself. The sublime is excited in me by the great stoical doctrine, Obey thyself. That which shows God in me, fortifies me. That which shows God out of me, makes me a wart and a wen."[22] Most concisely, the ethic is "self-reliance":

> Society everywhere is in conspiracy against the manhood of every one of its members. . . . The virtue in most request is conformity. Self-reliance is its aversion. It loves not realities and creators, but names and customs.
>
> Whoso would be a man must be a nonconformist. He who would gather immortal palms must not be hindered by the name of goodness, but must explore if it be goodness. Nothing is at last sacred but the integrity of your own mind.[23]

That Jesus is the *necessary* revealer of this gnosis is not as drastic a revision of this Romanticism as it might first appear. For Stevens, as for Emerson, Jesus is a "representative man," and such are important not for what they do for us, but for what they provoke us to do.[24] Accordingly, for Stevens, Jesus' teaching, rather than his passion, is salvific. While John's Jesus is the Passover lamb that takes away the sin of the world (John 1:29), its cross is also more revelatory than redemptive, because John sees the cross as Jesus' glorification, not his humiliation or passion (John 12:23–33). It returns him to the father and completes the Johannine revelation of life-conquering death (John 1:5; 3:14–16).[25] In short, John's cross is more about deification than redemption (John 14:1–7).

While John requires a transcendent revealer more than *The Greatest Story Ever Told*, we can overdo John's reliance on a supernatural revealer and Stevens's self-reliance. For John, Jesus is *monogenês*, the only begotten son (John 1:14; 3:16, 18), but those who hear God and respond positively to Jesus are also "from God" (John 8:39–47). In fact, John's Jesus once evades the charge of blasphemy by appealing to the scripture that calls those to whom the law came "gods" (John 10:31–39, citing Psalm 82:6). In the psalm, the "gods" are those whom God challenges (in divine counsel) on behalf of those they treat unjustly. As these gods are not those to whom Torah came, John's Jesus is adapting this text for John's rhetorical purpose, that is, to show that the divine revelation deifies its hearers. Thus, the Johannine *monogenês* creates other sons like himself—not friends or disciples (John 1:12–13)—who will follow Jesus in their own glorifying, death-denying deaths (John 13:36–14:7). Stevens's *The Greatest Story Ever Told* helps us to recover this aspect of John and to make some sense of the apparent contradiction between *monogenês* and the revelation's other divine children. John's Jesus, like Emerson's representative man, harmonizes this tension (mythically) by provoking Johannine mystics to realize their own greatness (divinity).[26]

More Fantastic Countries: The Exotic, Erotic Other

Jesus' example is important to Stevens because he feels that modernity has robbed us of some essential part of ourselves. "Trailing clouds of glory," we have lost our true selves in "the getting and spending" of modern industrialized, capitalist society. Accordingly, we need a revealer from elsewhere to call us to ourselves. The Jesus story is such a revelation (from afar). Stevens signals the story's alien nature by beginning and ending in an exotic Byzantine church. The contrast with DeMille and the biblical epics, in which Jesus is at one with an America audience, is dramatic. Here, Stevens's film differs even from Ray's *King of Kings*, because now the story of Jesus differs not just in time, but also in character, from everyday American reality.[27] In the sense of the strangeness of the Jesus tradition (or God), *Barabbas* is *The Greatest Story Ever Told*'s true precursor. Unlike the terrifying God of *Barabbas*, however, Stevens finds a romantically desirable other in the Jesus story.

Thus, in an interchange among members of the Sanhedrin, Sorak rejects the reports of Jesus' miracles as ridiculous tales for children. By contrast, Nicodemus avows a lasting fondness for children's stories and Joseph of Arimathea claims they have a scent of truth. The immediate segue to a smiling Jesus sitting among smiling children and then informing his disciples that the kingdom belongs to children completes Stevens's nostalgic configuration. By imagining the Jesus story as a children's story, Stevens simultaneously separates it (or acknowledges its separation) from ordinary adult reality and denies the hegemony of that adult reality.[28]

Thereby, Stevens nostalgically mythologizes the Jesus story. The contrast with Ray's historical approach could not be greater. Unlike history, myth is ritually connected to the present. Despite his (American) aversion to ritual, then, Stevens situates his movie in the church. This approach resembles that of Zeffirelli more than Ray, but as Zeffirelli imagines the Jesus story as the church's gospel truth, Stevens is even closer to Pasolini, who understands the tradition mythically. Like Pasolini, he reanimates the Jesus story because he is disenchanted with modern (bourgeois) society. Where Pasolini turns to peasants to recover myth, Stevens turns to American Romanticism and reads the Gospel as the story of the soul's adventure, a symbol of the divine creativity within us all.[29] Historically, scientifically, pragmatically, the Jesus story may be at risk, but as psychologically or romantically interpreted myth, it is eternally safe. Stevens, then, places the Jesus story in myth to protect it.

Like Bultmann, then, Stevens mythologizes the Jesus story to render it meaningful to moderns. Stevens simply mythologizes the Jesus story along Emersonian, rather than existentialist, lines.[30] Further, instead of rewriting the Jesus story as philosophical or sermonic *kerygma*, Stevens offers the Jesus story as a fantastic other world. In short, Stevens romances the Jesus story as an adventure for his audience (not his characters).[31] In typical romantic fashion, the idea is that the journey, even if only through film (or novel or poetry), will break the humdrum boundaries of everyday, modern living. Following Stevens's Jesus, we can wake up to the divine hero within and our adventure can begin.

Worlds Apart: Material Dualisms

Stevens does not, however, transport his audience to a metaphysically distinct other.[32] By contrast, John has, in theory, a metaphysically distinct, transcendent world above from which the revealer has come and to which he returns. That world above obscures John's own mythic nostalgia, as John's materially present other is actually the story of Jesus itself, not some transcendent realm. Like *The Greatest Story Ever Told*, John is nostalgically romancing that story in order to deny the normal adult reality of its readers.

According to some scholars, part of the historical situation of the Gospel of John was the Johannine community's expulsion from the synagogue.[33] At various points (see John 9:22, 12:42; 16:2), the gospel writes this recent event back into the Jesus story, mythically merging the past, the story, and the present. Thus, the Johannine Jesus speaks of the time of the readers as if it is already present to him (see John 13:7; 14:12–21, 25–30; 15:18–21, 26–27; 16:1–16, 19–28). Correspondingly, the narrator (retrospectively) interprets the time of Jesus in light of the post-Jesus knowledge of the Johannine mystics (see John 2:22; 7:39; 12:16, 36–43; 20:9).[34]

The gospel, then, tells two stories in one, the story of Jesus and the story of the Johannine community that identifies itself with and through the Jesus story.[35] By telling the story in this way, the gospel elides any distinctions between the stories of Jesus and the Johannine community. They are not worlds apart. The gospel's telling of the Jesus story turns the worldly ostracism (real or imagined) of the Johannine community into sectarian bliss and divine election. Rejected by the world, they are on the side of the Johannine revealer from above.[36]

The other world, then, that John connects its community with is the Jesus story, not the world above. John's audience leaves its normal adult world (or sees it differently) through the material device of John (which makes the romantic adventure of the Jesus story present). For John, the past is not dead and gone. Like the tinkling bell in Proust's memory and mammoth novel, the Jesus story tinkles on in John and its mystics. It is the notion of incarnate time (the past) in the Proust epigraph to this chapter that intrigues me, because John, too, has seemed to many readers—although not to gnostics—to speak of an incarnation. In light of Proust's *Remembrance of Things Past*, John actually incarnates the past Jesus story, not the world above, and its incarnation is actually an inlibriation (or inebriation?). The gospel's transcendence, then, is quite Proustian, because it extends Johannine mystics monstrously, "since, giant-like, reaching far back into the years, they touch simultaneously epochs of their lives—with countless intervening days between—so widely separated from one another in Time."[37]

Commonly, religion uses ritual to evoke and connect with its other world. At first glance, John has a rather cavalier attitude toward such matters. It does not narrate Jesus' baptism by John, although it has John remark upon it (John 1:32–33). It specifically denies that Jesus himself baptized (John 4:2). It does not bother to narrate the institution of the supper, although it has Jesus eating a final meal with his disciples and commenting on his betrayal (John 13). John has not, however, eschewed sacraments. Rather, John has dispersed reflection on Baptism (John 3:1–10) and Eucharist (John 2:1–11; 6:25–65) throughout the gospel. More importantly, John, rather than the sacraments, provides the material connection to the other. Reading John is the sacramental initiation to the Johannine mysteries (see John 14:26; 16:13).[38]

John's mysticism and nostalgia minimize apocalyptic eschatology (but see John 5:28–29; 6:39–40, 44, 54; 12:48). For John, life and judgment are present realities (John 3:18–21; 5:21–24). The crucial passage is, of course, Jesus' conversation with Martha (John 11:24–27). Accordingly, scholars often describe John's eschatology as "realized."[39] While apocalyptic (like Isaiah 24–27; Daniel 7–12; Revelation) typically transfers the mythic founding time—the creation of order out of chaos—to the future, John's romance with the past is a more traditional myth.

As we have seen, Stevens's *The Greatest Story Ever Told* also provides fantastic access to the other world of the Jesus story. Like John, the movie minimizes ritual (compare the repeated citations of Hosea 6:6) because it itself provides the cinematic equivalent of a ritual experience. Opening in a Byzantine church, the movie segues to its reprise of the Jesus story, and leaves that story to conclude in the same Byzantine church. The result is a "boxing" or "framing" of the story proper, an ecclesiastical contextualizing of the story. Within the movie itself, the church (or worship) becomes a pressure chamber through which the viewer enters and exits the alternate reality of the Jesus story. In short, Stevens's audience enters the movie twice, once when it comes into the theater and the movie begins and, again, when the camera moves from the church to the Jesus story proper. Stevens's film, then, has an uncanny resemblance to literary or cinematic fantasy, for, in most fantasy, the audience must follow some character through the looking glass, wardrobe, or some other portal to enter the fantastic realm.[40] For Stevens, the Jesus story is such a fantastic country and his movie the portal to it.

The exotic Byzantine church and the semi-ascetic teaching of Jesus are markers of this world's strangeness, but the ultimate fantastic "impossibility" lies in the distance between the metaphysical dualism of the Jesus story and Stevens's materialistic audience. Modern philosophy and science make John's (and the other gospels') dualism unpalatable.[41] Stevens's framing shrewdly handles this metaphysical problem, because the frame provides a material basis for John's dualism without articulating a belief in John's other world. Reading back and forth between *The Greatest Story Ever Told* and John suggests that John also has material bases for his dualism (and mysticism). In short, both film and gospel provide material bases for Romantic desires for and experiences of an exotic other.[42]

The Old, Old Story:
Familiarizing the Other; Mythic Naturalization

After moving the audience through the window of the church into the alternative reality of the Jesus story, Stevens familiarizes the exotic story. Again, Stevens's method is similar to fantasy, because the movie endeavors to play out the Jesus story in a way that seems realistic to the audience.[43] Stevens makes the audience at home by modernizing dialogue (his characters do not speak biblical

The mythic Western landscape.

English), by enlisting a cast of Hollywood stars, and by setting the story in the American West. Compared to previous Jesus films, the last move is the most innovative. The West's iconography naturalizes[44] Jesus as the American—or Western—hero. In short, *The Greatest Story Ever Told* is a Western,[45] the classic incarnation of one strand in the American myth, the notion of the frontier.[46] With the Western's frontier and its "others," Americans locate power, define themselves, and rejuvenate themselves.

The frontier is the classic other place in American mythology, the American alternative reality. Like the biblical notion of the wilderness, it is the place to meet the other, whether divine (desirable) or demonic (threatening). It is the place for hierophany and revelation. For American Romanticism, it is the place to confront nature and the native, or that which the Romantic needs in his/her ongoing battle with (industrial, bureaucratic) civilization.

Of course, in good mythic fashion, the native and the other are also to be resisted. Accordingly, the Western is a fruitful field for the binary oppositions of American mythology, including the individual and culture, freedom and restriction, integrity and compromise, nature and culture, and the West and the East.[47] As the place where these oppositions interact—intersecting in the hero—

the frontier West is a place of opportunity and risk, of romantic adventure and mythic violence. In fact, violence is endemic to the Western simply because it is the place where the binary oppositions of American mythology meet. The Western frontier, then, is not only the sacred place; it is also the *axis mundi,* the center where chaos becomes order.

Accordingly, the frontier is the crucible of national and individual identity. The Western's iconography of the lone individual etched against a panoramic Western background provides Americans with their dominant image of themselves, the individual at home in the natural world, yet violently opposed to the corrupting influences of civilization. At the same time, then, the Western provides Americans their mythic statement of bourgeois individuality and their cathartic relief from bourgeois society. In fact, the code of the West remains our cherished ideal. In the words of J. B. Books (John Wayne) in *The Shootist,* "I won't be wronged. I won't be insulted. I won't be laid a hand on. I don't do these things to other people and I require the same of them."[48] Not surprisingly, the result of such an ethic is often violence, and the Western often reflects upon justified violence, violence in a righteous cause (for example, *Shane, High Noon*), that is, a violence that reaffirms the cultural myth.

Such mythic (childish) simplicities reassure. The Western and its frontier rejuvenate Americans because that is where they belong. It is their "from whence," their Eden, and their "whither"; their Elysian Fields. It is the place where a man/woman can be free, natural, and innocent of society's corruptive influences. Not surprisingly, then, the journey there—even in a Winnebago or through a movie—is restorative.[49]

This American West is the mythic setting of *The Greatest Story Ever Told.* In particular, Jesus defines his character in the wilderness West and is empowered there—rather than at the baptism—in a defining contest with the (demonic, savage, or id-like) Dark Hermit. Thereafter, Jesus knows who he is and acts accordingly, regardless of the cost. Of course, he responds to those who "lay hands on him" in an uncharacteristically nonviolent manner for the Western hero. Further, Stevens cuts and dissolves from scene to scene to create oppositions typical of the Western. Most notably, he cinematically opposes the wilderness and the itinerant ministry of Jesus with the city/civilization and its rulers. Thus, act one ends with people outside the city shouting the news about the resurrection of Lazarus. When the Roman soldiers remove the people from the Temple and the city to maintain Roman order near the opening of act two, the dichotomy is quite clear. Not surprisingly, then, the authorities ultimately cast Jesus outside the city, and we actually see the crucifixion through the city gates. As Stevens films the individual of integrity (Jesus) versus a corrupt group (the authorities), he creates a pattern resonating deeply with the American myth. Thoroughly naturalizing the

Jesus story as an American Western/gospel,[50] Stevens renders the Jesus story as a new frontier, a site for power, identity, and rejuvenation. It becomes at least our "from whence"—our romanticized past—if not our "whither."

For John, the apparent functional equivalent of the frontier/wilderness is the world above,[51] but, as we have seen, John does not transport its audience to that world. Instead, John's Jesus comes from that world. For John, then, Jesus is the world above or, in Stevens's mythology, Jesus is the frontier. Of course, Stevens cannot "really" transmit his audience to the frontier either, because by the 1960s, it was a mythological place.[52] John and *The Greatest Story Ever Told* create stories, alternative (mythic) realities, which they use to critique the audience's normal reality. Where Stevens uses the medium of the Western frontier to transmit the Jesus story to the audience, John uses the medium of the Jesus story to suggest a mystic's transcendent world above. In one case, the Jesus story is the mythic goal. In another, it is the mythic means. Like the Western hero, of course, the Johannine Jesus mediates the oppositions between two different (and one [now] inaccessible) worlds.

Stranger Comes to Town

Of course, given their cultural locations, the two identify Jesus differently. For the movie, Jesus is the self-reliant Western hero who reveals each human's essential deity. For John, Jesus is the divine revealer descending from the world above. According to the prologue, Jesus—or, more accurately, the Word or the son—has descended from the father (John 1:10–14). In John 1:14, the Word becomes the "son," John's favorite title for Jesus thereafter, and John claims that this one reveals the glory, the visible presence of God (John 1:14).[53] All that John's Jesus ever truly reveals, however, is that he is the revealer, the access to the world above (John 1:51; 14:6). Neither the divine character nor the character of the world above is ever disclosed.[54] Not surprisingly, John can, on occasion, reduce the revelation to Jesus' simple "I am (he)" (John 8:24, 28, 58; 18:5, 9; compare 6:20).[55]

John introduces the ascent, the return to the father, more gradually (John 3:14), describing it variously as Jesus' lifting up, exaltation, return, or glorification. Further, John only gradually reveals that this glorified return is also Jesus' passion (John 6:62; 8:14, 28; 12:32–33). The climactic statement is John 12:32, with the Johannine narrator's clarification in 12:33: "'And I, when I am lifted up from the earth, will draw all people to myself.' He said this to indicate the kind of death he was to die." Thereafter, Jesus' private instructions for his disciples reiterate this interpretation (John 13–17).

Bultmann understood John's descending revealer in terms of gnostic redeemer mythology. For Bultmann, Gnosticism is a mythic "naturalization" of the Christian gospel.[56] That mythology expresses humanity's sense of alienation in the world and offers humans a *gnosis*, a liberating knowledge about their heavenly origins and the way out of this world. The full-blown gnostic myth—known only from the second century C.E.—is a cosmic and anthropological dualism valuing the spiritual and devaluing the physical world. The myth tells the story of a cosmic fall, in which spirit beings were trapped in the physical world, and offers the spirits' redemption through the agency of a descending revealer from the world of spirit/light.[57] Further, according to Bultmann, this dualistic worldview and its terminology is most apparent in the New Testament in John.[58] Since Bultmann, however, many scholars have rejected his analysis for a number of reasons.[59]

For our purposes, the precise historical milieu and the specific relationship of gnosticisms and christianities (note the plurals) are unimportant. What is important is that myths (note the plural) of descending-ascending revealers were common during the Hellenistic era, ranging from speculations about wisdom in certain forms of Judaism to emergent gnostic myths.[60] As Stevens does not really create a Western in *The Greatest Story Ever Told* but suggests it as a familiar mythic background so that the audience can assimilate his Jesus story, John does not really create a descending revealer myth, gnostic or otherwise. It merely suggests it.[61]

Thus, John offers no developed cosmology or anthropology. It provides no "back-story" about humanity's fall from a spirit world or about an overarching cosmological dualism. John's dualism is sociological. The distinction is less about spirit and flesh—despite Johannine words to that effect—and more about John's sectarian community and the larger social world that has rejected (and been rejected by) them.[62] In fact, John never truly stories the son's descent or ascent, beyond, of course, the ironic ascent of the passion. Despite the prologue, the descent is a fait accompli when the story begins. We never arrive at the world above. The Johannine story takes place wholly within a literary simulacrum of the audience's physical world. Everything revolves around the crisis brought by the revealer's presence in this world. The issue is whether others see Jesus as the one from above or not. The language about the one from above, then, identifies Jesus "as the Stranger *par excellence*" (especially John 8:23). Those who align with him, of course, also become strangers (sectarians) in the world.[63]

Incidentally (and ironically), the very idea of Jesus as stranger makes him quite familiar to modern audiences. It is not only that alienation and fears of ostracism are endemic to individualism; it is also that we have seen the story of the stranger come to town so many times in so many different movies, particularly Westerns.[64] The Western hero occupies iconographically a lonely space (frequently arrayed against monumental natural scenery) and, in terms of plot and character, the Western hero is a human caught between the conflicting interests of the frontier and civilization, or the old and new worlds.[65]

Stevens's *Shane* is a classic example. As the credits roll, the camera watches from afar as a lone rider (Shane), clad in buckskin, rides out of the mountains. In the first full scene, however, Stevens films a young boy, Joey, hunting deer in the river by his frontier homestead where he lives with his father (Joe Starrett) and his mother (Marian). Through Joey's eyes, Stevens's focalization of several critical points in the movie, we see Shane arrive at the homestead. Starrett, needing help around his place, offers Shane a job. Rather symbolically, Shane and Starrett remove a troublesome tree stump, and Shane, abandoning his gun and buckskins, gradually settles down.

Of course, this idyll cannot last. Soon, trouble comes to paradise as cattle ranchers try to drive the farmers from the valley. A farmer is killed; Starrett holds the farmers together; and the main rancher, fearing Shane's prowess, hires gun-slinging thugs. When Starrett decides to confront the rancher and his outlaws, Shane reluctantly realizes that he must act to save his adopted family. Knocking Starrett out in order to save him from a hopeless fight, he rides to town and, in a climactic showdown, defeats the outlaws. Interestingly, Stevens films the final showdown (as well as an earlier fistfight scene) from Joey's perspective. After the battle, Shane bids Joey goodbye. He cannot stay because "a man has to be what he is."

The parallels to John's stranger are obvious. Both are isolated figures caught between two worlds—whether the frontier and civilization or the world above and this world. Both heroes associate themselves with a small, endangered community that they both educate and deliver.[66] Both stories are set in the community's world, and both stories are told from the perspective of the community. Thus, John frequently comments on the post-passion/glorification setting, and Stevens focalizes *Shane* through Joey's eyes. In both cases, only the community sees the hero's (true) arrival and departure.

The introductions of *Shane* and John are also quite similar. We see both heroes—from afar—briefly in their native habitat before the story proper begins. In fact, *Shane's* introductory focus is closer to John than *The Greatest Story Ever Told* is. While the latter film's narrator quotes the Johannine prologue, it focalizes differently. Its church entrée serves to introduce us to the story's mythic world, not to bring the hero to a (mythic) simulacrum of ours. In short, in a sense, *The Greatest Story Ever Told* delivers us to the stranger's world, rather than bringing the stranger to us. All stories and movies actually represent, in discourse terms, a journey on the part of the audience, but that journey is not always a part of the story we read or see. *The Greatest Story Ever Told* "stories" the audience's journey. *Shane* and John do not.

Before we draw too fine a distinction here, however, we should remember that the difference is, in one sense, merely a matter of perspective. One story, *Shane* and John, is told from the perspective of the community redeemed. The other story, *The Greatest Story Ever Told*, is told from the perspective of the hero's journey. In *Shane* (and John), a gulf exists between the hero and the community even though the community becomes like the hero to some extent. Thus, Jarrett becomes his "own man" and Joey learns the myth of the loner and his gun. In *The Greatest Story Ever Told*, far less of a gap exists between the hero and others. The hero's journey is our own.

Actually, however, *Shane* and *The Greatest Story Ever Told* are simply different forms of the American myth. *Shane* is a good example of what we might call the apocalyptic form of the American myth.[67] *The Greatest Story Ever Told* is a more gnostic form of the American myth. John is itself a stranger visiting the American myth that may be read apocalyptically (*Shane*) or gnostically (*The Greatest Story Ever Told*). As a result, in American mythology, John becomes a mediating term. If salvation comes from outside in the apocalyptic myth as in *Shane* and from inside in the gnostic myth as in *The Greatest Story Ever Told* (and the Gospel of Thomas), John mediates with its glorified Jesus and indwelling paraclete. If *Shane* is a stranger-come-to-town story told from a communal perspective, and if *The Greatest Story Ever Told* is a someone-leaves-home story told from the hero's perspective, then John mediates with its strange revealer come to found the mystic sect and the sect members' own mystic journey (John 13:36–14:14; 17:24; 21:18–23).

Reading John in the Dark: Gnostic Jesuses

With its internalized interpretation of the Jesus story, *The Greatest Story Ever Told* tends toward Gnosticism.[68] For this film, Jesus is a matter of myth and privatized faith (or psychology). Notably, then, there is nothing specifically Jewish about this Jesus. He is, rather, the eternal Christ. As the monstrous, resurrected Christ of the finale demonstrates, he is not so much in the world as above it.

Similar tendencies toward Gnosticism appear in John. In effect, John's prologue renders the historical appearance of the Word as a temporary hiatus in the Word's story. John, then, is also mythic, and its Jesus is not truly a first-century Jew either. John's Jesus, too, is an eternal figure trailing clouds of glory. Like Stevens's Jesus, John's Jesus also calls his followers to recognize the divinity within. Although they must acknowledge Jesus as the one from above, that is only the first stage in their mystic journey. They truly understand *the glorified, not the earthly one* only when the indwelling divine instructs them (see John 2:22; 7:39; 12:16; 14:20–26; 16:4, 12–15). Then, they dwell mystically in Jesus and in

God (John 15:1–11; 17), and, like Jesus, in their own deaths they will mystically ascend (see John 13:36; 14:1–7; 17:24). Is John, then, gnostic? Scholars are widely divided.[69] What *The Greatest Story Ever Told* demonstrates, as the history of second/third-century interpretation already has, is that John can be read gnostically.

It is this potential that allows John its entrée into American myth and culture. John and *The Greatest Story Ever Told* meet at the juncture of the divine (American) individual:

> Freedom, in the context of the American Religion, means being alone with God or with Jesus, the American God or the American Christ. In social reality, this translates as solitude, at least in the inmost sense. The soul stands apart, and something deeper than the soul, the Real Me or self or spark, thus is made free to be utterly alone with a God who is also quite separate and solitary, that is, a free God or God of freedom. What makes it possible for the self and God to commune so freely is that the self already is of God; unlike body and even soul, the American self is no part of the Creation, or of evolution through the ages.[70]

Such individualism necessarily enshrines a sense of alienation that results in a fundamental restlessness. American religion becomes, then, "a severely internalized quest romance, in which some version of immortality serves as the object of desire."[71] As we have seen, John is about a similar mystic quest for deification (John 1:12–13; 3:16; 11:25–26). It is a mystic primer inviting others to an ascent—a call to glory—like Jesus'. All of this is important in America, because the American Jesus is also a glorified (resurrected) figure:

> The Southern Baptists in some sense take as their paradigm an interval about which the New Testament tells us almost nothing, the forty days the Disciples went about in the company of Jesus after his resurrection. I think that not only the Baptists but all adherents of the American religion, whatever their denomination, quest for that condition. When they speak, sing, pray about walking with Jesus, they mean neither the man on the road to eventual crucifixion nor the ascended God, but rather the Jesus who walked and lived with his Disciples again for forty days and forty nights. . . . the American walks alone with Jesus in a perpetually expanded interval founded upon the forty days' sojourn of the risen Son of Man. American Gnosticism escapes from time by entering into the life upon earth already enjoyed by the Man who died and then conquered death.[72]

This Jesus does not save. He imparts the knowledge of our own divinity. His only (or principal) difference from other Americans is that he has already risen. His importance is that we need not acknowledge our mortality.[73]

Reading John in the dark with *The Greatest Story Ever Told* intensifies John's gnostic and American potential. As this John is about the mystic's deification, the gospel becomes difficult to distinguish from the Gospel of Thomas and from popular American religion (and film). John's mythic Jesus lives as easily in Stevens's American West as he does in a mystic's first-century gospel (and can continue to make various cameo appearances as he does, for example, in *Play It to the Bone*). In sum, however, John lives on in America because Americans are gnostics (or immortals), not because they are orthodox (or evangelicals).

While John's dualistic worldview troubled early moderns, Stevens enables us to see John's dualism as a non-problem. Despite its pretensions, John does not make a transcendent world above present. John never stories the world above. Its story is Jesus. In short, John's dualism is quite material—so material, in fact, that it can hardly trouble the most rigorous modern materialist.

Cast into relief by Stevens's movie, however, John's metaphysical pretensions become quite evident. Unlike Stevens's movie, John makes a good deal of noise about a metaphysically distinct world above. In the dark, then, John becomes a mystic's primer. As such, John (like Thomas) becomes a precursor of modern Romantic religion, the so-called "inward turn."

Gnosticism, metaphysical dualism, and Romanticism do not separate moderns from John. Stevens negotiates all these difficulties. What Stevens cannot deal with in John (or ignores) is, however, also brought into the light when we read the gospel with the movie. In the dark, two features of John stand out nefariously.

First, John's deterministic worldview becomes inescapable. Those who do not accept the Johannine Jesus as the one from above are woefully human, sinfully culpable, *and supernaturally determined* (John 12:37–43). John writes this story too personally in the demonic Judas (John 6:70–71; 13:2, 27). John is so secure here that it does not even bother to distinguish the acts of the demonic and the acts of God/prophecy (compare John 13:8 with 13:2, 27). Stevens's creation of the Dark Hermit and his obscuring of Judas's motivation may serve to clear the reputation of his God and certainly serves to clear a space for human freedom, but it leaves John "on the hook" for a dastardly determinism.

Second, John's denunciation of the world also becomes glaringly obvious. John's sectarian community rejects the world (and the Jews whom it equates with the world) that rejects it. The final words of the pre-passion Jesus (John 13–17) articulate clearly the lines of mutual hostility, although only one side is allowed to speak. Like the synoptic apocalypses, these words precede, but answer, the passion.

Like Mark's apocalypse in particular, they voyeuristically condemn the world. Arguably, the world condemned is (merely) social, as the prologue identifies the God of creation and the God of salvation; nevertheless, John's mysticism and lack of a clear ethic indicate its separation from the world at large.[74] Notably, American Romantics, like Emerson, advance a more clearly defined ethic and seek rejuvenation in the natural world. Stevens's Edenic West—his celebration of "natural" beauty vis-à-vis civilization—casts the absence of such aesthetics in John into view. In short, even without a clearly defined metaphysical other, John abandons the world—if only in fantasy—far more than American Romantics (and film).

Notes

1. Marcel Proust, *Remembrance of Things Past,* 2 vols., trans. C. K. Scott Moncrieff (New York: Random House, 1934), 2:1122–23. Emphasis added.

2. See Raymond E. Brown, *The Gospel According to John,* 2 vols., *The Anchor Bible* (Garden City, N.Y.: Doubleday, 1970), I:cxxxviii–cxliv. For reading guides to John, see R. Alan Culpepper, *Anatomy of the Fourth Gospel: A Study in Literary Design* (Philadelphia: Fortress, 1983); and Jeffrey L. Staley, *The Print's First Kiss: A Rhetorical Investigation of the Implied Reader in the Fourth Gospel* (Atlanta, Ga.: Scholars, 1988).

3. See C. H. Dodd, *The Interpretation of the Fourth Gospel* (Cambridge: Cambridge University Press, 1968), 290, 400; and, quite concisely, Duling and Perrin, *The New Testament,* 425–40.

4. Chatman, *Story and Discourse,* 47–48. Henry James's *The Portrait of a Lady* is a classic example of a revelation plot. A critic once compared reading his novels to peeling an onion. One covers the same ground repeatedly to reach greater depths of character.

5. Culpepper, *Anatomy of the Fourth Gospel,* 89, asserts, "each episode has essentially the same plot as the story as a whole. Will Nicodemus, the Samaritan woman, or the lame man recognize Jesus and thereby receive eternal life? The story is repeated over and over. No one can miss it."

6. Some characters move toward Johannine faith (e.g., Nathaniel, Peter, Thomas, Mary, and Martha) and others defect (e.g., Peter, Judas) (ibid., 145–48). Raymond E. Brown, *The Community of the Beloved Disciple* (New York: Paulist, 1979), 59–91, explains the Johannine spectrum of characters in historical rather than literary terms.

7. John gradually reinterprets confessions (e.g., those in John 1) in light of its notion of Jesus as the one from above (John 6:66–71; 16:25–33). See Staley, *The Print's First Kiss,* 95–118; and Norman Petersen, *The Gospel of John and the Sociology of Light: Language and Characterization in the Fourth Gospel* (Valley Forge, Pa.: Trinity Press International, 1993), 23–53.

8. Stevens ends the wilderness incident with Jesus on a mountaintop to the accompaniment of triumphal music and a narrator intoning that all the tribes of the earth shall see the Son of Man coming in the cloud of heaven with power and great glory. Like John, then, *The Greatest Story Ever Told* "realizes" eschatology.

9. See Babbington and Evans, *Biblical Epics*, 143–46; and Tatum, *Jesus at the Movies*, 96–97. The epic genre further downplays Jesus' ethic. The movie cost twenty million dollars to produce, so Tatum, *Jesus at the Movies*, 97, jests, "Austerity never looked so good." Wood, *America in the Movies*, 165–88, identifies conspicuous waste as one of the appeals of the spectacle, biblical or otherwise.

10. Nicodemus's role is more ambiguous. When Caiaphas stacks the jury and tries the innocent at night (cf. John 7:50–51), the decent Nicodemus is aghast. Incidentally, this scene connects Nicodemus with "night" rather differently than John does (Stevens does not include Nicodemus's night visit to Jesus). Nicodemus, however, never clearly becomes a disciple. When Jesus replies, "I am," to Caiaphas's prodding query whether he is the Christ, the son of God, Nicodemus gulps hard and sits down even harder (cf. Mark 14:61–62). Whether this reaction represents sacred awe or a frustrated awareness that Jesus' fate is now sealed is not clear. Nicodemus's ambiguous role does nicely capture the Johannine notion of "secret disciples."

11. The blind man of John 9, not the Jewish authorities, sees Johanninely. In an amusing scene, the authorities admit that they do not know where Jesus is from (John 9:29), and the (healed) blind man tries vainly to instruct them (John 9:30–33)! Their blindness is culpable, not natural (like that in John 1–4), because they claim to see (John 9:41). Stevens expands this character by drawing on various gospel traditions. The blind man healed at Nazareth (who knew Jesus as a child) is one of three characters to proclaim Jesus as messiah outside the walls of Jerusalem. During the trial before the Sanhedrin, this blind man defends Jesus (transplanting John 9). While the religious leaders debate the point, the healed blind man asserts that Jesus is from God. Meanwhile, Peter denies Jesus in the courtyard outside.

12. Stevens is not as negative toward colonialism as Ray. Stevens's Romans are more circumspect; there are fewer bodies in his Temple. Stevens's weak Pilate, however, capitulates to the crowd. We last see him vainly washing his hands as a voiceover (in Pilate's voice) intones the line from the creed, "suffered under Pontius Pilate."

13. While Chronicles "clears" God's reputation, Stevens clears space for human freedom by effacing John's supernatural determinism. The Dark Hermit also serves, like Stevens's Sorak, to shift the blame from known biblical characters somewhat. He is the undeveloped precursor of Zeffirelli's Zerah.

14. If so, Stevens's Judas is the precursor of Jewison's Judas, not Zeffirelli's.

15. The movie's various teaching scenes piece together elements from various gospels. The traditional Sermon on the Mount appears just before Jesus withdraws for his final instruction of the disciples. That sermon does not dominate the film as much as the first "under the bridge" teaching or Jesus' preaching in the Capernaum synagogue and in the Jerusalem Temple. Stevens shortens the sermon to the beatitudes, the call to mission, and the Lord's Prayer (essentially Matthew 5:3–16; 6:1, 9–13). More importantly, Stevens's Jesus generally sounds Johannine. He does not parable, and he speaks primarily about himself and eternal life (not the kingdom).

16. The film uses Hosea 6:6 three times: 1) to distinguish John's message from that of the religious leaders; 2) to distinguish Jesus' viewpoint from that of the speaker in the Capernaum synagogue; and 3) to distinguish Jesus' Temple teaching from the Temple practices (see Stern,

Jefford, and DeBona, *Savior on the Silver Screen,* 136). An American (Protestant) audience might see this prophetic critique in law (Judaism) versus grace (Jesus and Christianity) terms. This repeated refrain might, then, lead to anti-Semitic readings.

17. This scene most clearly articulates Jesus' *semi*-ascetic teaching.

18. According to Forshey, *American Religious and Biblical Spectaculars,* 97, the movie script describes the Dark Hermit as Jesus' own inner voice. In the actual movie, however, John the Baptist looks much more like Jesus' inner voice. While we watch Jesus struggle in the wilderness, we hear John the Baptist preaching. We might see the wilderness scene as a psychological struggle between Jesus' id (the Dark Hermit) and his superego (the prophets) in which Jesus reaches maturity. Compare Donald Richie, *George Stevens: An American Romantic* (New York: Museum of Modern Art, 1970), 7–12, 52–73, who claims that Stevens's oeuvre is a struggle with the fundamental Romantic problem, life in a hostile world. Stevens's mature characters, like Shane and Jesus, forsake (adolescent) Romanticism to achieve maturity through self-knowledge and by "owning" their "outsider" status. Thus, in a famous scene in *Shane,* Shane differs from the cattleman with whom he struggles because he knows that his days are over.

19. Stevens's Jesus says this not once (as in John 18:36) but twice, both privately in Pilate's conference room and publicly in the *Ecce Homo* scene.

20. Stevens's inward focus differs notably from that of Zeffirelli and that of Krish and Sykes. Zeffirelli's *Jesus of Nazareth* (1977) offers the Jesus story popularly (*Jesus of Nazareth* is a made-for-television movie), but it also offers the story traditionally. See Chapter 2 above. Zeffirelli's Jesus demands a response from the heart, but this focus does not reject the apostolic, sacramental institution. It rejoins it versus its intellectual despisers. Notably, Zeffirelli's Judas is an intellectual. The inward focus of Krish and Sykes's *Jesus* (1979) is more akin to Johannine mysticism. Their film (or its use in a crusade setting) calls one to a personal, mystic connection with an otherworldly Jesus who dies to save. As we have seen before, Krish and Sykes read Luke Johanninely. In fact, their rhetorical approach is even closer to the Gospel of Thomas. For Thomas, the teaching of Jesus brings the mystic disciple into contact with the divine. For Krish and Sykes, their movie (or evangelistic sermons) brings the mystic into contact with Jesus' saving cross.

21. Richard Walsh, *Mapping Myths of Biblical Interpretation* (Sheffield: Sheffield Academic Press, 2001), 67. For a very brief description of Romanticism in literary terms, see Holman and Harmon, *A Handbook to Literature,* 415–17. I use "Romanticism" here to refer to the modern, sensitive individual's rejection of industrialized and capitalistic society in favor of an inner self or a nostalgic past. Compare expressive (and utilitarian) individualism in Bellah et al., *Habits of the Heart,* 33–35. The semi-ascetic cast to Stevens's Jesus may make him a more utilitarian than expressive individual. The Jesuses of Zeffirelli and Krish and Sykes are more clearly "expressive."

22. Ralph Waldo Emerson, "The Divinity School Address," in Ralph Waldo Emerson, *Self-Reliance and Other Essays* (New York: Dover, 1993), 108.

23. Ibid., 21.

24. See Ralph Waldo Emerson, *Representative Men* (Philadelphia: David McKay, 1893), 5–39. Emerson considers six representative figures: Plato, the philosopher; Swedenborg, the mystic;

Montaigne, the skeptic; Shakespeare, the poet; Napoleon; the man of the world; and Goethe, the writer. Reportedly, Emerson wanted to use Jesus as the mystic but feared public reaction.

25. Only after Jesus' glorification do the disciples understand Jesus' earthly life and sayings (e.g., John 2:22; 7:39; 12:16; 20:9).

26. Read with Stevens, John becomes less like the creeds and more like Thomas.

27. Stern, Jefford, and DeBona, *Savior on the Silver Screen*, 151–55, claim that *The Greatest Story Ever Told* failed financially because America had lost its (Protestant) Christian metanarrative. Stevens's framing of the Jesus story convinces me that he is aware of that cultural shift. Compare Richie, *George Stevens: An American Romantic*, 48–50, who comments on Stevens's "iconic" use of windows to leave the spectator outside the story. In the movie, Jesus often appears framed in doorways, gates, etc.

28. Not incidentally, Stevens offers the story of *Shane* largely through the eyes of a child (Joey, played by Brandon de Wilde). See below.

29. Compare Campbell, *Hero with a Thousand Faces*, 38–39, 251, 365–71; and *idem, Myths to Live By* (New York: Penguin, 1972), 13.

30. See Bultmann, "New Testament and Mythology."

31. The audience's "adventure" is like that of the disenchanted romance novelist in Zemeckis' *Romancing the Stone*, who finds an exotic, romantic adventure like that in her novels. Reportedly, tales of medieval knights fascinated Stevens. The buildings of the powers-that-be in *The Greatest Story Ever Told* do look like castles, and knightly fanfares often attend their presence on the screen.

32. Stevens's slow dissolves between scenes suggest "connections that are subjective, prophetic, elegiac, or magical"(Richie, *George Stevens: An American Romantic*, 44–45). They increase the ethereal (or otherworldly) quality of the movie.

33. See J. Louis Martyn, *History and Theology in the Fourth Gospel*, rev. ed. (Nashville, Tenn.: Abingdon, 1979); and Brown, *The Community of the Beloved Disciple*.

34. See Culpepper, *Anatomy of the Fourth Gospel*, 27–43. John's frequent use of the present tense also elides the distance between the story and the reader (ibid., 30–32).

35. The redaction critics see all the gospels in this "two-level" fashion.

36. Petersen, *The Gospel of John and the Sociology of Light*, 80–109, discusses John's linguistic creation of a sectarian community through "anti-language."

37. Proust, *Remembrance of Things Past*, 2:1124.

38. See Dodd, *The Interpretation of the Fourth Gospel*, 165, 420–23; Culpepper, *Anatomy of the Fourth Gospel*, 151–227; and Staley, *The Print's First Kiss*, 95–118.

39. See C. H. Dodd, *The Parables of the Kingdom*, rev. ed. (New York: Scribner's, 1961), 159; *idem, The Interpretation of the Fourth Gospel*, 6–7; and Bultmann, *Theology of the New Testament*, 2:37–40.

40. Fantasy is an aesthetic equivalent of the ritual experience in religion because it provides disjoints with "reality" or a "hesitation" between realities. Tzvetan Todorov, *The Fantastic*, trans. Richard Howard (Cleveland, Ohio: Case Western Reserve University Press, 1973), 25–43, argues that fantasy dwells in the hesitation between the marvelous and the uncanny, the consideration

whether the "madness" of the alternative reality is actually a "higher reason" (ibid., 40). The resolution of the dilemma ends the fantasy (ibid., 41–43).

41. Incredulity about miracle is a symptom of this metaphysical problem. Miracle is more foreign to the audience of *The Greatest Story Ever Told* than to that of *King of Kings*. Ray's Lucius provides a vehicle between the modern secular audience and the miraculous Jesus story. Stevens has no such intermediary. Miracle, save for psychosomatic healing, disappears. The larger-than-life resurrected Jesus is no exception, because that appearance simply segues to the painting of Jesus on the Byzantine wall. For Bultmann, "New Testament and Mythology," 38–43, Jesus died and rose into the faith of the church. For Stevens, Jesus died and rose into church art and into his film.

42. For Emile Durkheim, *The Elementary Forms of Religious Life*, trans. Karen E. Fields (New York: Free Press, 1995), 84–85, 94–108, 216–25, 424–25, society creates a sense of the sacred and of its ideal self through ritual experiences concentrating society and enthusing its members. The experience of the transcendent, then, has a material, social basis. In fact, society's effects on its members are the material basis of the notion of God (ibid., 208).

43. W. R. Irwin, *The Game of the Impossible: A Rhetoric of Fantasy* (Urbana, Ill.: University of Illinois Press, 1976), 9, claims that literary fantasy is "the persuasive establishment and development of an impossibility." To persuade, fantasy adapts readers' expectations about reality minimally, i.e., only as the central impossibility demands. In short, after the central impossibility, matters proceed realistically (ibid., 57–76).

44. Barthes, *Mythologies*, 129–31, argues that myth confers the status of the natural upon particular historical and political choices.

45. On the Western, see Jim Kitses, *Horizons West* (London: Thames & Hudson, 1969); John G. Cawelti, *The Six-Gun Mystique* (Bowling Green, Ohio: Bowling Green University Popular Press, 1971); idem, *Adventure, Mystery, and Romance: Formula Stories as Art and Popular Culture* (Chicago: University of Chicago Press, 1976), 192–259; Jane Tompkins, *West of Everything* (New York: Oxford University Press, 1992); and Ian Cameron and Douglas Pye, eds., *The Book of Westerns* (New York: Continuum, 1996).

46. See Robertson, *American Myth, American Reality*, 72–124; May, *The Cry for Myth*, 91–107; and, most concisely, Neale, *Genre and Hollywood*, 134–35.

47. See Kitses, *Horizons West*, 11; and Scott, *Hollywood Dreams and Biblical Stories*, 47–129.

48. Cited in Scott, *Hollywood Dreams and Biblical Stories*, 71–72.

49. Thoreau's *Walden* is a sophisticated form of this myth.

50. See Stern, Jefford, and DeBona, *Savior on the Silver Screen*, 157–60; Baugh, *Imaging the Divine*, 27; and David Jasper, "On Systematizing the Unsystematic: A Response," in March and Ortiz, eds., *Explorations in Theology and Film*, 236–41.

51. The American West and the biblical wilderness have certain mythic similarities, but John, in contrast to the Synoptic Gospels, does not make much of the wilderness.

52. In Hollywood movies, as in American mythology, the frontier has migrated from the West to the city to outer space and, most recently, to the machine (computer) world. If Stevens

had been a more recent Hollywood director, he might have made *Star Wars* or *The Matrix* instead of *Shane*. It is interesting to speculate how Lucas or the Wachowski brothers might imagine the alternative space of the Jesus story.

53. For a concise summary of Johannine titles for Jesus, see Petersen, *The Gospel of John and the Sociology of Light*, 58–59.

54. Bultmann, *Theology of the New Testament*, 2:66, famously says, "Thus it turns out in the end that Jesus as the Revealer of God *reveals nothing but that he is the Revealer.*" Wayne A. Meeks, "The Man from Heaven in Johannine Sectarianism," *Journal of Biblical Literature* 91 (1972): 57, describes Jesus' conversation with Nicodemus, for example, as "a *virtual* parody of a revelation discourse." Petersen, *The Gospel of John and the Sociology of Light*, 14, argues that John's use of synonyms for Jesus and God in the prologue so blurs the referents that all we can say is that "for John there is an Other that is the originator of the world and that It subsequently entered into the world in the form of the human being Jesus of Nazareth." Further, this other is not the God of everyday language because John redefines "God" to that not known apart from Jesus.

55. We could add the predicate nominative "I ams" as well (John 6:35, 51; 8:12; 9:5; 10:7, 9, 11, 14; 11:25; 14:6; 15:1, 5). They privilege the notion of Jesus as the access to the divine. Scholars generally consider the "I am" statements markers of divine revelation. See Bultmann, *Theology of the New Testament*, 2:64–66; Brown, *The Gospel According to John*, 1:525–32; and Petersen, *The Gospel of John and the Sociology of Light*, 57–61.

56. Bultmann, *Theology of the New Testament*, 1:164, calls this acculturation a "historical necessity."

57. Ibid., 1:164–67. Classic treatments of Gnosticism include Hans Jonas, *The Gnostic Religion*, 2nd ed. (Boston: Beacon, 1963); and Kurt Rudolph, *Gnosis: The Nature and History of Gnosticism* (San Francisco: Harper & Row, 1983). More concisely, see Koester, *Introduction to the New Testament*, 1:381–89.

58. Bultmann, *Theology of the New Testament*, 1:173; 2:11–14.

59. No evidence exists for the full-blown gnostic myth before John. Further, the Qumran discoveries and subsequent studies in Judaism have convinced many of the diverse and sometimes dualistic character of Second Temple Judaism. Finally, of course, many scholars are hesitant to admit that "heretical" thought could have a foothold within the New Testament canon. See Robert Kysar, *The Fourth Evangelist and His Gospel: An Examination of Contemporary Scholarship* (Minneapolis, Minn.: Augsburg, 1975), 104–46; and D. Moody Smith, "Johannine Studies," in Epp and MacRae, eds., *The New Testament and Its Modern Interpreters*, 271–96.

60. Charles H. Talbert, "The Myth of a Descending-Ascending Redeemer in Mediterranean Antiquity," *New Testament Studies* 22 (1976): 418–40, demonstrates this point convincingly.

61. Whether influenced by Gnosticism or not, John was certainly read gnostically. In addition to Brown, *The Community of the Beloved Disciple*, 145–64, see also Elaine H. Pagels, *The Johannine Gospel in Gnostic Exegesis: Heracleon's Commentary on John* (Nashville, Tenn.: Abingdon, 1973).

62. See Meeks, "The Man from Heaven in Johannine Sectarianism," 68–72; and Petersen, *The Gospel of John and the Sociology of Light*, 80–109.

63. This paragraph depends heavily on Meeks, "The Man from Heaven in Johannine Sectarianism," 44–72. The quote is from p. 50. For Meeks, Jesus is a wholly other stranger, an

enigma to those not Johanninely trained (ibid., 47, 55–60). This depiction makes Jesus remarkably like Rudolph Otto's "wholly other" (*The Idea of the Holy,* trans. John W. Harvey [New York: Oxford University Press, 1958], 25–30).

64. The individualist mythology supporting both the novel and modern film tends toward scenarios in which an individual confronts a group or in which an individual is "out of place" for some reason.

65. Cawelti, *Adventure, Mystery, and Romance,* 193–94. The main difference between the Western hero and John's Jesus here is the matter of setting (the Western frontier in the former case). It is precisely this difference that *The Greatest Story Ever Told* removes.

66. Religion and myth scholars have been particularly interested in *Shane,* and their critical comments often deal with the tension between the violent hero (Shane) and the hero who suffers violence (Jesus). See, e.g., Hill, *Illuminating Shadows,* 118–36; Scott, *Hollywood Dreams and Biblical Stories,* 47–67; Baugh, *Imaging the Divine,* 157–71; and Robert Banks, "The Drama of Salvation in George Stevens' *Shane,*" in Marsh and Ortiz, eds., *Explorations in Theology and Film,* 59–71. Richie, *George Stevens: An American Romantic,* 60–70, contends that this distinction is less important than the fact that both heroes act decisively and maturely.

67. See Walsh, "On Finding a Non-American Revelation," 1–6; and Jewett, *The Captain America Complex.* Incidentally, Eastwood's retelling of *Shane* in *Pale Rider* makes the apocalyptic motifs much more obvious.

68. See Baugh, *Imaging the Divine,* 30–32; Tatum, *Jesus at the Movies,* 94–96; and Stern, Jefford, and DeBona, *Savior on the Silver Screen,* 131–33, 145.

69. See Smith, "Johannine Studies," 283–88.

70. Harold Bloom, *American Religion: The Emergence of the Post-Christian Nation* (New York: Simon & Schuster, 1992), 15. Bloom admits that American religion's democratic and materialist tendencies distinguish it from ancient Gnosticism (ibid., 21–27, 260–65).

71. Ibid., 40.

72. Ibid.

73. Ibid., 65.

74. John's ethic is mysticism (abiding in Jesus), sectarian steadfastness in the face of the world's rejection, and communal love.

Chapter 8

Coming to America

The idea we have of ourselves as individuals on our own, who earn everything we get, accept no handouts or gifts, and free ourselves from our families of origin turns out, ironically enough, to be one of the things that holds us together. . . .

. . . The irony is that here, too, just where we think we are most free, we are most coerced by the dominant beliefs of our culture. For it is a powerful cultural fiction that we not only can, but must, make up our deepest beliefs in the isolation of our private selves.[1]

Coming to America

Neil Gaiman's *American Gods* imagines immigrants bringing their gods with them to America. As the immigrants acculturate, they adopt new American gods and leave their old gods behind. Forlorn and diminishing, these pathetic gods still inhabit the American mythscape.

This back-story gradually becomes clear as Gaiman tells the tale of Shadow, the hero of his novel. Shadow has troubles. Imprisoned for aggravated assault, he passes the time with Low Key, his cellmate, who introduces him among other things to Herodotus's notion that we should call no man happy before his death. The authorities release Shadow when his wife dies in a tragic accident. Released, he learns that his wife died in a compromising position with his best friend.

With little left to lose, Shadow reluctantly takes a job with a mysterious stranger, Mr. Wednesday. The past haunts Shadow, however, as his dead wife repeatedly visits him. Dreams of a mysterious buffalo-man (and others) also trouble him. In this fantastic world, Shadow is not surprised to learn that Mr. Wednesday is the American avatar of Odin and that his new job is to help Odin assemble a coalition of the old, fading gods whom Odin plans to lead in a last, desperate battle against the new gods—for example, gods of the media and consumer capitalism—that litter the American mythscape.

The story builds toward this Ragnarok when the new gods kill Mr. Wednesday during a truce. His murder motivates the wavering older gods to gather for war at Lookout Mountain, Georgia. Meanwhile, Shadow stands vigil for the dead Wednesday by hanging from a tree for nine days, a vigil that is certain death for a mere mortal. During his vigil, like Odin, Shadow gains knowledge. In particular, he learns that Odin is his father and that the god war is a con perpetrated by Odin and Loki (formerly Low Key), Shadow's old cellmate. The con's aim is a blood sacrifice designed to revive Odin's fading powers. Although Shadow dies, gods (Easter and Horus) revive him, and he stops Ragnarok by revealing the con.

Interestingly, among this eclectic pantheon, Jesus does not appear prominently. In an amusing scene, an Egyptian god explains, "That boy was one lucky son of a virgin. . . . Lucky, lucky guy. He could fall in a cesspit and come up smelling like roses." Jesus is not waning, so he does not need to join the battle. The gods take it phlegmatically enough, for they know that his success is relative. Thus, the Egyptian god continues, "So yeah, Jesus does pretty good over here. But I met a guy who said he saw him hitchhiking by the side of the road in Afghanistan and nobody was stopping to give him a ride. You know? It all depends on where you are."[2]

Recent international events have certainly underlined the point. Jesus is an American success story. As such, he has more in common with the hero of John Landis's *Coming to America* than with Gaiman's fading gods. Landis's movie features Eddie Murphy as Prince Akeem, a pampered, rich African royal who comes to America to escape an arranged marriage. He moves to Queens (of course) to find an independent American woman. In the process, he expresses his own individualism and finds a woman to match. Romantic love conquers all, and, as importantly, the arrogant young prince becomes a man of the people (he lives in a slum and works at McDowell's, a McDonald's copycat). This story is a romantic version of the prince and the pauper or a story of the creation of the American (upper) middle class, the very heart of American self-understanding.

Similar emphases dominate the Jesus movies. Since DeMille, these movies affirm the value of (and the values of) the middle class. The countercultural Jesuses of the 1970s only appear to be an exception, because they mainstream the counterculture. Further, in the Jesus movies, Jesus is always a man of the people. He always stands between the people and corrupt powers-that-be. This pattern is consistent with American populism generally and, of course, is clearly at home in Hollywood stereotypes. Again, romantic love triumphs in virtually every Hollywood movie. In Jesus movies, it simply takes a mystic form. The movies invite characters and audiences to attach to a personal god, Jesus. This erotic mysticism is particularly prominent in DeMille, Stevens, Krish and Sykes, and Zeffirelli. Scorsese, following the pattern of *Barabbas,* transforms the triumph to torment, but the erotic mysticism remains. Finally, at heart this erotic mysticism is simply one form of the expressive (Romantic) individualism so definitive of American myth and culture. Of course, some movies represent that expression as artistic (Arcand) or as ethical (Ray, Stevens, Pasolini), rather than as mystic.[3]

In short, the Jesus movies indicate Americans have Americanized Jesus. Jesus is the ideal American individual. Gaiman's *American Gods* acknowledges Jesus' American success, but its Shadow replaces Jesus as hero. As such, Shadow takes on some of the characteristics of the American Jesus. He is the lone hero standing against a mysterious, powerful, and corrupt group. Furthermore, he finds self-knowledge in the midst of an apocalyptic crisis. He learns to express himself in the midst of the individual's final *agon*, the struggle with his/her own death. As he overcomes his death, he finds himself and realizes what the buffalo has been telling him all along, "This [America] is not a land for gods."[4] The land and the self-reliant people are sufficient. For American individuals, gods are problems to be overcome. With notable artistic revisions,[5] then, Gaiman's Shadow embodies the characteristic features of the American Jesus. He is a true, triumphant individual.

Jesus: True, Triumphant Individual

In America, that which is ultimately and finally sacred is the individual.[6] The individual is the source of power and meaning in our culture. Further, individualism is our defining mythic identity. Each of us expresses that identity simply by "being ourselves." The absurdity—as the epigraph from Bellah and his associates indicates—is patent: we all claim to be unique. Of course, such absurdity does not trouble mythology or religion, because the absurd is their métier. Thus, religion renders the profane—in this case, the mundane, common individual— a special hierophany.[7] The absurdity of American individualism, then, is an important marker of its sacred centrality in American myth and culture.

The Jesus movies dwell in these sacred precincts. As we have seen, they offer privatized versions of religious faith and piety (DeMille, Stevens, Krish and Sykes, Zeffirelli, Scorsese) or they depict expressive individualism in some other form (Ray, Pasolini, Arcand). In this regard, *The Greatest Story Ever Told* may be the quintessential American Jesus movie, because it expresses most blatantly the sacred— and gnostic—individual. For DeMille, Krish and Sykes, Zeffirelli, and Scorsese, a sacred other is more necessary. For Ray, Pasolini, and Arcand, the individual stands *humanly* alone. For Stevens, the other is our own internal and true self, the god within. In *The Greatest Story Ever Told*, we are like Jesus (and Lazarus and Judas), if not Jesus ourselves, because of our fundamentally divine nature.

Of course, apocalyptic is as important as Gnosticism in American movies and in the American Jesus. Vis-à-vis the self, the divine, immortal American individual is quite gnostic. Vis-à-vis the world, American individualism often expresses itself apocalyptically, because individualism is an inherently agonistic mythology.[8] The individual forms himself or herself in conflict with others (or internalized versions of the other). Almost any novel or movie—the modern art forms—provides examples. Further, every conflict for the individual is always "final" or apocalyptic, because the whole world hangs in the balance when the individual—the sacred itself—is at risk.

Once again, the Jesus movies play out this apocalyptic pattern. Jesus is invariably the hero standing alone against a powerful, corrupt group and maintaining his integrity to the death. He defines himself in a fatal conflict with the powers-that-be, so his death expresses his essential identity.[9] Often, resurrection or some other indication of Jesus' triumph and continuing iconic significance testifies to his victory over his opponents[10] and publicly vindicates Jesus. The Christ-figure films and the biblical epics are blatant examples of this apocalyptic triumph. In the former case, the hero may die, but his cause triumphs, for example, in Luke's memory in Cool Hand Luke, in the inmates' restored dignity in One Flew over the Cuckoo Nest, and in the salvation of America in End of Days. In the epics, Christianity triumphs over (or, more accurately, Christianizes) the Roman Empire. Thus, American apocalypses never bring in fundamentally new worlds. Instead, they restore the threatened world in which we already live. From Shane to End of Days, they restore and legitimize American society. More importantly, of course, they assert the value and dignity of the individual, both in the hero and the other—often a woman or child—for whom the hero acts.[11]

The apocalyptic tendencies in the Jesus movies also demonstrate that Americans will not abide a weak Jesus. They expect Jesus and their other heroes to triumph even if they have to die to do so. Our daily frustrations—not the least of which is our inability to be individuals—demand conquering heroes. No wonder, then, that Scorsese's The Last Temptation of Christ was not well received. Scorsese's tormented Jesus is too much like us. His triumph is too muted and his struggle too prominent. He is no apocalyptic conqueror. In fact, despite the struggle over the flesh and the spirit and his triumph over the flesh on the cross, this Jesus is also insufficiently aware of the divinity within him.

Once again, Stevens's Jesus is more triumphantly American. He defines himself in conflict, first with the Dark Hermit and then with the powers-that-be. Not surprisingly, then, for Stevens, Jesus' apocalyptic triumph as the Son of Man occurs on a mountain in the wilderness after this wilderness temptation. Similarly, the resurrection—an apocalyptic motif—of Lazarus and of Jesus himself bookends his conflict with the powers-that-be. Certainly, Stevens's movie meditates on John—the American gospel—and, therefore, is more gnostic than apocalyptic; however, as in John, apocalyptic remnants remain. In Shane,

Stevens reverses the ratio, with apocalyptic dominating and Gnosticism becoming an undercurrent.

Given its combination of apocalyptic and gnostic elements, we may again consider *The Greatest Story Ever Told* the American Jesus movie. Generally speaking, the others fail to capture either the gnostic or apocalyptic elements in American mythology. Stevens's precursor in this regard was DeMille's *The King of Kings*. By the 1960s, however, DeMille's understanding of Jesus was too Puritan for American audiences. To use Bellah's categories, Americans had moved from utilitarian individualism to expressive individualism.[12] To use our categories, changing features in society—for example, the move from a production-oriented society to a consuming society—had reinvigorated Romantic elements in American individualism. Expressive individualism, then, ruled the day. DeMille's Jesus simply was not Romantic enough. He was also too specifically (Protestant) Christian. In the 1960s, America became increasingly secular. Accordingly, Stevens's movie did not have great economic success. The Jesus movies after Stevens that have portrayed a "religious" Jesus, whether ecumenical (Zeffirelli) or evangelical (Krish and Sykes), have not displaced Stevens's American Jesus for that reason alone. Like DeMille, they are too clearly religious and not generically expressive (Romantic, gnostic) enough.[13] The Jesuses of Jewison, Greene, and Scorsese fail for another reason. They are too weak for American tastes. They are not sufficiently apocalyptic and triumphant. Ironically, the foreign filmmakers, Pasolini and Arcand, depict more American Jesuses. Their Jesuses are apocalyptic individuals.

Jesus in American Religion and Myth Revisited

As we saw in Chapter I, the Jesus movies function religiously in American civil religion or in the individual's privatized notions of religious faith. That the American Jesus appears in both apocalyptic and gnostic forms simply refines those earlier insights.

American civil religion expresses the distinctly American faith and practice (although, as we have seen, that faith differs over time). It renders sacred the land and people of America at the price of devaluing other nations and peoples. Any civil religion exists inherently in tension, if not outright conflict, with others. While not always in conflict, it always teeters on the edge of children-of-light-versus-children-of-darkness language. Civil religion comes consciously to the fore, understandably, whenever its adherents feel the divine nation threatened from within or without. Accordingly, it often speaks from the very brink of chaos. American civil religion is thus inherently apocalyptic, and when it imagines Jesus, it does so apocalyptically.

Privatized religious experiences—with little or no social import—tend toward gnostic understandings of the self and Jesus. Such experiences provide mystic union with a divine revealer or mystic knowledge of the deity within. In either case, the individual expresses herself/himself. Not surprisingly, such images have dominated American Jesus movies since the 1960s. The breakdown of modern (American) metanarratives and the turn to self-expression in the 1960s and 1980s in particular have all privileged the individual's self-expression (and the gnostic Jesus). It remains to be seen whether recent threats and renewed patriotism will return the apocalyptic Jesus to prominence in American mythology.

That popular culture, media, and religion express a Jesus of that culture is hardly surprising. What we should take note of is that, in American religion and mythology, Jesus represents the (an?) American ideal, not American reality. We imagine in Jesus the self that we Americans would be. Vis-à-vis the world and others, he is apocalyptically triumphant. He is first among others. Vis-à-vis the self, he is not only righteous and pure, but divine. He is best. In short, as we have already observed, the American Jesus is the true, triumphant individual. That Jesus is the American mythic ideal explains how a pacifistic, semi-ascetic Jew can be the supreme icon of a capitalist empire. If Americans are imperialists, Jesus is righteously violent or even pacifistic. If Americans are capitalists, Jesus is ascetic, semi-ascetic, or at least cavalier about economic matters. By imagining our American selves vis-à-vis Jesus, we purify ourselves. If we do not give up empire and capitalism, we salve our guilt by expressing our commitment to an ideal that we would live by, if only we did not have to live in the real world. Of course, we also use that ideal to legitimate—if only because we are self-consciously aware of—our capitalist empire. In short, with the American Jesus, we claim that we do empire and capitalism right. From the canonical Gospels to DeMille to Young, Jesus (even the Jesus of international directors) is on our side.

I do not mean this analysis altogether negatively. It is "natural" mythic work: "Thus each successive epoch of theology found its own thoughts in Jesus; *that was, indeed, the only way in which it could make Him live.*"[14] The emphasized material underlines the crucial point: Jesus, of the movies or of the Gospels, is an empty signifier who needs a context, history, culture, and so forth in order to mean. In America, apart from some (heroic) prophetic or poetic feat, Jesus means Americanly. If he does not speak individualistically, whether apocalyptically or gnostically, he would not be heard or he would be interpreted as so speaking anyway. The foreign films are wonderful examples. In America, Pasolini and Arcand tell stories of the pure, lone individual engaged in apocalyptic conflict with corrupt, corporate powers. They may well speak differently elsewhere. In America, however, American myth consumes the other and regurgitates the American.[15]

In America and in the Jesus movies, Jesus functions mythically. He incarnates (and connects us with) the source of power in American culture, the individual. He expresses American self-identity, both in its apocalyptic and gnostic forms. He harmonizes tensions in our society and in our psyches by easing the gap between our reality and our ideals. The result legitimates our selves and society. He does all of this myth work by being the iconic form of the true, triumphant American individual.

This mythic ideal eases our social and psychological dis-ease. Thus, according to Lévi-Strauss, myth resolves the tensions caused by the binary oppositions bedeviling a particular culture. While the basic opposition is Hamlet's "to be or not to be," myth generates "an unlimited series of other binary distinctions which, while never resolving the primary contradiction, echo and perpetuate it on an ever smaller scale. . . ."[16] Thereby, myth provides the illusion that this and other contradictions can be overcome.[17] Myth, then, draws a cover—even if it is only a "moth-eaten musical brocade"—over our deepest fears. For triumphant American individuals, the apocalyptic Jesus salves fears of loss, of frustration, of tragedy, and of death. For true American individuals, the gnostic Jesus salves our fear of failing to "be true to ourselves." For Americans, as May observes, the myth of individualism charts a safe haven (a being) between our twin (non-being) terrors of absorption and ostracism. No wonder, then, that we have so much trouble relating to another as genuinely other, dealing with failure, and even imagining death. No wonder, then, that our heroes die so that we will not and that they express themselves even if we cannot be so true.[18]

Ironically, then, our individualism is not heroic. With our myth of individualism, we do not become heroes, but conformists. What Jasper says of Hollywood, I would extend to the entire American myth-making enterprise (a.k.a., our culture):

> Hugely systematic as a commercial enterprise and oblivious of the human waste which it [Hollywood cinema] casts in its wake, the popular cinema nevertheless trades in the myths of the "unsystematic"—the maverick hero, the individual who defeats the corrupt corporation, the ugly duckling who becomes the beautiful princess. All, however, are ultimately conformists.[19]

In short, in our myth we are individuals because we cannot cope with the idea of our non-being and because "individualism" is our defense—however illusory—against forces larger than we are.[20] Asserting our individuality, we huddle together.

Individualism is nothing less than the standard (mythic) means of coping in our society (and with our society). Cohen and Taylor capture this myth concisely:

"I escape, therefore I am," is ultimately the only ontological message we can manage. An ideology of bourgeois individualism this certainly is and it would be absurd to claim that we are not prone to it ourselves or that it should not be subjected to the same relentless relativism to which we have exposed other ideologies. Such bourgeois individualism—the obstinate clinging on to the idea of a separate self—is decadent and reactionary; its radicalism is expressive rather than instrumental, the limitations of any cultural rather than structural politics. . . .

. . . We have described rather than transcended the ruinous preoccupations of a society which celebrates the value of the unique individual identity, a self-consciousness which our society has developed almost to the point of the pathological.

But it is the only world we seem to know.[21]

It is actually, then, no surprise that individualism survives. Our entire culture foists it on us. The very act of asserting our individuality makes us at home in America. In fact, individualism sometimes seems a "bread and circus" program keeping us securely in place as consumers, as it is primarily what we consume that differentiates us from other American individuals. The American Jesus belongs to this whole mythic process and to our collaboration with it. Only dinosaurs, seers, and the disenfranchised bother to worry.

A More Parabolic Jesus:
Loosing Jesus or a Non-American Jesus

I am not any of those, although I feel more paleographic every day, but clearly mythic univocity (or mythic imperialism) troubles me. Our world is too pluralistic and we ourselves are too fragmented for triumphant, true individualism to go unchallenged. Within that existing myth, then, I find myself looking for parable. As I have suggested, for my purposes, parable is a story alongside (or within) culture's dominant myth. This notion, which recalls the etymological meaning of parable as "cast alongside," has been explicated well by Crossan. The parable I look for, then, is not an antimyth, but the "dark night of story," the edge of myth.[22] I look for a Jesus, then, that stands parabolically alongside the American myth of the triumphant, true individual (Jesus).

The quest for such a figure is part of the impetus of the historical Jesus movements. Too often, however, the historical Jesus simply becomes an antimyth. If so, the process simply repeats—in a scholarly way, of course—the drive toward the myth of (expressive) American individualism (self-identity). In short, we—American scholars—do the "historical Jesus" in order to promote ourselves agonistically against our culture, our tradition, or our colleagues. With our Jesuses, we legitimate our positions of power and prestige. That our scholarly Jesuses are typically countercultural reflects, among other things, our own sense of social dislocation.[23] We are retainers, not the powers-that-be. With our countercultural Jesuses, then, we reap the benefits of our culture while disavowing the hand that feeds us and reveling in our sense of disenfranchisement. We would not be popular (in theory at least) for power or money, because if we were popular, we would not be true to ourselves. Of course, then, we do not esteem the Jesus of any popular Jesus movie. That simply is not done. Ironically, however, this sectarian or cynical revelry renders us "true Americans." In our eschewals of the popular, in our esteem for the "unsystematic" Jesus, we are simply writing and starring in our own Hollywood gospel. Thereby, we act out the myth of the lone, good individual striving against some mysterious, evil group (for example, Hollywood or the church) and become triumphant and true Americans.

Such Jesuses are hardly parabolic. The parabolic Jesus is not an antimyth, a truth, or a legitimating force (even for scholars). The parabolic Jesus is the "dark night" of all such claims. In parable, the mythic, "musical brocade" has to slip more completely. The best way to achieve such parables, I think, is to remember that we are in conversation, even when we monologue, and that our religious/mythic acts are interpretations, not the truth. To this end, perhaps, we should disavow Jesus altogether. We can have a Jesus other than ourselves, a non-American Jesus, only by loosing/losing Jesus. We have to see Jesus as only passing through (America).

Scholars often express a concern that Jesus will be lost in the unending production and consumption of images. The problem is rather that one Jesus might dominate the field and establish the empire of some particular scholar, guild, church, or country. Scholarly fears about losing Jesus are really desires for a "real Jesus" beyond semiotics and culture. Such real Jesuses are covert rhetoric for someone's ideology. Versus such ideologues, multiple Jesuses are serendipitous. The multiple historical Jesuses at least had this merit. They meant that the church could no longer contain and control Jesus.

The merit of the Jesus movies is that now neither scholars nor the churches can control Jesus. The movies set Jesus loose in culture (as the vernacular translations of printed Bibles once did). They render Jesus indigestible by any particular ideology. Thus, for example, *The Last Temptation of Christ* critiques previous Jesus films and rejects the gnostic Jesus of American popular religion. That stance renders it unpalatable to popular audiences. Similarly, *Monty Python's Life of Brian* refuses to let the church's Christ and the Gospels stand as the only reading of early Christian events. For Christian tradition, that film is a distasteful account of multiple messiahs, of misunderstood events (rather than miracles), of misunderstood sayings (rather than stately sayings), and of multiple, competing religions (rather than one, true church). In a different vein, the humor of this film unsettles the stomach of (deadly) serious scholars. *Jesus of Montreal* provides even more problems for scholarship by exposing scholarship's frequent and manifestly false claims to objectivity and certainty. Further, Arcand's wonderful film provides by itself a salvific plethora of jostling Jesuses.

If we are worried, however, that all these Jesuses simply come from one provider—whether Hollywood, America, or modern consumer capitalism—two points may settle our queasiness. First, VCR and DVD technology—like the printed, vernacular Bibles—makes film's multiple images of Jesus continually available and individually usable. Accordingly, and second, we do not have to passively consume these Jesuses. We can interpret. By reading the Jesus movies in conversation with the Gospels and with American culture (and scholarship), I have tried to render all these Jesuses unconsumable by any one ideology. Theoretically, such comparison protects each Jesus' rough, historic particularity and leaves open the possibility of parable, as well as myth.

To ease my own anxieties about mythic univocity further, I will close by reflecting on the possibility of a non-American Jesus. In brief, the non-American Jesus would not be (apocalyptically) triumphant nor (gnostically) true. The non-American Jesus would be mortal or would, at least, affirm his mortality. That such a Jesus is largely unthinkable in America has nothing to do with our (ecclesiastical) creedal convictions. It has everything to do with our myth of individualism. It is the resurrected Jesus that matters to Americans because that Jesus signifies our own triumph and immortality.[24]

More than the scholars—who have treated the resurrected Jesus as a metaphysical rather than an ethical problem—the Jesus movies have made a start here.[25] Scorsese's Jesus is particularly helpful. His Jesus, who has important precursors in the Jesuses of Jewison and Greene, is embarrassingly riven and indecisive. He is hardly the triumphant, true individual with whom Americans like to identify. For us, he is an all-too-human Jesus.

Other movies are also helpful because they remind us that Jesus is not unique. In particular, Ray and Monty Python profane Jesus by focusing on other crosses. Thus, their Jesus is only one victim among many of the Pax Romana. Similarly, Pasolini renders Jesus a peasant among other peasant victims of imperial and bourgeois society. In fact, with enough nonpassive attention, all the Jesus movies (even DeMille and Stevens?) might reveal non-American (parabolic) Jesuses alongside the mythic Jesuses so readily available on their surfaces. If so, those Jesuses may look more like Gaiman's Shadow, Camus' Sisyphus, or Arcand's Daniel than the resurrected Jesus of American mythology. It would need to be a Jesus able to face mortality and perhaps a

Jesus even happy[26] with mortality to efface America's triumphant and true individualism. If a parabolic Jesus lives in America, he will have to be less triumphant and true; that is, he will have to be less literally American. Only a metaphoric (different) Jesus can be parabolic.[27]

Accordingly, I would like to keep more than one story (and one Jesus). I see no reason to insist on a harmony of the gospels (or of the movies). I prefer to think of the gospels—and to include Thomas and others—rather than to think of *the Gospel* according to. . . . And, I would like to confess that I like Jesus movies (to my family's dismay) and like reading them alongside the Gospels. My personal favorite is Arcand's *Jesus of Montreal* simply because of its embarrassing plethora of jostling Jesuses. A close second is *Monty Python's Life of Brian,* a film that I (petulantly) insist on seeing as a Jesus film. It is the fact that Brian is and is not Jesus that intrigues me. That he is "not Jesus" territory makes him a wonderful map for Jesuses. The inclusion in the same film of a cameo appearance by an epic (or creedal) Christ, whom the crowd misunderstands, is a crowning achievement in Jesus studies as well as in Jesus films. Finally, and not surprisingly, Griffith continues to interest me. Despite his stories alongside, however, he is unfortunately only telling one story. He has, in effect, created a film version of the canonical four Gospels. But what if he had placed four different— even discordant—Jesus stories alongside one another? What kind of parabolic possibilities would that offer?

Notes

1. Bellah et al., *Habits of the Heart,* 62, 65.

·2. Neil Gaiman, *American Gods* (New York: HarperCollins, 2001), 161–62.

3. Notably, foreign films figure prominently in these alternatives.

4. Gaiman, *American Gods,* 192. See also ibid., 397–402, 430.

5. The interplay between European and American Indian mythology is fairly common in American culture. The Western is one genre that frequently brings these mythologies together. See Pirsig, *Lila,* 44–48, 301–4, for a broader discussion. The European mythology typically prominent is, of course, Christianity. King's *Green Grass, Running Water* is an amusing send-up of the typical mythic dialogue here as well as an amusing Indian correction of Christian mythology. In this context, Gaiman's most interesting artistic revision is a mythic replacement of Christian with Norse mythology. As a result, he brings Norse and American Indian mythology into dialogue. This connection allows for a more satisfying treatment of death than is typical of either the American Jesus or Hollywood. Both Shadow and his wife have to come to terms— like the heroes of ancient, Greek, and Norse mythology—with their own death. By contrast, the American Jesus—and many Hollywood heroes—makes it possible for us to reach our happy

endings without pain, toil, suffering, and tragedy. This "metaphysical optimism" borders on the "bottom line" in American mythology. Thus, my students frequently do not believe in God, Jesus, etc., but they always believe in their immortal soul.

6. See Bellah et al., *Habits of the Heart,* 142–63. According to these authors, our cultural conversation traditionally included biblical, republican, and individualist strands, but only the last remains a major factor. Thus, their works strive to engender a conversation that transcends individualism (ibid., 27–51, 275–96).

7. See Eliade, *The Sacred and the Profane,* 201–13.

8. On the apocalyptic nature of American mythology/religion, see Jewett, *The Captain America Complex;* Albanese, *America: Religions and Religion,* 283–343; and Walsh, "On Finding a Non-American Revelation."

9. Interestingly, the foreign directors are most forthright here. See Stack, *Pasolini on Pasolini,* 56–57; and Loiselle, "I Only Know Where I Came from, Not Where I Am Going," 157.

10. *Godspell, Jesus Christ Superstar,* and *Life of Brian* are notable exceptions here.

11. American movies often willingly sacrifice groups or numbers of people to affirm the sanctity and worth of the individual. *Saving Private Ryan* and *Dinosaur* come to mind as examples.

12. According to Peter Homans, "Puritanism Revisited: An Analysis of the Contemporary Screen-Image Western," *Studies in Public Communication* 3 (Summer 1961): 73–84, the Western combines Puritan ideology with the romance genre. The classic Western hero has Stoic or Puritan qualities. Bellah calls such individualism "utilitarian." By contrast, the Jesus films, after the epics, have tended toward expressive individualism. On these types of individualism, see Bellah et al., *Habits of the Heart,* 32–35. That volume traces the move from utilitarian individualism (read "Puritan" or "Stoic") to expressive (read "Romantic") individualism. Bellah and his associates also claim that our public, working lives are governed by utilitarian individualism and our private lives by expressive individualism. This fissure is a harbinger of the postmodern disappearance of the stable individual self.

13. Zeffirelli is also too institutional (apostolic) for American sectarians, and Krish and Sykes too stridently evangelical. Americans readily accept only capitalist evangelists.

14. Schweitzer, *The Quest of the Historical Jesus,* 4. Emphasis added.

15. This Americanization of culture is a particular concern of the Canadian Arcand. See Wilkins, "No Big Picture"; and Stern, Jefford, and DeBona, *Savior on the Silver Screen,* 321–33.

16. Claude Lévi-Strauss, *The Naked Man,* trans. John and Doreen Weightman (New York: Harper & Row, 1981), 694.

17. Ibid., 659. By applying Lévi-Strauss's understanding of myth to Hollywood movies, Scott, *Hollywood Dreams and Biblical Story,* provides enlightening insights into American mythology.

18. I do not know whether to sing—with due mythic fervor—"The Old Rugged Cross" or "My Heroes Have Always Been Cowboys."

19. Jasper, "On Systematizing the Unsystematic," 235–36. He also observes that cinema turns the Christian Gospel into *The Greatest Story Ever Told,* i.e., the story of mid-1960s America.

20. According to Ernest Becker, *The Denial of Death* (New York: Free Press, 1973), 47, 51, 55, 268–85, those of us who cannot heroically confront our own death live via some "vital" or "life lie," like the myth of individualism. Lévi-Strauss, *The Naked Man*, 625–26, 687–95, calls "individualism" the "spoilt child" of modern philosophy and claims that it stands (mythically) in the way of our acceptance of our non-being.

21. Stanley Cohen and Laurie Taylor, *Escape Attempts: The Theory and Practice of Resistance to Everyday Life*, 2nd ed. (London: Routledge, 1992), 236.

22. See Crossan, *The Dark Interval*, 60, which is, of course, this book's epigraph.

23. See Jeffrey L. Staley, *Reading with a Passion: Rhetoric, Autobiography, and the American West in the Gospel of John* (New York: Continuum, 1995), 14–15.

24. See Bloom, *American Religion*, 40. May, *The Cry for Myth*; and Becker, *The Denial of Death*, both identify mortality as the problem that American (or modern mythology) does not grapple with seriously.

25. Crossan, *Jesus: A Revolutionary Biography*, 123–58, is a notable exception. My point is not whether the resurrection is metaphysically possible or not. My point is the ethical—or mythical—consequences of the assertion/proclamation of the resurrection.

26. I refer, of course, to Camus' remark, "One must imagine Sisyphus (read, "Jesus") happy" (*The Myth of Sisyphus*, 123). Obviously, this happiness differs markedly from the superficial happiness of Young's always-resurrected Jesus.

27. See Smith, *Map Is Not Territory*, 291: "Religion is the quest, within the bounds of the human, historical condition, for the power to manipulate and negotiate ones [*sic*] 'situation' so as to have 'space' in which to meaningfully dwell." Obviously, I am closing with rhetorical pleas for my position and am fully "in" the scholarly myth. I hope I have seen the parabolic edge and have arrived at "comic" rather than "apocalyptic" eschatology. On this point, see Crossan, *Raid on the Articulate*.

Appendix:
Portraying the Sacred in Film

Paul Schrader (*Transcendental Style in Film*) and Margaret Miles (*Seeing and Believing*) have made the strongest statements against the religious epics' portrayal of the sacred; nevertheless, both still hope that film may function religiously. Schrader believes that an austere style of film (typical of Ozu, Bresson, Dreyer) can generate a "hierophany" by bringing humans to a sense of limit or incongruity (that "negatively" suggests transcendence). Similarly, Miles feels that film can "learn" techniques to portray religious experience (after all, it already knows how to portray love). More importantly, Miles avers that (any?) film can function religiously as it becomes part of religious activity; that is, critical discussion or pious discipline.

Clearly, my sentiments lie with Miles. I do not expect a hierophany of the wholly other of Western monotheism in film. I do think, however, that film already has techniques—including (the) realistic photography (of talismans), special effects, spectacle, and theatrical "faces"—by which it alludes to the sacred, to what may be thought to provide power or meaning. Interestingly, the analysis of the bureaucracy of the sacred by various scholars indicates that religion has long had similar "techniques" for suggesting the sacred—talismans, stories of miracles, provision of alternative realities through ritual (and other means), and the experience of (and means for creating) creature consciousness. Figure 5 connects these "techniques" (in both film and religion) with a scholar who has analyzed such techniques in religion (full references to these works are in the selected bibliography) and with examples from Jesus films (or religious epics).

Adele Reinhartz ("Scripture on the Silver Screen") provides numerous examples of talismans in film. Michael Wood (*America in the Movies*, 165–88) discusses film's spectacles as alternative realities akin to those of religious ritual. Bryant ("Cinema, Religion, and Popular Culture") discusses film as ritual experience. With respect to special effects, Eli Cross (Peter O'Toole as the director in *The Stunt Man*) says it all: "If God could do the tricks that we can do he'd be a happy man."

Notably, with respect to Jesus films, Jesus is *only one* signifier (of the sacred) among many. Often, he is not even the most important signifier. Spectacle, special effects, and film's alternative realities need Jesus only as window dressing.

Figure 5: Techniques for Portraying the Sacred

Technique	Scholar	Example
Talismans	Van der Leeuw's fetishes	The robe in *The Robe;* water in *Ben-Hur;* the Bible in *The Apostle;* the ubiquity of the cross and cruciform shapes
Spectacle	Berger's sacred canopy or Ellwood's "alternative reality" of ritual	The epic style of DeMille, Ray, and Stevens; the "church" enclosure of Stevens's film; the musical genre of Jewison and Greene; the interlacing of ancient and modern stories in Griffith and Arcand
Special effects	Eliade's hierophany	The risen, "heavenly" Christ at the end of DeMille, Stevens, and Krish and Sykes; Pasolini's "exploding" tomb
Theatrical faces	Otto's *mysterium tremendum et fascinans*	Awed faces, terror, and worship (of Christ) in the religious epics; Zeffirelli's apostolic church story

They are themselves more important signifiers, gesturing at the "real" power behind the films—whether capitalism, entertainment, or mysticism. Talismans rely more heavily on Jesus as a signifier; however, Jesus is replaceable by robe, cup of water, and his story/tradition (variously told). In fact, the biblical epics are clearly more comfortable using symbolic replacements of Jesus. They are happier with Jesus' shadow than with Jesus. Jesus is most important as the signifier of the sacred when figures respond to him as the sacred other who causes conversion or degradation. Even here, however, he is remarkably vacuous, because this technique switches attention from Jesus to the story of other characters. As a result, Jesus tends to get lost (see Chapter 2).

Film's techniques signify a sacred palatable to Western monotheism only when the viewer imports the "meanings" of traditional Western religion. In a pluralist society and outside traditional myth-ritual complexes (see Walsh, "Recent Fictional Portrayals of God"), that meaning is hardly certain. *Barabbas, Monty Python's Life of Brian,* and *Jesus of Montreal* play in this pluralist cultural situation.

Arguably, of course, film can signify any sacred. The film medium, however, suits polytheism, pantheism, or materialism better than monotheism. The "cult" of celebrities is akin to polytheism. Film's realistic photography certainly hallows the material world and might suggest either pantheism or materialism. The use of film in capitalist consumerism, of course, ultimately signifies materialism above all else. Given its American cultural (and mythic) location, as we have seen, Hollywood film also frequently configures present American culture and individuals as sacred. Film can, however, also (through special effects and spectacle) attribute sacred power to some "other," although it generally signifies this other rather ambiguously (see Chapters 1 and 2 above). These diverse significations are, however, not exclusive. Thus, a particular film may suggest various locations of the sacred. Martin, *Images and the Imageless,* 59–111, has a very helpful taxonomic analysis of film genres and their "typical" sacred significations.

Movies Cited

Accattone. Pier Paolo Pasolini (director). 120 mins. Brandon Films, 1968 (1961).

American Beauty. Sam Mendes (director). 121 mins. DreamWorks SKG, 1999.

The Apostle. Robert Duvall (director). 134 mins. October Films, 1997.

Barabbas. Richard Fleischer (director). 144 mins. Columbia Pictures, 1962.

Being There. Hal Ashby (director). 130 mins. United Artists, 1979.

Ben-Hur. William Wyler (director). 212 mins. Metro-Goldwyn-Mayer, 1959.

The Big Chill. Lawrence Kasdan (director). 105 mins. Columbia Pictures, 1983.

Blazing Saddles. Mel Brooks (director). 93 mins. Warner Brothers, 1974.

Bonnie and Clyde. Arthur Penn (director). 111 mins. Warner Brothers/Seven Arts, 1967.

Bronco Billy. Clint Eastwood (director). 116 mins. Warner Brothers, 1980.

Butch Cassidy and the Sundance Kid. George Roy Hill (director). 110 mins. Twentieth Century Fox, 1969.

Chinatown. Roman Polanski (director). 131 mins. Paramount Pictures, 1974.

El Cid. Anthony Mann (director). 182 mins. Allied Artists Pictures, 1961.

City of Joy. Roland Joffé (director). 132 mins. TriStar Pictures, 1992.

Coming to America. John Landis (director). 116 mins. Paramount Pictures, 1988.

Contact. Robert Zemeckis (director). 143 mins. Warner Brothers, 1997.

Cool Hand Luke. Stuart Rosenberg (director). 126 mins. Warner Brothers, 1967.

Dances with Wolves. Kevin Costner (director). 183 mins. Orion Pictures, 1990.

Dead Poets Society. Peter Weir (director). 128 mins. Buena Vista Pictures, 1989.

The Decline of the American Empire (Déclin de l'empire américain, le). Denys Arcand (director). 101 mins. Cineplex Odeon Films, 1986.

Demetrius and the Gladiators. Delmer Daves (director). 101 mins. Twentieth Century Fox, 1954.

Dinosaur. Eric Leighton and Ralph Zondag (directors). 82 mins. Buena Vista Pictures, 2000.

End of Days. Peter Hyams (director). 121 mins. Universal Pictures, 1999.

eXistenZ. David Cronenberg (director). 97 mins. Dimension Films, 1999.

The Fall of the Roman Empire. Anthony Mann (director). 188 mins. Paramount Pictures, 1964.

Final Fantasy: The Spirits Within. Hironobu Sakaguchi and Moto Sakakibara (directors). 106 mins. Columbia Pictures, 2001.

Fried Green Tomatoes. Jon Avnet (director). 130 mins. Universal Pictures, 1991.

From the Manger to the Cross. Sydney Olcott (director). Kalem, 1912.

Gladiator. Ridley Scott (director). 155 mins. DreamWorks Distribution LLC, 2000.

The Gods Must Be Crazy. Jamie Uys (director). 109 mins. Twentieth Century Fox Film Corporation, 1984 (1980).

Godspell. David Greene (director). 103 mins. Columbia Pictures Corporation, 1973.

The Gold Rush. Charles Chaplin (director). 82 mins. United Artists, 1925.

The Gospel According to St. Matthew. Pier Paolo Pasolini (director). Continental, 1966 (1964).

Grand Canyon. Lawrence Kasdan (director). 134 mins. Twentieth Century Fox, 1991.

The Great Dictator. Charles Chaplin (director). 124 mins. United Artists, 1940.

The Greatest Story Ever Told. George Stevens (director). 260 mins. United Artists, 1965.

Hamlet. Franco Zeffirelli (director). 130 mins. Warner Brothers, 1990.

The Handmaid's Tale. Volker Schlöndorff (director). 108 mins. Home Box Office, 1990.

He Who Must Die (Celi qui doit mourir). Jules Dassin (director). 122 mins. Kassler Films, 1958 (1957).

High Noon. Fred Zinnemann (director). 85 mins. United Artists, 1952.

In the Bedroom. Todd Field (director). 130 mins. Miramax Films, 2001.

Intolerance: Love's Struggle through the Ages. D. W. Griffith (director).

Iris. Richard Eyre (director). 91 mins. Miramax Films, 2001.

Jesus (The Public Life of Jesus: A Documentary). John Krish and Peter Sykes (directors). 117 mins. Warner Brothers, 1979.

Jesus. Roger Young (director). 173 mins. CBS TV, 1999.

Jesus Christ Superstar. Norman Jewison (director). 108 mins. Universal Pictures, 1973.

Jesus of Montreal. Denys Arcand (director). 118 mins. Orion Classics, 1990 (1989).

Jesus of Nazareth. Franco Zeffirelli (director). 371 mins. National Broadcasting Company, 1977.

Johnny Guitar. Nicholas Ray (director). 110 mins. Republic Pictures, 1954.

The King of Kings. Cecil B. DeMille (director). 112 mins. Kino, 1927.

King of Kings. Nicholas Ray (director). 168 mins. Metro-Goldwyn-Mayer, 1961.

Knock on Any Door. Nicholas Ray (director). 100 mins. Columbia Pictures, 1949.

Kundun. Martin Scorsese (director). 128 mins. Buena Vista Pictures, 1997.

The Last Temptation of Christ. Martin Scorsese (director). 164 mins. Universal Pictures, 1988.

Little Buddha. Bernardo Bertolucci (director). 140 mins. Miramax Films, 1993.

Mamma Roma. Pier Paolo Pasolini (director). 110 mins. Meridian Video, 1995 (1962).

The Matrix. Andy Wachowski and Larry Wachowski (directors). 136 mins. Warner Brothers, 1999.

Mean Streets. Martin Scorsese (director). 110 mins. Warner Brothers, 1973.

Michael. John Turtletaub (director). 123 mins. Buena Vista Pictures, 1996.

Modern Times. Charles Chaplin (director). 87 mins. United Artists, 1936.

Monty Python's Life of Brian. Terry Jones (director). 94 mins. Orion Pictures, 1979.

Mr. Deeds Goes to Town. Frank Capra (director). 115 mins. Columbia Pictures, 1936.

Mulholland Drive. David Lynch (director). 146 mins. Universal Pictures, 2001.

Nazarín. Luis Buñuel (director). 94 mins. Connoisseur Video, 1968 (1958).

One Flew over the Cuckoo's Nest. Milos Forman (director). 133 mins. United Artists, 1975.

Pale Rider. Clint Eastwood (director). 115 mins. Warner Brothers, 1985.

Parable. Rolf Forsberg and Tom Rook (directors). 22 mins. No production company listed, 1964.

Phenomenon. Jon Turteltaub (director). 123 mins. Buena Vista Pictures, 1996.

Play It to the Bone. Ron Shelton (director). 124 mins. Buena Vista Pictures, 1999.

Pleasantville. Gary Ross (director). 124 mins. New Line Cinema, 1998.

Powder. Victor Salva (director). 111 mins. Buena Vista Pictures, 1995.

The Prince of Egypt. Brenda Chapman, Steve Hickner, and Simon Wells (directors). 90 mins. DreamWorks SKG, 1998.

Quo Vadis? Mervyn LeRoy (director). 171 mins. Metro-Goldwyn-Mayer, 1951.

Raiders of the Lost Ark. Stephen Spielberg (director). 115 mins. Paramount Pictures, 1981.

The Rapture. Michael Tolkin (director). 100 mins. New Line Cinema, 1991.

Rebel without a Cause. Nicholas Ray (director). 111 mins. Warner Brothers, 1955.

The Return of Martin Guerre (Le Retour de Martin Guerre). Daniel Vigne (director). 122 mins. European International, 1983 (1982).

La ricotta. Pier Paolo Pasolini (director). A short film included in *RoGoPaG.*

The Robe. Henry Koster (director). 135 mins. Twentieth Century Fox, 1953.

RoGoPaG (Laviamoci il cervello). Jean-Luc Godard, Ugo Gregoretti, Pier Paolo Pasolini, and Roberto Rossellini (directors). 122 mins. Cineriz, 1962.

Romancing the Stone. Robert Zemeckis (director). 105 mins. Twentieth Century Fox Film, 1984.

Run Lola Run (Lola Rennt). Tom Tykwer (director). 80 mins. Sony Picture Classics, 1999 (1998).

Santa Fe. Andrew Shea (director). 97 mins. Nu Image, 1997.

Saving Private Ryan. Steven Spielberg (director). 170 mins. Paramount Pictures, 1998.

Seven Years in Tibet. Jean-Jacques Annaud (director). 139 mins. TriStar Pictures, 1997.

Shane. George Stevens (director). 118 mins. Paramount Pictures, 1953.

The Shootist. Don Siegel (director). 100 mins. Paramount Pictures, 1976.

Snatch. Guy Ritchie (director). 102 mins. Sony Pictures Entertainment, 2000.

Sommersby. Jon Amiel (director). 114 mins. Warner Brothers, 1993.

Star Wars: Episode IV: A New Hope. George Lucas (director). 121 mins. Twentieth-Century Fox Film, 1977.

Star Wars: Episode VI: Return of the Jedi. Richard Marquand (director). 134 mins. Twentieth-Century Fox Films, 1983.

Star Wars: Episode II: Attack of the Clones. George Lucas (director). 143 mins. Twentieth-Century Fox Film, 2002.

Stigmata. Rupert Wainwright (director). 103 mins. Metro-Goldwyn-Mayer, 1999.

The Stunt Man. Richard Rush (director). 131 mins. Twentieth Century Fox, 1980.

Sullivan's Travels. Preston Sturges (director). 90 mins. Paramount Pictures, 1942.

The Tao of Steve. Jenniphr Goodman (director). 87 mins. Sony Pictures Classics, 2000.

Taxi Driver. Martin Scorsese (director). 113 mins. Columbia Pictures, 1976.

The Ten Commandments. Cecil B. DeMille (director). 220 mins. Paramount Pictures, 1956.

The Thirteenth Floor. Josef Rusnak (director). 100 mins. Columbia Pictures, 1999.

True Grit. Henry Hathaway (director). 128 mins. Paramount Pictures, 1969.

The Truman Show. Peter Weir (director). 103 mins. Paramount Pictures, 1998.

Uccellacci e uccellini. Pier Paolo Pasolini (director). Brandon Films, 1967 (1966).

La Última Cena. Tomás Gutiérrez Alea (director). 120 mins. Tricontinental Film Center, 1978 (1976).

Unforgiven. Clint Eastwood (director). 131 mins. Warner Brothers, 1992.

Il Vangelo secondo Matteo (The Gospel According to St. Matthew). Pier Paolo Pasolini (director). Continental, 1966 (1964).

Viridiana. Luis Buñuel (director). 90 mins. Kingsley-International Pictures, 1962 (1961).

The Wild Bunch. Sam Peckinpah (director). 134 mins. Warner Brothers/Seven Arts, 1969.

Witness. Peter Weir (director). 112 mins. Paramount Pictures, 1985.

55 Days at Peking. Nicholas Ray (director). 150 mins. Allied Artists Pictures, 1963.

Selected Bibliography

Further Reading in Religion, Gospels, Jesus, and Film

Aichele, George. *The Control of Biblical Meaning: Canon as Semiotic Mechanism*. Harrisburg, Pa.: Trinity Press International, 2001.

————. *Jesus Framed*. London: Routledge, 1996.

————. *Sign, Text, Scripture: Semiotics and the Bible*. Sheffield: Sheffield Academic Press, 1997.

————. "Translation as De-Canonization: Matthew's Gospel According to Pasolini." *Cross Currents* 51, no. 4 (Winter 2002): 524–34.

Aichele, George, and Richard Walsh, eds. *Screening Scripture: Intertextual Connections between Scripture and Film*. Harrisburg, Pa.: Trinity Press International, 2002.

Albanese, Catherine L. *America: Religions and Religion*. 2nd ed. Belmont, Calif.: Wadsworth Publishing Company, 1992.

Andrew, Geoff. *The Films of Nicholas Ray: The Poet of Nightfall*. London: Charles Letts & Co., 1991.

Babbington, Bruce, and Peter William Evans. *Biblical Epics: Sacred Narrative in Hollywood Cinema*. Manchester and New York: Manchester University Press, 1993.

Bach, Alice, ed. *Biblical Glamour and Hollywood Glitz*. Semeia 74. Atlanta, Ga.: Scholars Press, 1996.

Barański, Zygmunt G. "The Texts of *Il Vangelo secondo Matteo*." *The Italianist* 5 (1985): 77–106.

Barr, David. *New Testament Story: An Introduction*. 3rd ed. Belmont, Calif.: Wadsworth Group, 2002.

Barthes, Roland. *Mythologies*. Translated by Annette Lavers. New York: Hill & Wang, 1972.

Baugh, Lloyd. *Imaging the Divine: Jesus and Christ-Figures in Film*. Kansas City, Mo.: Sheed & Ward, 1997.

Bellah, Robert N., Richard Marsden, William M. Sullivan, Ann Swindler, and Stephen M. Tipton. *Habits of the Heart: Individualism and Commitment in American Life*. Berkeley: University of California Press, 1985.

Benjamin, Walter. *Illuminations*. Edited by Hannah Arendt. Translated by Harry Zohn. New York: Harcourt, Brace & World, 1968.

Berger, John. *Ways of Seeing*. New York: Penguin Books, 1977.

Berger, Peter L. *The Sacred Canopy: Elements of a Sociological Theory of Religion*. Garden City, N.Y.: Anchor Books, 1969.

The Bible and Culture Collective. *The Postmodern Bible*. New Haven, Conn.: Yale University Press, 1995.

Blonsky, Marshall. *American Mythologies*. Oxford: Oxford University Press, 1992.

Bloom, Harold. *American Religion: The Emergence of the Post-Christian Nation*. New York: Simon & Schuster, 1992.

Borg, Marcus. *Jesus: A New Vision*. San Francisco: Harper & Row, 1985.

Bryant, M. Darrol. "Cinema, Religion, and Popular Culture." In *Religion in Film*, edited by John R. May and Michael Bird, 101–14. Knoxville, Tenn.: University of Tennessee Press, 1981.

Bultmann, Rudolf. "New Testament and Mythology." In *Kerygma and Myth: A Theological Debate*, edited by Hans Werner Bartsch and translated by Reginald H. Fuller, 1–44. New York: Harper & Row Publishers, 1961.

————. *Theology of the New Testament*. 2 vols. Translated by Kendrick Grobel. New York: Charles Scribner's Sons, 1955.

Butler, Ivan. *Religion in the Cinema*. New York: A. S. Barnes & Co., 1969.

Cameron, Ron. *The Other Gospels*. Philadelphia: The Westminster Press, 1982.

Campbell, Joseph. *The Hero with a Thousand Faces*. Princeton, N.J.: Princeton University Press, 1972.

————. *Myths to Live By*. New York: Penguin Books, 1972.

Cawelti, John G. *Adventure, Mystery, and Romance: Formula Stories as Art and Popular Culture*. Chicago: University of Chicago Press, 1976.

Chatman, Seymour. *Story and Discourse: Narrative Structure in Fiction and Film*. Ithaca, N.Y.: Cornell University Press, 1978.

Cosandey, Roland, André Gaudreault, and Tom Gunning, eds. *Une Invention Du Diable?* Sainte-Foy: Les Presses De L'Université Laval, 1992.

Crossan, John Dominic. *The Dark Interval: Towards a Theology of Story*. Niles, Ill.: Argus Communications, 1975.

————. *The Historical Jesus: The Life of a Mediterranean Peasant*. San Francisco: HarperSanFrancisco, 1991.

————. *Raid on the Articulate: Comic Eschatology in Jesus and Borges*. San Francisco: Harper & Row, 1976.

Culpepper, R. Alan. *Anatomy of the Fourth Gospel: A Study in Literary Design*. Philadelphia: Fortress Press, 1983.

Davies, Philip R. "Life of Brian Research." In *Biblical Studies/Cultural Studies: The Third Sheffield Colloquium*, edited by J. Cheryl Exum and Stephen Moore, 400–14. Sheffield: Sheffield Academic Press, 1998.

Detweiler, Robert. "Christ and the Christ Figure in American Fiction." *The Christian Scholar* 47, no. 2 (1964): 111–24.

Doty, William. *Mythography: The Study of Myths and Rituals*. 2nd ed. Tuscaloosa: University of Alabama Press, 2000.

Duling, Dennis C., and Norman Perrin. *The New Testament: Proclamation and Parenesis, Myth and History*. 3rd ed. Fort Worth, Tex.: Harcourt Brace College Publishers, 1994.

Durkheim, Emile. *The Elementary Forms of Religious Life*. Translated by Karen E. Fields. New York: Free Press, 1995 [1912].

Eliade, Mircea. *The Sacred and the Profane: The Nature of Religion.* Translated by Willard R. Trask. New York: Harcourt Brace & World, 1959.

Ellwood, Robert S., Jr. *Introducing Religion: From Inside and Outside.* 3rd ed. Englewood Cliffs, N.J.: Prentice Hall, 1993.

Ford, James L. "Buddhism, Christianity, and *The Matrix:* The Dialectic of Myth-Making in the Contemporary Cinema." *The Journal of Religion and Film* 4, no. 2 (October 2000): n.p. [cited on 15 August 2001]. Available from http://www.unomaha.edu/~wwwjrf/articles.htm

Forshey, Gerald E. *American Religious and Biblical Spectaculars.* Westport, Conn.: Praeger, 1992.

Frei, Hans. *The Eclipse of Biblical Narrative.* New Haven, Conn.: Yale University Press, 1974.

Frye, Northrop. *The Great Code.* New York: Harcourt Brace Jovanovich, 1982.

Geertz, Clifford. *The Interpretation of Cultures.* New York: Basic Books. 1973.

Girard, René. *The Scapegoat.* Translated by Yvonne Freccero. Baltimore, Md.: Johns Hopkins University Press, 1986.

Greeley, Andrew M. "Images of God in the Movies." *The Journal of Religion and Film* 1, no. 1 (April 1997): n.p. [cited on 15 August 2001]. Available from http://www.unomaha.edu/~wwwjrf/articles.htm

Greene, Naomi. *Pier Paolo Pasolini: Cinema as Heresy.* Princeton, N.J.: Princeton University Press, 1990.

Harrington, Daniel J., S.J. "The Jewishness of Jesus." *Bible Review* 3 (1981): 33–41.

Hill, Geoffrey. *Illuminating Shadows: The Mythic Power of Film.* Boston: Shambhala Publications, 1992.

Holloway, Ronald. *Beyond the Image: Approaches to the Religious Dimension in Cinema.* Geneva: World Council of Churches, 1977.

Hurley, Neil P. "Cinematic Transfigurations of Jesus." In *Religion in Film,* edited by John R. May and Michael Bird, 61–78. Knoxville: University of Tennessee Press, 1981.

Jasper, David. "On Systematizing the Unsystematic: A Response." In *Explorations in Theology and Film: Movies and Meaning,* edited by Clive Marsh and Gaye Ortiz, 235–44. Oxford: Blackwell, 1997.

Jewett, Robert. *The Captain America Complex.* 2nd ed. Santa Fe, N.M.: Bear & Co, 1984.

Jewett, Robert, and John Shelton Lawrence. *The American Monomyth.* Garden City, N.Y.: Anchor Press, 1977.

Johnson, Luke Timothy. *The Real Jesus: The Misguided Quest for the Historical Jesus and the Truth of the Traditional Gospels.* San Francisco: HarperSanFrancisco, 1997.

Kelber, Werner. *Mark's Story of Jesus.* Philadelphia: Fortress Press, 1979.

Kermode, Frank. *The Genesis of Secrecy: On the Interpretation of Narrative.* Cambridge, Mass.: Harvard University Press, 1979.

Kingsbury, Jack Dean. *Matthew as Story.* 2nd ed. Philadelphia: Fortress Press, 1988.

Kinnard, Roy, and Tim Davis. *Divine Images: A History of Jesus on the Screen.* New York: Citadel Press, 1992.

Kitses, Jim. *Horizons West.* London: Thames & Hudson, 1969.

Kloppenborg, John S. *The Formation of Q: Trajectories in Ancient Wisdom Collections*. Studies in Antiquity and Christianity. Philadelphia: Fortress Press, 1987.

Kloppenborg, John S., Marvin W. Meyer, Stephen J. Patterson, and Michael G. Steinhauser. *Q-Thomas Reader*. Sonoma, Calif.: Polebridge Press, 1990.

Koester, Helmut. *Ancient Christian Gospels: Their History and Development*. Philadelphia: Trinity Press International, 1990.

———. *Introduction to the New Testament*. 2 vols. Philadelphia: Fortress Press, 1982.

Kreidl, John Francis. *Nicholas Ray*. Boston: Twayne Publishers, 1977.

Kreitzer, Larry. *Gospel Images in Fiction and Film: On Reversing the Hermeneutical Flow*. Sheffield: Sheffield Academic Press, 2001.

Lévi-Strauss, Claude. *Myth and Meaning*. Toronto: University of Toronto Press, 1978.

Lincoln, Bruce. *Theorizing Myth: Narrative, Ideology, and Scholarship*. Chicago: University of Chicago Press, 1999.

Livingston, James C. *Anatomy of the Sacred: An Introduction to Religion*. 3rd ed. Englewood Cliffs, N.J.: Prentice-Hall, 1998.

Loiselle, André. "'I Only Know Where I Come from, Not Where I Am Going': Conversations with Denys Arcand." Translated and edited by André Loiselle. In *Auteur/Provocateur: The Films of Denys Arcand*, edited by André Loiselle and Brian McIlroy, 136–61. Westport, Conn.: Greenwood Press, 1995.

Loiselle, André, and Brian McIlroy, eds. *Auteur/Provocateur: The Films of Denys Arcand*. Westport, Conn.: Greenwood Press, 1995.

Lyden, John. "To Commend or to Critique? The Question of Religion and Film Studies." *The Journal of Religion and Film* 1, no. 2 (1997): n.p. [cited on 15 August 2001]. Available from http://www.unomaha.edu/~wwwjrf/tocommend.htm

Mabee, Charles. *Reimaging America: A Theological Critique of the American Mythos and Biblical Hermeneutics*. Macon, Ga.: Mercer University Press, 1985.

Mack, Burton L. *The Lost Gospel: The Book of Q and Christian Origins*. San Francisco: HarperSanFrancisco, 1993.

———. *A Myth of Innocence: Mark and Christian Origins*. Philadelphia: Fortress Press, 1988.

———. *Who Wrote the New Testament? The Making of the Christian Myth*. San Francisco: Polebridge Press, 1995.

Malbon, Elizabeth Struthers. *In the Company of Jesus: Characters in Mark's Gospel*. Louisville, Ky.: Westminster John Knox Press, 2000.

———. *Narrative Space and Mythic Meaning in Mark*. San Francisco: Harper & Row, 1987.

Malone, Peter. "Jesus on Our Screens." In *New Image of Religious Film*, edited by John May, 57–71. Kansas City, Mo.: Sheed & Ward, 1997.

———. *Movie Christs and Antichrists*. New York: Crossroad Publishing Company, 1990.

Marsden, George M. *Religion in American Culture*. San Diego, Calif.: Harcourt Brace Jovanovich, 1990.

Marsh, Clive, and Gaye Ortiz, eds. *Explorations in Theology and Film: Movies and Meaning*. Oxford: Blackwell, 1997.

Martin, Joel W., and Conrad E. Ostwalt Jr., eds. *Screening the Sacred: Religion, Myth, and Ideology in Popular American Film*. Boulder, Colo.: Westview Press, 1995.

Martin, Thomas M. *Images and the Imageless: A Study in Religious Consciousness and Film*. 2nd ed. London: Associated University Presses, 1991.

May, John R., and Michael Bird, eds. *Religion in Film*. Knoxville: University of Tennessee Press, 1981.

May, Rollo. *The Cry for Myth*. New York: Dell Publishing, 1991.

Medved, Michael. *Hollywood vs. America*. New York: HarperPerennial, 1991.

Meeks, Wayne A. "The Man from Heaven in Johannine Sectarianism." *Journal of Biblical Literature* 91 (1972): 44–72.

Meier, John P. *A Marginal Jew: Rethinking the Historical Jesus*. 3 vols. Garden City, New York: Anchor Books, 2001.

———. *The Vision of Matthew: Christ, Church, and Morality in the First Gospel*. New York: Paulist Press, 1979.

Miles, Margaret R. *Seeing and Believing: Religion and Values in the Movies*. Boston: Beacon Press, 1996.

Moore, Stephen D. *Literary Criticism and the Gospels: The Theoretical Challenge*. New Haven, Conn.: Yale University Press, 1989.

Neale, Steve. *Genre and Hollywood*. London: Routledge, 2000.

Nelson, John Wiley. *Your God Is Alive and Well and Appearing in Popular Culture*. Philadelphia: The Westminster Press, 1976.

Nineham, Denis. *The Use and Abuse of the Bible*. New York: Macmillan, 1973.

O'Brien, Tom. *The Screening of America: Movies and Values from Rocky to Rain Man*. New York: Continuum, 1990.

Otto, Rudolph. *The Idea of the Holy*. Translated by John W. Harvey. New York: Oxford University Press, 1958.

Patterson, Stephen J. *The Gospel of Thomas and Jesus*. Sonoma, Calif.: Polebridge Press, 1993.

Pelikan, Jaroslav. *Jesus through the Centuries: His Place in the History of Culture*. New Haven, Conn.: Yale University Press, 1985.

Perrin, Norman. *Jesus and the Language of the Kingdom: Symbol and Metaphor in New Testament Interpretation*. Philadelphia: Fortress Press, 1976.

Pervo, Richard I. *Profit with Delight: The Literary Genre of the Acts of the Apostles*. Philadelphia: Fortress Press, 1987.

Petersen, Norman. *The Gospel of John and the Sociology of Light: Language and Characterization in the Fourth Gospel*. Valley Forge, Pa.: Trinity Press International, 1993.

Pippin, Tina. *Apocalyptic Bodies: The Biblical End of the World in Text and Image*. London/New York: Routledge, 1999.

Postman, Neil. *Amusing Ourselves to Death: Public Discourse in the Age of Show Business*. New York: Penguin Books, 1986.

Rank, Otto. *The Myth of the Birth of the Hero and Other Writings*. New York: Vintage Books, 1964.

Reinhartz, Adele. "Scripture on the Silver Screen." *The Journal of Religion and Film* 3, no. 1 (1999): n.p. [cited 24 April 2001]. Available from http://www.unomaha.edu/~wwwjrf/scripture.html

Rhoads, David, and Donald Michie. *Mark as Story: An Introduction to the Narrative of a Gospel*. Philadelphia: Fortress Press, 1982.

Richie, Donald. *George Stevens: An American Romantic*. New York: Museum of Modern Art, 1970.

Robertson, James Oliver. *American Myth, American Reality*. New York: Hill & Wang, 1980.

Rumble, Patrick, and Bart Testa. *Pier Paolo Pasolini: Contemporary Perspectives*. Toronto: University of Toronto Press, 1994.

Sanders, E. P. *Jesus and Judaism*. Philadelphia: Fortress Press, 1985.

Schneidau, Herbert N. *Sacred Discontent: The Bible and Western Tradition*. Berkeley: University of California Press, 1976.

Schrader, Paul. *Transcendental Style in Film: Ozu, Bresson, Dryer*. Berkeley: University of California Press, 1972.

Schweitzer, Albert. *The Quest of the Historical Jesus: A Critical Study of Its Progress from Reimarus to Wrede*. Translated by W. Montgomery. New York: Macmillan Publishing, 1968.

Schweitzer, Robert Fred. *The Biblical Christ in Cinema*. Ph.D. Diss., University of Missouri, 1971.

Scott, Bernard Brandon. *Hollywood Dreams and Biblical Stories*. Minneapolis, Minn.: Fortress Press, 1994.

Segal, Robert A. *Theorizing about Myth*. Amherst: University of Massachusetts Press, 1999.

Smith, Jonathan Z. *Drudgery Divine: On the Comparison of Early Christianities and the Religions of Late Antiquity*. Chicago: University of Chicago Press, 1990.

————. *Map Is Not Territory: Studies in the History of Religion*. Leiden: E. J. Brill, 1978.

Stack, Oswald. *Pasolini on Pasolini: Interviews with Oswald Stack*. Bloomington: Indiana University Press, 1969.

Staley, Jeffrey L. *The Print's First Kiss: A Rhetorical Investigation of the Implied Reader in the Fourth Gospel*. Atlanta, Ga.: Scholars Press, 1988.

————. *Reading with a Passion: Rhetoric, Autobiography, and the American West in the Gospel of John*. New York: Continuum International Publishing Group, 1995.

Stern, Richard C., Clayton Jefford, and Guerric DeBona, O.S.B. *Savior on the Silver Screen*. Mahwah, N.J.: Paulist Press, 1999.

Talbert, Charles H. *Literary Patterns, Theological Themes, and the Genre of Luke-Acts*. Missoula, Mont.: Scholars Press, 1974.

Tannehill, Robert. *The Narrative Unity of Luke-Acts: A Literary Interpretation*. 2 vols. Minneapolis, Minn.: Fortress Press, 1990.

Tatum, W. Barnes. *Jesus at the Movies: A Guide to the First Hundred Years*. Santa Rosa, Calif.: Polebridge Press, 1997.

Telford, William R. "Jesus Christ Movie Star: The Depiction of Jesus in the Cinema." In *Explorations in Theology and Film: Movies and Meaning*, edited by Clive Marsh and Gaye Ortiz, 115–39. Oxford: Blackwell, 1997.

Testa, Bart. "Arcand's Double-Twist Allegory: *Jesus of Montreal*." In *Auteur/Provocateur: The Films of Denys Arcand*, edited by André Loiselle and Brian McIlroy, 90–112. Westport, Conn.: Greenwood Press, 1995.

————. "To Film a Gospel . . . and Advent of the Theoretical Stranger." In *Pier Paolo Pasolini: Contemporary Perspectives*, edited by Patrick Rumble and Bart Testa, 180–209. Toronto: University of Toronto Press, 1994.

Tolbert, Mary Ann. *Sowing the Gospel: Mark's World in Literary-Historical Perspective*. Minneapolis, Minn.: Fortress Press, 1989.

Tompkins, Jane. *West of Everything*. New York: Oxford University Press, 1992.

Van der Leeuw, G. *Religion in Essence and Manifestation*. 2 vols. Translated by J. E. Turner. New York: Harper & Row, 1963.

Vaux, Sara Anson. *Finding Meaning at the Movies*. Nashville, Tenn.: Abingdon Press, 1999.

Walsh, Richard. "Ancient Biblical Worlds and Recent Magical Realism: Affirming and Denying Reality." In *The Monstrous and the Unspeakable: The Bible as Fantastic Literature*, edited by George Aichele and Tina Pippin, 135–47. Sheffield: Sheffield Academic Press, 1997.

————. "On Finding a Non-American Revelation: *End of Days* and the Book of Revelation." In *Screening Scripture: Intertextual Connections between Scripture and Film*, edited by George Aichele and Richard Walsh, 1–23. Harrisburg, Pa.: Trinity Press International, 2002.

————. *Mapping Myths of Biblical Interpretation*. Sheffield: Sheffield Academic Press, 2001.

————. *Reading the Bible: An Introduction*. Notre Dame, Ind.: Cross Cultural Publications, 1997.

————. "Recent Fictional Portrayals of God, or: Disney, Shirley MacLaine, and Hamlet." In *Culture, Entertainment, and the Bible*, edited by George Aichele, 44–65. Sheffield: Sheffield Academic Press, 2000.

————. "Tragic Dimensions in Mark." *Biblical Theology Bulletin* 19 (July 1989): 94–99.

Wilder, Amos Niven. *Early Christian Rhetoric: The Language of the Gospel*. Cambridge, Mass.: Harvard University Press, 1971.

————. *Jesus' Parables and the War of Myths: Essays on Imagination in the Scripture*. Philadelphia: Fortress Press, 1982.

Wilken, Robert L. *The Myth of Christian Beginnings*. Garden City, N.Y.: Doubleday, 1971.

Wood, Michael. *America in the Movies*. 2nd ed. New York: Columbia University Press, 1989.

Wright, N. T. *Christian Origins and the Question of God*. 2 vols. Minneapolis, Minn.: Fortress Press, 1997.

Ziolkowski, Theodore. *Fictional Transfigurations of Jesus*. Princeton, N.J.: Princeton University Press, 1972.

Index of Names and Movies